Making Sense of
AUTISM

Nashville-based artist, Grace Walker Goad, is 12
and has moderately functioning autism. Since her
talent for creating visual art was discovered at age four,
she has studied with several private art teachers and
art therapists. Grace's art has been shown on
Capitol Hill in Washington, D.C., in New York City,
and in many locations in Nashville, Tennessee.
Her art (including the painting on the cover, "Boy")
can be viewed online at her web site
(http://www.gracegoad.com).

Making Sense of
AUTISM

by

Travis Thompson, Ph.D.

·P A U L·H·
BROOKES
PUBLISHING Co.®

Baltimore • London • Sydney

Paul H. Brookes Publishing Co.
Post Office Box 10624
Baltimore, Maryland 21285-0624

www.brookespublishing.com

Typeset by Spearhead Global, Inc., Bear, Delaware.
Manufactured in the United States of America by
Versa Press, Inc., East Peoria, Illinois.

The case studies in the book represent real situations, but the names and
identifying details have been changed to protect the privacy of the individuals.

The cover design entitled "Boy" is by Grace Goad; the photographs of Grace Goad (page
ii) are courtesy of Lawrence Ballew and Bill Bangham. Photographs on the frontispiece
are used courtesy of Kammy N. Kramer, Christine Majowski, Rebecca L. Thompson, and
the Wisconsin Early Autism Project.

Second printing, February 2012.

Library of Congress Cataloging-in-Publication Data

Thompson, Travis.
  Making sense of autism / by Travis Thompson.
    p.   ; cm.
  Includes bibliographical references and index.
  ISBN 978-1-55766-915-5   (alk. paper)
  1. Autism.   2. Autism in children.   I. Title.
  [DNLM: 1. Autistic Disorder—diagnosis.   2. Autistic Disorder—therapy.
WM 203.5 T477 2007]   I. Title.
RC553.A88T4568 2007
618.92′85882—dc22   2007007705

British Library Cataloguing in Publication data are available from the British Library.

Contents

About the Author

Travis Thompson, Ph.D., Professor, Department of Pediatrics at the University of Minnesota School of Medicine, Autism Program, MMC 486 Mayo, 420 Delaware, Minneapolis, Minnesota 55455

Dr. Travis Thompson with his grandson Michael Rodriguez, who has an autism spectrum disorder. Michael attends a regular education classroom in West Orange, New Jersey.

Dr. Thompson completed his doctoral training in psychology at the University of Minnesota. He did postdoctoral work at the University of Maryland and spent a year at Cambridge University in the United Kingdom doing research and a year as a visiting scientist at the National Institute on Drug Abuse in Rockville, Maryland. Dr. Thompson was director of the John F. Kennedy Center for Research on Human Development at Vanderbilt University and director of the Institute for Child Development at the University of Kansas Medical Center, a clinical, training, and research institute. He served as the executive program director of a nonprofit community-based early intervention program for children with autism spectrum disorders in Minneapolis from 2003 to 2005.

Dr. Thompson has served on several National Institutes of Health research review committees, and chaired the committee that reviews applicants for Collaborative Programs of Excellence in Autism awards. He has been a member of American Psychological Association task forces concerned with the practice of psychology and psychopharmacology and is a past president of the Behavioral Pharmacology Society, the Division of Psychopharmacology and Substance Abuse, and the Division of Mental Retardation and Developmental Disabilities of the American Psychological Association. Dr. Thompson has received numerous awards, including The Arc USA Distinguished Research Award, the Academy on Mental Retardation Life Time Research Award, the Don Hake Award of the American Psychological Association, and the Edgar A. Doll Award for his contributions to facilitating the transfer of research on intellectual and developmental disabilities into practice. He has published more than 220 journal articles and chapters as well as 26 books dealing with developmental disabilities, psychopharmacology, and related topics. Dr. Thompson co-authored the first textbook on behavioral pharmacology and has spoken in more than 41 states and 15 countries about autism spectrum disorders and other developmental disabilities and psychopharmacology.

Preface

The original title of this book was to have been *Oughtism,* based on the intense need for control, structure, and predictability that drives so many of the actions of people with autism spectrum disorders (ASDs). Their lives are consumed by the need to regulate their world so that it conforms to what they think it ought to be. There was concern, however, that the title might confuse readers casually searching through book titles, assuming that the book was about moral philosophy rather than a pervasive developmental disability. Although the title has changed, the book's content and intent have not. It is still a book about children with ASDs. Leo Kanner, the man who provided the first detailed clinical description of austism spectrum disorders, wrote of these children,

> *Changes of routine, of furniture arrangement, of a pattern, of the {form} in which every-day acts are carried out, can drive him {the child with an ASD} to despair. The dread of change and incompleteness seems to be a major factor in the explanation of the monotonous repetitiousness and the resulting limitation in the variety of spontaneous activity. (1943, pp. 245–246)*

Autism spectrum disorders present a growing challenge to health care workers, educators, service agencies, and, most of all, parents. More professionals in more settings are being called on to provide appropriate services to children with unusual, puzzling, and often difficult behavioral challenges. Parents have become increasingly aware of the importance of obtaining effective services for their children with ASD diagnoses as early as possible, and they want to know where to turn for reliable information.

An enormous amount of research concerning the causes and underlying neurobiological and genetic underpinnings of these conditions—and their complex array of cognitive, communication, social, emotional, and behavioral expression—has emerged over the past decade. Under the auspices of funding from the National Institutes of Health, the Centers for Disease Control and Prevention, and the U.S. Department of Education, researchers have studied literally thousands of children and youth with ASDs in an effort to improve diagnostic, treatment, and educational methods. The flood of new findings is encouraging, but it also presents daunting challenges to those who attempt to keep abreast of burgeoning research discoveries. Practitioners and parents often find it difficult to understand the information published in journals and research monographs. Matters had been made more difficult by researchers focusing on the specific issue they were studying (e.g., molecular genetic mechanisms) or a particular classroom application;

there was little cross-talk among disciplines. That situation has improved with the creation of the National Institutes of Health Collaborative Programs of Excellence in Autism, subsequently called the Autism Centers of Excellence, which has brought together researchers in 10 major medical and behavioral science centers to promote collaboration designed to overcome some of the problems. And although there has been improvement, there continues to be limited interaction among practitioners, educational researchers, and those in the biomedical and more basic behavioral science fields. The present volume grew out of nearly four decades of experience integrating information from these various perspectives and translating it into a common vocabulary that can be understood by professionals, parents, and university students.

A variety of experiences formed the foundation for this book. On several occasions, I had the good fortune to chair the National Institutes of Health committee that reviewed grant applications for Autism Centers of Excellence. The amount of exciting research being done by these remarkable centers to solve the problems posed by ASDs has been a real eye opener. Through participating in interdisciplinary diagnostic evaluations, such as those conducted by the Autism Program at the University of Minnesota Department of Pediatrics, I have become cognizant of the complexity of differential diagnoses and the wide variety of presentations of ASDs and related disabilities. Through consulting with classroom teachers in dozens of public schools who were trying to meet the educational needs of children with ASDs, I have come to appreciate their dedication and creativity as well as the frustrations and practical dilemmas they face. In addition, a clearer picture of the reality of parenting a child with an ASD emerged from working directly with a great many families of children with ASDs in the course of supervising home-based intensive early intervention services. Most of the stories about children and families discussed in this book are based on individuals with whom I have worked, although the names and other details are changed to protect their privacy. The book's focus is on children with ASDs who are approximately 2 to 6 or 7 years of age, the period in which it appears most possible to prevent the emergence of severe autism symptoms through effective intervention.

My career has been divided among research, teaching/training, and clinical practice. To be a good teacher, one must have a voracious appetite for learning. Over many years, I have conducted more than 70 training workshops on autism, mostly under the auspices of Behavioral Intervention Specialists, Inc., a staff training organization based in Oxford, Mississippi. Through addressing a wide range of audiences, as well as training graduate students, I've learned the importance of presenting complex interdisciplinary information so that it is clearly understood. This book reflects the confluence of those experiences, providing an integrated account of autism spectrum disorders.

Parents desperately want to feel hopeful about the future of their young children with ASDs, and they also want to receive the truth from someone they trust.

Professionals seek to understand what is known in ways they can grasp, even if the information comes from a field other than their own. They want to know when a treatment is effective or ineffective and when the outcomes to date have been equivocal. Parents and professionals are eager to hear about emerging research that remains to be corroborated. Findings may be promising, even exciting, but more work often needs to be done before one can honestly present the information as based on solid evidence. I have attempted to make evidence-based practice the backbone of the information presented here. In some cases, sufficient information is currently unavailable, and I have alerted the reader to those limitations. When procedures discussed are based on clinical experience rather than controlled research studies, I have made that known as well.

It will be clear to the reader of this book that I have been greatly affected by the children and families with whom I have worked. They have all faced formidable challenges and have suffered. The children have been tormented by confusion and anxiety, their mothers have experienced moments of depression, and their fathers have felt anguished over what to do to make their children whole again. A caring professional's effectiveness depends on maintaining objectivity coupled with a compassionate understanding of what a child and his or her family are experiencing. When there are triumphs, the child and family celebrate them. When little progress is being made, the professional is tempted to make excuses or to report negligible improvements to buoy up discouraged parents. But parents nearly always know who has been honest and objectively helpful and compassionate, and who has misled them by offering disingenuous balm to temporarily assuage their pain.

My thanks go to the children and their families who have allowed me to be part of their lives, and to the outstanding therapists and classroom teachers with whom I have had the good fortune to work. To my colleagues Jodi Dooling-Litfin, Patricia Dropik, Theresa Estrem, Caroline Moniza, Tim Moore, Michael Reiff, Robin Rumsey, Campbell Thompson, and Kristie Thompson, from whom I have learned so much about improving the lives of children with autism spectrum disorders, I am most grateful. I am especially thankful to my wife Anneke Thompson and daughter Andrea Thompson, special education teachers who have shared their practical wisdom as teachers of children with ASDs. To my former colleague Dale Osterman, my thanks for his support and for teaching me what it means to manage. I am also indebted to Dr. Walt Antonow, whose organization, Behavior Intervention Specialists, Inc., sponsors my autism workshops throughout the country. Thanks also to Grace Goad for permitting me to use her painting "Boy" for the cover of the book.

Finally, many thanks to Rebecca Lazo, Acquisitions Editor for Paul H. Brookes Publishing Co., who supported my efforts to see this book to fruition, and to Trish Byrnes, Production Editor, whose skillful editorial work improved the manuscript immeasurably.

To Anneke, for her loving support, and to our grandson Michael,
who helped us understand what a child with autism means to a family

1

Is It Oughtism or Autism?

Imagine what it would be like to realize that your 2-year-old child is slipping away before your eyes and there seems to be nothing you can do about it. That is what happened to Ross and Beth, whose son Matt was between 5 and 6 years old when his parents first talked with me about him. Their palpable sadness pervaded the room as we talked. Ross offered me a tape recording of Matt talking and singing nursery rhymes when he was little more than 2 years old. His high-pitched, sing-song "A, B, C, D, E, F, G ..." reminded me of my own daughter's voice at that age. When Beth and Ross spoke of Matt, it was in the past tense, almost as though they were talking about a deceased child. Beth handed me a recent photograph of Matt—his pale blue eyes stared at me from the photograph above his quizzical smile, with one corner of his mouth turned up and the other turned slightly downward. His sandy blond hair was the same color as his father's. Ross and Beth had noticed that around 3 years of age, Matt's speech had slowed to a trickle and eventually stopped. He spent hours staring at his fingers and gazing out the window at branches of trees weaving in the breeze. He rocked incessantly, and began screaming and having tantrums for no apparent reason. He seemed frustrated, almost as though nothing was the way it ought to be. He lost his daily living skills, some of which he had learned a year before. His outbursts lasted for a half an hour to an hour, during which he bit, hit, and kicked his parents and periodically banged his head against hard surfaces. Although the changes seemed rapid between 2 and 3 years of age, his parents recalled that Matt was always different. From a very early age he spent an inordinate amount of time rocking in his crib, bumping his head against the headboard, and he didn't seem to like being held. But his loss of skills occurred much more rapidly during his toddler years. As I listened to Beth and Ross's story, I could only imagine the anguish they must have felt.

SOMETHING IS WRONG, BUT WHAT?

Regressive autism, like Matt's, occurs in about 20%–30% of individuals with an autism diagnosis; the cause of regression with associated loss of skills is unknown. For the other 70%–80%, signs of an autism spectrum disorder were usually apparent within the first 6 months of life. Ross and Beth recalled that their son cried incessantly, often for no apparent reason. It was impossible to comfort him, and holding him did no good. When picked up, he stiffened instead of conforming to the shape of his mother's arms. Parents of a child who will later receive an ASD diagnosis nearly always recognize something is wrong with their child, but they don't know what. The mother of a daughter with autism recalled that she was very fussy about flavors and textures of food, spitting up and vomiting much more often than her older siblings had. When she learned to sit, she rocked and sometimes hit her head against the headboard of the crib repeatedly until picked up and moved. She repeated the sounds of words, but didn't seem to use them to communicate. Instead, she sat staring at a spot of sunlight on a shiny surface, repeatedly saying "bop, pop, bop, pop." When a daily routine unexpectedly changed (e.g., her blue blanket wasn't out of the dryer and it was nap time), she screamed inconsolably. If her father tried to redirect her to another blanket or her favorite stuffed toy, she hit, kicked, and tried to bite him.

Feeling Alone

Before a child is diagnosed with an autism spectrum disorder (ASD), parents experience anguish and guilt about the reasons for their child's unusual behavior. They are criticized even by the people closest to them, who often assume the child's behavior problems are the result of inappropriate parenting. The child's tantrums often occur at inopportune times, and the repetitive behavior seems inexplicable. When an outburst occurs during a trip to the shopping mall, it seems that every eye is turned on the child and his or her parents, who feel that they are being judged for not stopping the tantrum—"What in the world are they doing to that child?"—or offered advice—"You should be firmer with the child!" The child's pediatrician recognizes something is amiss but seems reluctant to assign a diagnosis, instead suggesting that she will monitor the child's development more closely. Parents try everything they've read in child-rearing book, but nothing solves the problem. Old friends stop calling to get together because they can no longer tolerate the child's tantrums. Grandparents offer to hire a babysitter for the child when their son and daughter-in-law come for Sunday dinner, so that they will be spared another intolerable tirade by their grandson. Many parents of young children with ASDs feel progressively isolated from friends and family, and they feel misunderstood, judged, and utterly alone.

It is important for parents to realize that what they are seeing isn't just the "terrible 2s," and that they need to seek outside assistance for their child. I have never met a couple who was prepared to parent a child with an ASD. Everything one does to comfort, teach, and support the development of a typical child seems to backfire when applied to a child with autism. Picking a child up to comfort him when he is in the midst of a tantrum only makes matters worse. Sending a 4-year-old to his room when he is being destructive is rewarding to the child, who would rather be left alone to rock and weave his head from side to side. Trying to explain to the young girl with an ASD why she shouldn't climb on the kitchen table is fruitless. She puts her fingers in her ears and screams. She doesn't understand what her parents are saying, and she doesn't want her preferred routine (climbing on top of furniture) to be interrupted.

Early Autism Screening

During the first 3 years, children make regular visits to their pediatrician or family practice doctor. When doctors indicate to a child's parents that they are concerned that there may be a problem, evidence shows that parents generally take the doctor's concern seriously and are likely to act on it. As a result, it is important that doctors caring for young children use each well child visit to screen for signs of an ASD. They already weigh and measure growth, which is charted and compared with typical development. Well visits also provide opportunities to screen for and chart a child's social, emotional, and cognitive development, and several programs have been developed in the United States, Canada, the United Kingdom, and other countries to prepare doctors and their nurses to conduct simple screening tests for signs of an ASD. Screening tests are brief tools that sort children who probably have delays in development, learning, and behavior from children who probably don't. Screenings *do not give a diagnosis* but only tell whether there is a reasonable chance of a problem. Screenings can be simple, taking just a few minutes, and are effective because they are based on well-established developmental milestones.

Parents often suspect that something may be wrong with their child's development even before the doctor mentions it. There are several tools parents can use that will provide potentially important information about their child's development. The Ages & Stages Questionnaires developed by Diane Bricker and her colleagues (Bricker, Squires, & Mounts, 1999) can be obtained through the publisher, Paul H. Brookes Publishing Co., or in many bookstores. It consists of 30-item questionnaires to be completed at designated intervals. Filling out a questionnaire takes 10–15 minutes. The questionnaire covers five key developmental areas: communication, gross motor, fine motor, problem solving, and personal–social. Scores suggesting that there may be a problem should be discussed with the child's doctor.

Web-based screening tools are available for parents as well. The FOREPATH web site (http://www.forepath.org/) provides a measure called *PEDS: Parents' Evaluation of Developmental Status.* PEDS consists of questions concerning language, emotional and social skills, and fine and gross motor skills. The researchers who developed PEDS have devised cutoff scores that indicate a child may or may not have a developmental delay. After completing the PEDS basic screening, parents can then administer the Checklist for Autism in Toddlers (CHAT) that focuses specifically on signs of ASDs in very young children. If scores indicate that there is a likely delay, the parents should make an appointment with their child's doctor to discuss the results of the screening.

First Signs (http://www.firstsigns.org/) is a national nonprofit organization that offers a wide variety of excellent resources to parents, doctors, and other professionals for detecting the first signs of autism and other developmental disorders. The goal of First Signs is to improve screening and practices and to lower the age at which young children are identified with ASDs and other developmental disorders. First Signs offers screening manuals and training videotapes to doctors and other professionals who are involved in early autism screening. They emphasize that there are a variety of ways that physicians can seamlessly weave a developmental screening into a well visit. A parent might fill out a screening form in the physician's waiting room, at home before a well visit, or with the assistance of a nurse, physician, or other professional in the examination room. The red flags that should alert parents and pediatricians of a possible problem are

- No big smiles or other warm, joyful expressions by 6 months of age or thereafter

- No back-and-forth sharing of sounds, smiles, or other facial expressions by 9 months of age or thereafter

- No babbling by 12 months

- No back-and-forth gestures, such as pointing, showing, reaching, or waving by 12 months

- No words by 16 months

- No two-word meaningful phrases (without imitating or repeating) by 24 months

- Any loss of speech or babbling or social skills at any age

A recent study by Zwaigenbaum and colleagues (2005) at McMaster University indicated that it is possible to detect signs of ASDs as early as one year of age. Unusual eye contact, lack of visual tracking, prolonged latency to disengage visual attention, failure to orient to name, lack of imitation, lack of social smiling, passivity at 6 months, lack of social interest and affect, peculiar sensory-oriented behaviors, extreme distress reactions at 12 months, a tendency to fixate on particular objects in the environment for prolonged periods, and decreased expression of positive affect by 12 months were all predictive of a later autism diagnosis. These signs combined with delayed expressive and receptive language were especially predictive of a later autism diagnosis among young children who had an older sibling with an ASD.

Obtaining a Diagnosis

A critical first step is obtaining an accurate diagnosis. Although it has been more than 200 years since autism was first described, and more than 60 years since the first modern clinical diagnostic criteria for autism and Asperger syndrome were published, there is still no biological diagnostic test for autism. There have been literally thousands of studies dealing with different aspects of ASDs. A great deal has been learned, but there is still no blood, x-ray, genetic, or other biomedical test for autistic disorder, Asperger syndrome, or pervasive developmental disorder not otherwise specified (PDD-NOS)—the three main categories making up ASDs. They continue to be behaviorally defined syndromes. Scientists are actively studying biological differences among individuals with various ASDs compared with matched controls in search of a screening tool. Some differences occur with high frequency; however, the tests have not been standardized to distinguish ASDs from comparison groups of children with other developmental problems. Most medical tests, such as functional brain imaging, are far too expensive for routine screening of every child who exhibits autism-like behavior. One of the main reasons that no single biological test has been found that distinguishes children with autism from those with other developmental disabilities is that autism is not a single condition. It is a family of conditions, sharing some features in common but differing considerably in other ways.

Differentially Diagnosing ASDs

There are two types of ASD identification: school and medical. A school identification of autism is sufficient for a child to receive special education services; however, reimbursement for specialized therapies and services outside of school (e.g., private speech, occupational, or behavioral therapy) requires a medical diagnosis. In many school districts, autism specialists receive training in autism diagnosis. School personnel attend workshops on how to screen for and diagnose autism. Sometimes their training is adequate, but at times it is insufficient for a proper diagnosis. Some staff members are unaware of the difference between assessments meant to screen for autism and those specifically for diagnosis. Screening instruments, such as the Childhood Autism Rating Scale or the CHAT are intended to determine whether a child *may* have autism, not to diagnose autism. If a screening assessment yields a score for a child in the "probable autism" range, the child should be referred for a more thorough diagnostic assessment.

The gold standard diagnostic instrument is the Autism Diagnostic Observation Schedule (ADOS), which was designed to assess core features of autism that are matched with the criteria in the *Diagnostic and Statistical Manual of Mental Disorders (DSM-IV-TR)* of the American Psychiatric Association. Some psychologists and school personnel attend workshops on using the ADOS to diagnose autism. Typically during such a 1-day workshop, those in attendance obtain practice applying the instrument to a single child. This is a good start, but it may not provide sufficient experience to validly employ the ADOS with a range of children varying in intellectual ability, severity of symptoms, and possible confounding problems (e.g., anxiety disorder, language disabilities). Valid use of the ADOS for differential diagnosis requires extensive experience and calibration of diagnostic decisions with an experienced practitioner who is certified in administering the ADOS. Often, several months of practice assessing a dozen or more children with varying signs and symptoms who have been referred with probable ASDs is required to reliably and validly use the ADOS for diagnosis. Schools also routinely assess children referred for possible autism for speech and sensory-motor problems used in developing the child's individualized education program (IEP).

Medical diagnosis is usually done by a pediatrician or psychiatrist specializing in children's developmental problems. In some states, licensed psychologists with training in autism diagnosis may also conduct assessments that meet the criteria for medical diagnosis if they are certified by the state department of mental health and developmental disabilities and medical insurance companies. Many general pediatricians have little or no experience with autism because they have been trained to function as internists for children. It is important that parents seek a referral to a pediatrician who specializes in developmental disorders, usually a developmental pediatrician. While most child psychiatrists have some experience with autism, some specialize instead in attention-deficit/hyperactivity disorder (ADHD), childhood depression, anxiety disorders, or conduct disorders. Their experience may not prepare them to differentially diagnose ASDs. Again, in seeking a referral, it is important that parents determine the child psychiatrist's area of specialization before making an appointment for a diagnostic assessment.

Pediatricians and psychiatrists who specialize in ASDs usually work closely with a licensed psychologist who has been trained in administering and interpreting a battery of assessments (including the ADOS) that are necessary to arrive at a differential diagnosis (i.e., to make certain that the signs they are seeing are specific to autism and not caused by another condition). In many practices specializing in autism, a licensed speech-language pathologist (SLP) conducts an independent assessment that plays an important role in differentiating specific language impairment (SLI) from the communication problems often seen in autism. After the physician has obtained a history from the child's parents and interacted with the child, and the psychologist and the SLP have completed their assessments, the three professionals meet to compare their observations and findings before arriving at a final diagnosis. The physician reviews his or her own DSM-IV diagnostic checklist with the psychologist's ADOS findings and the speech-language assessment results obtained by the SLP. Only by integrating the various assessments can there be reasonable certainty about the diagnosis.

Parents reasonably wonder why assessments conducted by different clinicians occasionally yield different conclusions. Differentiating Asperger syndrome or PDD-NOS, for example, from an SLI combined with anxiety disorder can be difficult. Unless a thorough battery of appropriate assessments is done, it is easy to arrive at an incorrect diagnosis. Medical diagnoses conducted by clinics that specialize in ASDs employ more comprehensive batteries of medical screening, cognitive, language/communication, emotional, behavioral, and neuropsychological assessments that are more likely to reveal other problems (e.g., SLI, ADHD, obsessive-compulsive disorder [OCD], temporal lobe seizure disorder) that may resemble features of autism but require different intervention strategies. It is also possible that some diagnostic assessments are influenced by the availability of services within those regions to accommodate children with ASDs. Children may be less likely to receive a diagnosis of autism if there are limited specialized services for children with ASDs in a geographic area. Such areas may have few personnel trained and experienced in autism. Independent assessments by psychologists, pediatricians, or child psychiatrists and their SLP colleagues associated with specialty clinics may be less likely to be influenced by the types of services available in arriving at a diagnosis.

Develop a Circle of Support

Once a diagnosis is obtained, the child's parents should share that information with the child's teachers, grandparents and other relatives, neighbors, and friends. Parents can obtain pamphlets about autism from the local or state chapter of the Autism Society that explain the condition, its characteristics, expectations, and coping strategies. By providing friends and family members with objective information from outside autism experts, parents will begin to better understand the child with ASD and the parents' predicament. Parents' sense of isolation will diminish accordingly. By inviting friends and relatives to attend a meeting of the local Autism Society, parents will expose their immediate support group to information provided by other parents and professionals experienced in autism. Grandparents are often especially effective caregivers for children with autism. They bring the wisdom that comes with experience, and at times may find it easier to be more patient with the child than the child's own parents. Chief Joseph, the remarkable statesman of the Nez Percés people, said, "Let us put our minds together, and see what we will make for our children." The more people parents can bring into their circle of support, the better. Parents should explain their son or daughter's condition to their minister or rabbi, to the librarian at the nearby public library where they check out books for the child, and the staff at the YMCA where the child goes swimming on Saturdays. When behavioral eruptions occur, which they inevitably will from time to time, it is best to have everyone on the same team.

OUGHTISM: UNDERSTANDING CHILDREN WITH AUTISM SPECTRUM DISORDERS

The most important thing that parents, teachers, and other caregivers can do to help a child with autism develop is to try to see the world through the child's eyes. For children with ASDs, very little in the world around them is the way it ought to be. Taking time to gain an appreciation for the way your child, client, or student sees the world is invaluable in understanding their often puzzling behavior and more rationally developing educational, medical, and other intervention plans. Some days it may seem that children with ASDs wake up in the morning wondering what they can do to drive their parents and teachers crazy. In reality, children with ASDs are doing their best to make their world understandable, predictable, and tolerable—the way it *ought* to be (at least from their perspective). Our job is to figure out how to make their world more manageable by understanding why they are doing what they're doing and teaching them more effective ways of overcoming the problems they encounter. The world is very confusing and at times scary for children and youth with ASDs. They don't understand what people say to them and the meaning behind people's actions. They don't understand what will occur, in which order it will occur, or when it will occur. The most fundamental problem each person with autism faces is how to gain control over a disorderly world. They need their environment to be predicable. When a child with an ASD screams, cries, has tantrums, or slaps his or her own face, it is often intended to make his or her parents stop making demands. Children with autism don't understand what is being said to them and they fear that it involves some change they are unable to tolerate. If a daily routine is changed, their aggression is intended to make their parents restore it the way it *ought* to be—from their perspective.

Many parents and teachers feel that they are losing control of the situation if they are unable to insist that the child with an ASD obey them—usually immediately. Ordering the child to do things, or not do things, and expecting prompt compliance will inevitably result in frustration for everyone involved and, very likely, a fracas. Each successive altercation over "who's in control here" will make matters worse.

One of the more effective ways to gain control over the behavior of a child with an ASD is often to relinquish some control over things that matter greatly to the child and are relatively unimportant to you. By teaching a child legitimate ways of controlling his or her world, even if some of the things that seem important to them don't make much sense to you, the child will feel more secure. He or she will no longer need to throw a tantrum, hit or bite, or otherwise harm him- or herself to make the world change. By providing the child with ways of gaining some control over the timing of when things are done and some details of how they are done, and giving them appropriate ways to communicate their need to leave disturbing situations, parents, teachers, therapists, and other caregivers, you will gain the child's trust and in the long run have a more loving and effective relationship with the child.

Searching for Help

When I first met Ross and Beth nearly 40 years ago, very little was known about autism. They wondered what was wrong with Matt. Beth spent hours poring over her pregnancy with Matt, almost day by day, to see if she had taken medicine she shouldn't have or was exposed to an unknown toxin that might have caused Matt's condition. Matt's pediatrician referred Matt's parents to a child psychiatrist, who expressed special interest in his parents' sex life and asked probing questions about whether Matt had been planned or was the result of an unwanted pregnancy. They were angry and humiliated by his questions but most of all felt a growing sense of hopelessness. Matt was taken to a pediatric neurologist who said that Matt had mental retardation and there wasn't much that could be done for him. A university clinical psychologist was the first to mention autism to Matt's parents. The psychologist said there wasn't very much known about autism at that time, but that perhaps I could help them. That was shortly after Ross and Beth had reluctantly placed Matt in a state-operated institution for people with mental retardation. Matt lived in a newer building for children and adolescents called a Learning Center. At the time, Ross made a promise to himself and Beth: "We'll do whatever is necessary to bring Matt home from that place."

Matt's parents and I visited him in his residence, a one-story building on the outskirts of a small town, 2½ hours north of his home—an encounter that was terribly difficult for Matt's parents. Matt, who was 6 years old, had scratches and bruises on his hands and arms and a large bruise on his knee, the result, the staff said, of falling during an attempt to climb on top of furniture. Matt approached his parents without looking directly at them, flicking his fingers in front of his eyes, and moving his head strangely from side to side. He made no attempt to talk with them nor did he attempt to take their hands or otherwise interact with them. His mother put her arm around him, but Matt turned away, seemingly indifferent to his mother's gesture. The staff clearly liked Matt and tried to reassure his parents about how well he was doing. As she wiped tears from her eyes, Beth pleaded, "What can we do, my God, what can we do? There must be something better than this. Is there no way to help Matt?"

Matt appeared utterly frustrated about something, but what? His activity level was phenomenal. He never stopped moving. He climbed on, under, and over furniture. He picked up toys and puzzle pieces, skillfully twirling them like a juggler, often glancing in another direction as he did so. He appeared to want something, but what? One almost had the impression that he was trying to make sense out of an incomprehensible situation. He picked up puzzle pieces and sniffed them instead of looking at them. Instead of looking directly at objects, he tilted his head to one side and seemed to study them out of the corner of his eye. At other times staff members attempted to encourage Matt to participate in a game or activity, but Matt turned away abruptly with what appeared to be an angry expression on his face. At one point when a staff member was particularly persistent, Matt began slapping his own face, harder and harder until someone restrained him, saying "No, Matt, no hitting." Matt's mother left the room when she heard the first slap.

Early the following Friday morning, Matt's parents drove the 130 miles to pick him up from the state-operated residence and bring him home for the weekend. I met them at their house and noticed that Matt seemed calmer than he had been at the institution but difficult to engage. He showed no reaction when spoken to and walked aimlessly from room to room, stopping to stare out the window. I held out two of his favorite snacks, M&Ms and sugar-coated cereal. He studied them briefly and then snatched some cereal and ran away to consume it. He must have learned that habit in the institution in which food theft by peers was common. He returned within a few minutes and this time looked more carefully at the two snacks, different items in each hand. He selected one and immediately put it in his mouth. I said, "Good job, Matt." He showed no reaction to my comment. When Matt returned, I closed both of my hands concealing the snack items in each. This time he grabbed one hand and turned it over. As I opened my hand, he studied three Cracker Jacks and then grabbed the other hand, prying it open. It contained M&Ms. Matt grabbed the pieces of candy and placed them his mouth and walked away more slowly, making a humming sound. After a few minutes he returned and seemed to be looking for something—my hands. I held my hands behind my back. "Want a treat, Matt?" I asked. He tried to pull my hand from behind my back. I placed both hands in front of him, each enclosing a snack. "What do you want, Matt?" He touched my hand and I immediately turned it over revealing two M&Ms. He quickly picked them up, this time very deftly with one finger and his thumb. His fine motor dexterity was impressive. I continued holding out the other hand enclosing another treat. "What do you want, Matt?" I asked. He touched my hand, and I immediately turned it over so he could retrieve several Cracker Jacks. "Good job, Matt," I said. He glanced up at me briefly, expressionless, and walked away.

We took a short break and I suggested to Matt's mother that she cut out the logo from the front of the cereal box and the M&M logo from the candy container and paste them on two pieces of cardboard. I placed them on the table in front of Matt and held my hands above each card. The left hand containing two M&Ms was above the M&M card, and the right hand containing several pieces of cereal was above the logo of the cereal. "What do you want, Matt?" I asked. He touched my hand containing the cereal and I promptly opened it. He shoved it away seemingly in irritation and immediately grabbed the other hand. He retrieved the M&Ms and ate them. Matt had clear preferences. I pointed to both cards and said, "What do you want, Matt?" He looked puzzled at first and made an odd sound, similar to the rising inflection when asking a question. Then he touched the M&M card and I opened my hand containing the M&M. He was catching on to the idea that a picture could represent something he wanted. Matt understood what I meant when I asked, "What do you want?" and he used a simple gesture of pointing at the picture to say, "I want M&Ms." That was the beginning of Matt's communication.

Soon, instead of providing edible rewards, we showed Matt pictures of items or activities he might like and asked the same question, "What do you want, Matt?" When he pointed to the picture, he was tickled, given his favorite toy, or his favorite song was turned on so he could hear it, depending on the picture to which he pointed. After several hours practicing making requests by touching a picture of what he wanted, I left, suggesting to Matt's parents that they continue to work on using pictures to communicate with Matt for the rest of the weekend. On Sunday afternoon, Matt was returned to the institution for another week, which to Beth and Ross seemed an eternity.

I called the following Monday, and Beth reported that early Sunday morning, Matt had had a terrible tantrum and bit his father's hand. Matt had apparently wanted something but there was no picture that represented it. When they were unable to figure out what he wanted, he became increasingly angry—screaming, throwing things, and finally biting his father. "I don't know if we can do this, Travis," Matt's mother said. "Ross has a lot of trouble keeping his cool when Matt acts like that, and I can't blame him."

That Monday evening I had coffee with them at their home and we discussed the incident. "Just when I thought we were making progress, everything fell apart," Ross said. "It must be terribly frustrating," I replied. Actually, Matt was doing much better, despite the tantrum and outburst. It was just that he thought his parents ought to understand what he wanted, now that they were beginning to communicate with him. The problem was that there was no symbol that represented what he wanted. Over the coming weeks, we worked together to teach Matt new skills that were useful at home and improved his communication. By trial and error his parents developed an inventory of activities and items he most often wanted and created picture cards representing each. Later his picture menu included going swimming at the YMCA, going with his mother to the library, playing a game with his sister, and various community activities. Eventually, he used a communication board with pictures of the 8–10 items or activities he most often requested. Matt's frustration was clearly fading, and his interest in his family was increasing.

At times Matt brought his picture card menu to his mother with a disturbed expression on his face. He waved the card in agitation and made a very unhappy sound, half a cry and half an angry growl. That was our clue that what he wanted wasn't on the picture menu. That was when Matt's parents came up with the idea of asking him to point at what he wanted. He led them to the room in which the item he wanted was located (in the kitchen) and pointed with a sweep of his hand toward cupboards above the refrigerator. His mother climbed on a stool and opened the cabinet doors and Matt very animatedly pointed at the bag of popcorn seeds. Though it was only 9 A.M., his mother popped popcorn for Matt. As they sat together at the kitchen table, Beth rubbed Matt's arm as he wolfed down the popcorn. Matt had begun to smile at his parents, which was one of those special occasions Beth would always remember.

After 2 months of weekend visits, Matt came home for good. We had used each weekend visit to practice new skills and conduct refreshers on those previously acquired. Ross and Beth were becoming more confident that they could help Matt learn and manage his behavior problems. They had previously lost confidence in their ability to parent Matt. Over the next year Matt continued to make progress, but gains alternated with periods of turmoil and disappointment. Matt liked to help his mother prepare dinner, and she allowed him to stir melting butter into hot peas and pour milk or juice. Matt was fascinated by shining objects or surfaces and twirled his mother's keys and balanced a spoon on its handle and made it spin. His skill at spinning things without them falling over was uncanny. Beth had to watch Matt closely to prevent him from burning himself when she was cooking because he liked to lean over boiling water or a sizzling frying pan and watch the bubbles dance on the surface.

During one of my visits to their home, Beth asked me if it were true that children with autism don't bond with their mothers, as she had read in an article in a magazine. Before I could answer, Ross interjected, "Watch this," and Beth shouted upstairs, "Matt, it's time for bed." Matt came bounding down the stairs, two steps at a time, and plopped himself down beside his mother on the sofa. She opened a children's book and began reading. With her first words, he leaned his head against her shoulder and she put her arm around him. He flicked a puzzle piece in his hands, but listened attentively at the same time. The words in the book were more complicated than he could fully understand, but the act of reading with the rising and falling intonation of Beth's voice and the vibrations from her body as she read seemed comforting to Matt. It was a remarkably affectionate scene, reminiscent of the comfort a newborn infant receives from hearing his or her mother's heartbeat while being held at her breast. When Beth reached the last page and closed the book, Matt jumped down off the sofa as if a starter's gun had sounded and ran upstairs to his bedroom. "I guess that answers the question about whether children with autism bond with their mothers," I said. Beth beamed as she walked upstairs to tuck Matt in.

Matt grew up at home as a member of his family. He attended special education classes for students with severe disabilities, and when he left school, he worked in a sheltered workshop. His life at home was often uneventful, but periodically his behavior worsened. Whether due to physical illness or other changes in his life, Matt occasionally became aggressive. He was treated with psychotherapeutic medications and his parents received periodic consultation from a behavior therapist. When Matt reached his early 20s, he moved into a group home with several other young men with autism and group-home parents who helped guide the young men, assuring their safety and well-being. Matt regularly participated in community activities such as swimming at the YMCA, going on outings to the zoo, and fishing with his father. In some respects, Matt had a surprisingly typical life despite his severe disability.

Matt initially had no idea how to interact with people or how to communicate. He engaged in rigid, highly repetitive behavior, like rocking or flicking his fingers in front of his eyes. If anyone interrupted his repetitive movements he had a tantrum. Not all children with autism are as severely affected as Matt. Some children repeat words or phrases, enjoy being held by their parents, and are rigid in more subtle ways. Many have preferred daily routines and become upset if they are changed. Others begin talking at the same age as their brothers and sisters begin talking, but they have a limited understanding of how language functions even though they are able to produce words. Because of this collection of similar symptoms and signs, which vary greatly in intensity from child to child, autism is called a syndrome.

The primary focus of this book is on younger children with ASDs, those from 2 to 6 or 7 years of age, the period of greatest developmental malleability. Later sections of the book address mental health problems often seen in elementary- and middle-school-age children with ASDs, as well as autism seen in other neurodevelopmental disorders. The goal is to integrate what is known about the neurobiology of autism with behavioral, educational, and pharmacological interventions. This is not a cookbook. It does not prescribe specific techniques or procedures; rather, it examines principles underlying those procedures and practices.

2

Autism Spectrum Disorders

ORIGINS OF AUTISM DIAGNOSIS

Autism was first recognized as a distinct disability over two centuries ago by a physician in Aveyron, in southwestern France. Jean Itard was widely recognized in France for his work on deafness and being the first to describe Tourette's syndrome. Today he is most often remembered for providing the first detailed description of a youth with autism. But it would be over 140 years after Itard's publication of his *De l'éducation d'un homme sauvage, ou des premier développements physiques et moraux du jeune sauvage de l'Aveyron"* (Itard, 1801/ 1962) before explicit clinical diagnostic criteria were provided for these puzzling disabilities. In this chapter the origins of autism clinical investigation are discussed, followed by an examination of the modern diagnostic criteria.

IN THE BEGINNING: JEAN ITARD AND VICTOR

Alarm bells have been sounding about a recent "autism epidemic" featured in newspaper headlines and on the covers of national magazines, suggesting that autism is a new problem. In fact, Jean Itard was the first professional person to describe a case of autism in detail in 1801. Three French hunters were exploring a wooded area in southern France when they came upon a young boy. He was naked and dirty and his body was covered with scratches and scars. The boy ran from them, but he was caught when he stopped to climb a tree. The hunters brought him to a nearby village and turned him over to the care of a widow. As the story of his capture spread, local residents reported that a young naked boy had been seen in the woods on and off for several years. There were rumors that he howled like an animal, and as a result some called him the wolf child. It was presumed that he had lived alone for some time, and that he had survived by eating whatever he could scavenge or catch, including vegetables and fruit he pilfered from farmhouses near the forest (Itard, 1801/1962).

The boy escaped from the widow and spent the next winter roaming the woods alone. He was eventually recaptured and placed in custodial care. An official in the French government heard about him and suggested that he be taken to Paris where he could be studied as an example of the human mind in its primitive state (Itard, 1801/1962). Several prominent Parisian physicians who examined him concluded that he was not "wild" at all; their collective opinion was that the boy was mentally deficient and had been abandoned by his parents, which was not an uncommon occurrence at that time.

The boy was brought to Itard, who argued that the boy's apparent mental deficiency was due to a lack of human interaction. Moreover, he believed that this could be overcome with training and education. He brought the boy, whom he eventually named "Victor," to The National Institution for Deaf-Mutes, and devoted the next five years to an intensive educational program. This was the first example of what later came to be called an individualized education program (IEP; Gaynor, 1973; Humphrey, 1962; Pinchot, 1948). Itard focused on communication and socialization, teaching Victor to communicate using wooden or cardboard symbols to represent things or activities he wanted. Victor learned quickly as long as consistent methods were used. Although Victor never became sociable, he learned to tolerate social interactions with people who were familiar to him.

Itard's contributions were remarkable. He recognized that Victor was not like the "feeble-minded" children he had encountered; his deficits were much more specific. Itard recognized the three core features of what Leo Kanner would later call infantile autism: lack of understanding of social relationships; lack of understanding of and use of language; and fixed repetitive routines, which if interrupted lead to emotional outbursts. He was the first physician to claim that an enriched environment could compensate for developmental delays caused by heredity or previous deprivation. Up to that time, it was assumed that people with intellectual disabilities were uneducable, but Itard's work gave hope that effective intervention might be possible. Itard recognized that Victor's inability to make his wishes known created the most serious practical problems for the boy, and he taught the youth to use icons to communicate, similar to the modern Picture Exchange Communication System (PECS). For many years, iconic communication was called the Itardian Communication Method. Though Itard later concluded that his effort to cure Victor had failed, in reality, he made one of the most important contributions in the history of developmental disabilities.

IDENTIFICATION OF CLINICAL SYNDROMES: LEO KANNER AND HANS ASPERGER

Leo Kanner

Leo Kanner, who was born in Klekotow, Austria, in 1894, was the first modern clinically trained professional to identify the combination of characteristics that became known as early infantile autism. Kanner had received his medical training in Europe before immigrating to the United States in 1924 when he became an assistant physician in Yankton, South Dakota. In 1930, Kanner was recruited by the Johns Hopkins University School of Medicine where he established the nation's first child psychiatric service. In the late 1930s, Kanner saw eight boys and three girls who had previously been described as mentally defective or schizophrenic, but who had distinctively different features. He wrote about them in his remarkably astute paper *Autistic Disturbances of Affective Contact* in 1943, as revealed by several excerpts:

The children did not use {language} for the purpose of communication.... When sentences are finally formed, they are for a long time mostly parrot-like repetitions of heard word combinations. They are sometimes echoed immediately, but they are just as often "stored" by the child and uttered at a later date. One may, if one wishes, speak of delayed echolalia (Kanner, 1943, p. 243).

There is a limitation in the variety of his spontaneous activities. The child's behavior is governed by an anxiously obsessive desire for the maintenance of sameness that nobody but the child himself may disrupt on rare occasions. Changes of routine, of furniture arrangement, of a pattern, of the {form} in which every-day acts are carried out, can drive him to despair.... The dread of change and incompleteness seems to be a major factor in the explanation of the monotonous repetitiousness and the resulting limitation in the variety of spontaneous activity (Kanner, 1943, p. 245).

The children's relation to people is altogether different...upon entering the office {the children} immediately went after blocks, toys, or other objects, without paying the least attention to the persons present. It would be wrong to say that they were not aware of the presence of persons. But the people, so long as they left the child alone, figured in about the same manner as did the desk, the bookshelf, or the filing cabinet (Kanner, 1943, p. 246).

It is not easy to evaluate the fact that all of our patients have come of highly intelligent parents. This much is certain, that there is a great deal of obsessiveness in the family background...for the most part, the parents, grandparents, and collaterals are persons strongly preoccupied with abstractions of a scientific, literary, or artistic nature.... We must, then, assume that these children have come into the world with innate inability to form the usual, biologically provided affective contact with people, just as other chil-

dren come into the world with innate physical or intellectual handicaps
(Kanner, 1943, p. 250).

In his singularly perceptive article, Leo Kanner provided the first detailed clinical description of autism as a clinical syndrome, including the three cardinal features: 1) lack of interest in affective relationships with people, 2) lack of use of speech for the purposes of communication, and 3) fixed repetitive routines, which, if disrupted, cause tantrums. Moreover, he implied that some of these features appeared to be inherited from their parents. Kanner mistook the children's reluctance to enter into social interactions for a preference for "aloneness," borrowing from the term Bleuler had applied to schizophrenia (Kanner, 1943, p. 242). In all likelihood, social interactions that were imposed upon the children were just one more disruption of preferred routines, and represented communication demands that could not be met and were therefore assiduously avoided.

Hans Asperger

Hans Asperger was born in Vienna in 1906 and trained as a pediatrician with a special interest in children with disabilities. In 1944, he published a paper describing four boys he identified as having an unusual pattern of behavior and abilities that he called "autistic psychopathy" (i.e., autism = self; psychopathy = personality disease [Asperger, 1944]). Apparently, Kanner and Asperger did not know each other and happened upon the term *autism* independently. The behavior pattern Asperger identified included lack of empathy, little ability to form friendships, one-sided conversations, intense absorption in special interests, and clumsy movements. Asperger's paper was published in German and was not widely read in the English-speaking world until it was brought to light by English psychiatrist Lorna Wing in 1981 and subsequently translated by Uta Frith in 1991. Children with Asperger syndrome do not exhibit clinically significant general delay in language (e.g., single words used by age 2 years, communicative phrases used by age 3 years) or delay in cognitive development or in the development of age-appropriate self-help skills, adaptive behavior (other than in social interaction), and curiosity about the environment in childhood. Though children with Asperger syndrome may have an extensive vocabulary, it often sounds pedantic. They are exceedingly literal, having great difficult understanding figures of speech or metaphors. As a result, others may see them as humorless, or having a very juvenile sense of humor. They have difficulty understanding facial expressions and usually exhibit poor eye contact. People with Asperger syndrome often have difficulty grasping subtle aspects of social interactions, including posture, body language, and social context. Though Asperger believed his patients would grow up to lead relatively typical lives, most young adults with Asperger syndrome have considerable difficulty with interpersonal situations that demand a more sophisticated understanding of social relationships.

MODERN DIAGNOSTIC CRITERIA

Autism spectrum disorders are a family of closely related conditions that are considered syndromes. In this section, the current diagnostic criteria for the three major ASDs are discussed as well as the importance of accurate diagnosis for understanding a child's needs, planning, and intervention.

Autism Spectrum Disorders

Autism is not a single, unified condition. It is a family of closely related disabilities that overlap but are not identical. In medicine, the term *syndrome* refers to the association of several features, signs, symptoms, or characteristics that often occur together, so that the presence of one feature alerts the clinician to the presence of the others. The term *syndrome* derives from the Greek and means "run together," as the features do. A condition is called a syndrome when the reason the features occur together has not yet been discovered. AIDS, or acquired immune deficiency syndrome, was recognized before the human immunodeficiency virus (HIV) was first described. Severe acute respiratory syndrome (SARS) is a more recent example that was later found to be caused by the coronavirus.

Sometimes a familiar syndrome name continues to be used even after an underlying cause has been found. Many syndromes are named after the physicians who were credited with first reporting the association; these are *eponymous syndromes.* In other instances, disease features or presumed causes, or sometimes references to geography or history, can lend their names to syndromes (e.g., Jerusalem syndrome, Sick Building syndrome).

Diagnostic and Statistical Manual of Mental Disorders

The *Diagnostic and Statistical Manual of Mental Disorders (DSM),* published by the American Psychiatric Association (APA), is the handbook used most often in diagnosing mental disorders in the United States and internationally. A DSM diagnosis is required for reimbursement of health care services by Medicaid, state agencies, and private medical insurers. *The International Statistical Classification of Diseases and Related Health Problems (ICD)* is a commonly used alternative in other parts of the world. ICD diagnostic codes are also used in the United States for administrative and laboratory purposes. The first DSM was published in 1952, and the diagnostic criteria have been revised three times. The DSM-IV was published in 1994 and revised in 2000, making the DSM-IV-TR the current version. The fifth revision of DSM is scheduled to be published in 2012.

Within the DSM system, autistic disorder, Asperger syndrome, and pervasive developmental disorders not otherwise specified (PDD-NOS) all fall under the umbrella of pervasive developmental disorders. PDDs are distinguished from specific developmental disorders (SDD). The 10th revision of the ICD includes four categories of SDD: specific developmental disorders of speech and language, specific developmental disorders of scholastic skills, specific developmental disorders of motor function, and mixed specific developmental disorders. On the other hand, PDDs are a group of disorders characterized by broad delays in the development of multiple basic functions including socialization and communication combined with narrow repetitive interests and behavioral routines. PDDs are often apparent in infancy and nearly always have an onset prior to 3 years of age. A growing body of evidence indicates PDDs are neurodevelopmental disorders caused by errors in the developing nervous system.

Of the three major sub-categories of PDDs, *autistic disorder* is often considered to be the most severe because it involves disabilities in all three domains: communication, socialization, and fixed repetitive interests and routines. However, severity of autism manifestations depends on the intellectual ability of the affected person. People diagnosed with autistic disorder with above average intellectual ability may compensate for some of these limitations; however, they typically have significant problems in relationships with others and in effective communication. Their narrow and fixed interests may be partially controlled so as not to be as intrusive in daily life, but they are nonetheless limiting.

The criteria for diagnosis of autistic disorder according to the current version of DSM are as follows:

DSM-IV-TR Diagnostic Criteria for 299.00 Autistic Disorder[1]

Individuals with autistic disorder typically exhibit impairments in more domains of functioning and experience more limitations than those with Asperger's Disorder and PDD-NOS. Even individuals with a high-functioning autistic disorder exhibit more language and social impairments than children and youth with other PDDs.

A. A total of six (or more) items from 1, 2, and 3, with at least two from 1, and one each from 2 and 3.

   1. Qualitative impairment in social interaction, as manifested by at least two of the following:

      • Marked impairment in the use of multiple nonverbal behaviors such as eye-to-eye gaze, facial expression, body postures, and gestures to regulate social interaction

---

[1]DSM-IV-TR diagnostic criteria on pages 20–23. American Psychiatric Association. (2000). *Diagnostic and statistical manual of mental disorders: DSM-IV-TR* (4th ed., text revision). Washington, DC: Author; used by permission.

- Failure to develop peer relationships appropriate to developmental level

- Lack of spontaneous seeking to share enjoyment, interests, or achievements with other people (e.g., lack of showing, bringing, or pointing out objects of interest)

- Lack of social or emotional reciprocity

2. Qualitative impairments in communication as manifested by at least one of the following:

- Delay in, or total lack of, the development of spoken language (not accompanied by an attempt to compensate through alternative modes of communication such as gesture or mime)

- In individuals with adequate speech, marked impairment in the ability to initiate or sustain a conversation with others

- Stereotyped and repetitive use of language or idiosyncratic language

- Lack of varied, spontaneous make-believe play or social imitative play appropriate to developmental level

3. Restricted repetitive and stereotyped patterns of behavior, interests, and activities, as manifested by at least one of the following:

- Encompassing preoccupation with one or more stereotyped and restricted patterns of interest that is abnormal either in intensity or focus

- Apparently inflexible adherence to specific, nonfunctional routines or rituals

- Stereotyped and repetitive motor mannerisms (e.g., hand or finger flapping, twisting, or complex whole-body movements)

- Persistent preoccupation with parts of objects

B. Delays or abnormal functioning in at least one of the following areas, with onset prior to age 3 years:

1. Social interaction

2. Language as used in social communication

3. Symbolic or imaginative play

C. The disturbance is not better accounted for by Rett's disorder or childhood disintegrative disorder.

DSM-IV-TR Diagnostic Criteria for 299.80 Asperger's Disorder

Many people with Asperger's disorder (or syndrome) are integrated into the broader community despite social and language difficulties and restricted interests. Often their success depends on finding a niche that tolerates, or sometimes benefits from, their single-minded and often didactic focused interests. The primary feature that distinguishes people with Asperger's disorder from those with autistic disorder or PDD-NOS is their seemingly typical language development in childhood and academic skills similar to typical peers. Although the onset of language tends to occur at about the same age as that for their siblings and peers, it often has a more formal, almost pedagogic quality and tends to be more literal. They often understand the literal meaning of most words but not the words' social implications. Family members and associates often report being frustrated with people with Asperger's disorder because of their unwillingness or inability to engage in the give and take of a reciprocal conversation, instead repeatedly returning to a topic that only they find captivating.

A. Qualitative impairment in social interaction, as manifested by at least two of the following:

1. Marked impairment in the use of multiple nonverbal behaviors such as eye-to-eye gaze, facial expression, body posture, and gestures to regulate social interaction

2. Failure to develop peer relationships appropriate to developmental level

3. Lack of spontaneous seeking to share enjoyment, interests, or achievements with other people (e.g., lack of showing, bringing, or pointing out objects of interest to others)

4. Lack of social or emotional reciprocity

B. Restricted repetitive and stereotyped patterns of behavior, interests, and activities, as manifested by at least one of the following:

1. Encompassing preoccupation with one or more stereotyped and restricted patterns of interest that is abnormal either in intensity or focus

2. Apparently inflexible adherence to specific, nonfunctional routines or rituals

3. Stereotyped and repetitive motor mannerisms (e.g., hand or finger flapping, twisting, or complex whole-body movements)

4. Persistent preoccupation with parts of objects

C. The disturbance causes clinically significant impairment in social, occupational, or other important areas of functioning.

D. There is no clinically significant general delay in language (e.g., single words used by age 2 years, communicative phrases used by age 3 years).

E. There is no clinically significant delay in cognitive development or in the development of age-appropriate self-help skills, adaptive behavior (other than in social interaction), and curiosity about the environment in childhood.

F. Criteria are not met for another specific pervasive developmental disorder or schizophrenia.

DSM-IV-TR *Diagnostic Criteria for 299.80 Pervasive Developmental Disorder, Not Otherwise Specified*

Pervasive developmental disorder not otherwise specified (PDD-NOS) refers to a severe and pervasive impairment in the development of reciprocal social interaction or verbal and nonverbal communication skills, or when stereotyped behavior, interests, and activities are present. However, the criteria are not met for a specific PDD, schizophrenia, schizotypal personality disorder, or avoidant personality disorder. For example, this category includes "atypical autism"—presentations that do not meet the criteria for autistic disorder because of late age of onset, atypical symptomatology, or subthreshold symptomatology, or all of these. When a PDD diagnosis is incorrectly made (e.g., a child actually has an anxiety disorder or obsessive compulsive disorder [OCD], and has a significant language disability, but *not* an ASD), the most common misdiagnosis is PDD-NOS.

WHY DOES DIAGNOSIS MATTER?

It is important that a child who is suspected of having an ASD is evaluated by one or more professionals with substantial experience with autism, ideally a pediatrician or child psychiatrist, and a licensed psychologist who specializes in autism. There are important implications of an autism spectrum diagnosis. First, parents will be able to better understand their child, their unusual behavior, and not misinterpret noncompliance and behavior outbursts. Second, it provides a basis for developing an intervention strategy, beginning with intensive early intervention (if the child is 5 years old or younger), including speech/communication therapy. An ASD diagnosis is also helpful in establishing expectations for a child's progress. It is not unusual for a child with an ASD to show limited progress for several months and then suddenly begin improving rapidly. Moreover, it is useful to school personnel in better understanding the student and in developing an IEP for the child. Children with high-functioning autism or Asperger syndrome are often confusing to general education teachers because they may display precocious spoken vocabularies and an ability to read words beyond their age level, but they may also have limited comprehension. Finally, in older children with more challenging behavior, a diagnosis is helpful in considering the best combination of functional behavioral intervention and medication treatment, if necessary. A practical consideration is that, in most states, reimbursement for services outside of school requires a medical diagnosis of an ASD by a qualified physician or psychologist who is certified to make such diagnoses.

PROBLEMS WITH DIAGNOSIS

Many years ago I enrolled in an evening class devoted to designing and constructing leaded, stained-glass windows. I became utterly entranced with the wonderfully textured and colored glass and different types of lead, copper, and other materials and the processes involved in creating stained-glass windows. I couldn't stop thinking about and seeing stained-glass windows at every turn. Over the next several years, I spent nearly every Saturday working on windows of my own design, having been taken under the wing of professional artists at a commercial stained-glass studio. I began noticing stained-glass windows in buildings I'd driven past many times but never noticed before. I became aware of bad reproductions of Tiffany and Frank Lloyd Wright windows, and noticed shoddy solder-joints and poorly selected glass for specific designs. I attended conferences, visited studios of famous stained glass artists, and saw an endless world of possibilities for architectural art glass. I had been transformed by my experience with leaded and copper foiled glass panels.

People who have had little previous experience with children with autism and who then delve into their world often undergo a similar transformation. One suddenly becomes aware of behavioral nuances one hadn't previously noticed, such as the odd way some children with autism cock their heads to one side and peer at objects out of the corner of their eye. At first many newcomers to the field begin seeing autism signs right and left whenever a child exhibits behavior that appears unusual, such as flapping their hands when they are excited or covering their ears when a fire truck drives by. If a child cries when he or she is asked to put away toys, or seems to enjoy spending time alone in his or her room, we begin wondering about autism. We think: Maybe he has an intolerance for changes in routine or maybe she prefers social "aloneness"—classic autism signs. Increased awareness of autism and its characteristics, combined with greater scrutiny of subtle features of young children's behavior, has led some people to see autism where another problem may exist, or, in some cases, where there may just be variations on typical development.

It is likely that some of the increase in autism diagnoses stems from selective attention to features in a child's behaviors that conform to a preexisting hunch that a child has autism. The more experience one has with children with autism who differ widely in their presentation, including intellectual level and degree of disability in the three core domains, the greater care one takes in arriving at a diagnosis. One also comes to realize that it is as important to learn to rule out other conditions that may resemble autism as it is to conclude that a child truly meets the diagnostic criteria for one of the ASDs.

Because ASD is not a single condition, there is great variability in presentation. The best current evidence indicates that ASDs exist on a continuum, with degrees of disability depending on the specific brain dysfunction each child experiences. Autistic disorder, Asperger syndrome, and PDD-NOS tend to recur within the same family, which should not occur if they are qualitatively different conditions. A growing body of research indicates that there are problems in four to five brain areas that make it difficult for people with ASDs to process specific kinds of information. Depending on which areas are affected most, a child may have language that appears typical, but may lack empathy and an ability to socially reciprocate. Other children may be affectionate but have difficulty verbally expressing themselves. This variability often puzzles people who have limited experience working with children and youth with autism and who may expect every individual with an ASD to resemble Dustin Hoffman in *Rain Man*. An autism spectrum diagnosis cannot predict with accuracy how a given individual will respond to a specific treatment, but it cannot predict which treatments are likely to be the most successful. After treatment or educational intervention has been underway for several months, experienced professionals can often provide parents with an estimate of the rate of progress they can expect.

CONDITIONS THAT RESEMBLE AUTISM SPECTRUM DISORDERS

Many children are referred for evaluation in autism clinics because someone believes they exhibit autism symptoms, but actually do not have an autism spectrum disorder. A pediatrician, teacher, friend, or relative of the child's parents may notice that the child seems unusually shy, seldom interacting with peers. Other children may have poor language skills, may periodically line up toys in a row, or twirl them, or may rock or flap their hands when they are excited. While these can be signs of autism, there is more to an ASD diagnosis. Several conditions that can be mistaken for an ASD are discussed below.

Global Developmental Delay

Some children suffer damage to their developing nervous system that affects many brain structures similarly. Many of the commonly recognized genetic syndromes fall into this category (e.g., Down syndrome, phenylketonuria [PKU]). Other developmental delays are caused by toxin exposure during pregnancy (e.g., fetal alcohol syndrome, infections such as cytomegalovirus). Typically, people with global developmental delays have similar degrees of disabilities in most psychological domains and in their day-to-day adaptive skills. They seldom display significant deficits or impairments in the three core autism features: communication, socialization, and fixed repetitive interests and routines. Some people with global developmental delays may also meet the diagnostic criteria for autism because of damage to some of the same brain structures that are dysfunctional in autism, but that is not typical.

Attention-Deficit/Hyperactivity Disorder

Approximately one in 20 children have a developmental disability involving impairments in attention (only), impairments in activity level (only), or both. To be diagnosed as having attention-deficit/hyperactivity disorder (ADHD), a child must exhibit at least 8 of the following 14 characteristics for a duration of at least 6 months with onset before 7 years of age:

1. Often fidgets with hands or feet or squirms in seat

2. Has difficulty remaining seated, be easily distracted, have difficulty following through on instructions, talk excessively, or when required to do so

3. Is easily distracted by extraneous stimuli

4. Has difficulty awaiting turns in games or group situations

5. Often blurts out answers to questions before they have been completed

6. Has difficulty following through on instructions from others (not due to oppositional behavior or failure of comprehension)

7. Has difficulty sustaining attention in tasks or play activities

8. Often shifts from one uncompleted activity to another

9. Has difficulty playing quietly

10. Often talks excessively

11. Often interrupts or intrudes on others, e.g., butts into other children's games

12. Often does not seem to listen to what is being said to him or her

13. Often loses things necessary for tasks or activities at school or at home (e.g., toys, pencils, books)

14. Often engages in physically dangerous activities without considering possible consequences

Accordingly, there are three types of ADHD: hyperactive, inattentive, and both hyperactive and inattentive. Children with ADHD of the combined type usually have the greatest difficulties.

Children with ADHD seldom lack the ability to use language appropriately. They usually understand emotions and empathize with others, and it is unusual for them to exhibit extreme intolerance for unexpected changes in routines. But because many children with ASDs are more active than their same-age peers and often have difficulty paying attention to tasks that aren't interesting to them, parents and some professionals may suspect that their child has ADHD. Technically, according to the DSM-IV, a diagnosis of ASD and ADHD should not be assigned to the same child. However, as a practical matter, some children with ASDs appear to have the signs and symptoms of ADHD, and they respond favorably to the same medications as children with ADHD who do not have an autism diagnosis.

Specific Language Impairment

Specific language impairments (SLIs) are communication disorders that affect more than 1 million students in the public schools. SLPs may use other names to refer to SLIs (e.g., developmental language disorder, language delay, developmental dysphasia). Children with SLI may not produce any words until they are nearly 2 years old. At age 3, they may talk but they can't be understood. As they grow, they will struggle to learn new words, make conversation, and sound coherent. A child with SLI scores within the typical range for nonverbal intelligence, and hearing loss is not present. Emerging motor skills, socioemotional development, and the child's neurological profile are all typical. A child with a speech disorder makes errors in pronouncing words or may stutter. Studies have found that most children with SLI do not have a speech disorder (Leonard, 1998; Rice, 2002). Rather, SLI is a *language disorder.* This means that the child has difficulty understanding and using words in sentences. Both receptive and expressive skills are typically affected. Children with SLIs who also have significant anxiety problems may be misdiagnosed with PDD-NOS. A thorough evaluation by a licensed SLP is an essential step in differential diagnosis.

Landau-Kleffner Syndrome

Landau-Kleffner Syndrome (LKS) is a rare childhood neurological disorder characterized by the sudden or gradual development of aphasia (the inability to understand or express language) and an atypical electroencephalogram (EEG). LKS affects the parts of the brain that control comprehension and speech. The disorder usually occurs in children between the ages of 5 and 7 years. Usually, children with LKS develop typically but then lose their language skills for no apparent reason. Although many of the affected individuals have seizures, some do not. The disorder is difficult to diagnose and may be misdiagnosed as autism, PDD-NOS, hearing impairment, learning disability, auditory/verbal processing disorder, ADHD, mental retardation, childhood schizophrenia, or emotional/behavioral problems. Treatment for LKS usually consists of medications (e.g., anticonvulsants, corticosteroids) and speech therapy, which should be started early.

Obsessive-Compulsive Disorder

Obsessive-compulsive disorder (OCD) is an anxiety disorder in which a child has obsessive (repetitive, distressing, intrusive) thoughts and related compulsions (tasks or rituals) that attempt to reduce the obsessions. The typical individual with OCD performs tasks (or compulsions) to seek relief from obsessions. To other people, these tasks may appear odd and unnecessary, and at times even humorous, as with the television character Adrian Monk. As a police detective, Monk encounters disturbingly disorderly and unpredictable situations. As a result, he is plagued by phobias and almost everything causes him angst: germs, heights, and so forth. However, rituals are no laughing matter to the person suffering from OCD. A younger child with OCD may have persistent thoughts that harm will occur to himself or a family member (e.g., an intruder entering an unlocked door or window). The child may compulsively check all the doors and windows of his home after his parents are asleep in an attempt to relieve anxiety. The child may then fear that he may have accidentally unlocked a door or window while last checking and locking, and then must compulsively check over and over again. For the child with OCD, such tasks can feel critically important, and must be performed in particular ways to ward off dire consequences and to stop stress from building up. Children with OCD do not have basic communication or social reciprocity difficulties. Indeed, they are often much attuned to others' emotions. Although they engage in specific, ritualistic routines, they rarely exhibit the types of repetitive behavior (e.g., hand flapping, finger flicking) that are common in children with ASDs. Children with OCD are often treated with the same types of medications as adults with the disorder, often successfully.

AUTISM PREVALENCE

Studies conducted by the U.S. Centers for Disease Control and Prevention, using the current criteria for diagnosing autism and ASDs such as Asperger syndrome and PDD-NOS, found prevalence rates for ASDs between 2 and 6 per 1,000 individuals. Therefore, it can be surmised that between 1 in 500 (2/1,000) to 1 in 166 children (6/1,000) have an ASD. Before 1990, the prevalence was estimated at 4–6 per 10,000 (or 1 per 2,000). The reasons for the increase in prevalence are controversial. In 1994, ASDs were the 10th most common disability in children ages 6–21 served by special education. Between 1994 and 2003, the number of children being classified as having an ASD had increased six-fold from 22,664 to 141,022. Although it is clear that more children are getting special education services for autism than ever before, it is important to remember that this classification was only added in the early 1990s and the growth of children classified may be due in part to the addition of this as a special education category (Centers for Disease Control and Prevention, 2006; Rutter, 2005).

The introduction of broadened ASD diagnostic criteria in 1994 when the 4th revision of the DSM was published, the introduction of the autism diagnostic inventory (a research assessment) in 1997, and the introduction of ADOS in 1999 contributed to the increase in diagnosis of ASDs. These new criteria were influential in two respects. First, they spelled out in greater detail the diagnostic features of Asperger syndrome and PDD-NOS, milder forms of ASD that may have received a different diagnosis previously. Second, many more professionals were trained to use these diagnostic tools, making it more likely that a child who might have an ASD would be seen by a professional trained to make such a diagnosis.

Autism and Vaccines

An article was published in the prestigious English medical journal *Lancet* in March 1998 proposing a link between measles-mumps-rubella (MMR) vaccination and autism. The appearance of that article was followed by a series of letters and responses from researchers and clinicians that appeared in *Lancet* and the *British Medical Journal* presenting evidence suggesting there was no such connection (Horton, 2004; Kaye et al., 2001; Taylor et al., 1999). The controversy, sparked by what appeared to be a disagreement among professionals, created widespread public alarm, especially among parents in the autism advocacy community. An investigation of the chief author of the initial *Lancet* article was launched when all of his co-authors wrote a retraction and the journal expunged the discredited paper. The fact that a vaccination can produce an exaggerated immune response in some people, and in the case of live vaccines can lead to meningitis or encephalitis, has been known for many years. MMR vaccination specifically can produce joint and limb complaints, convulsions with high fever, and mumps (when the Urabe strain-containing MMR vaccine is used) in a small percent of children receiving the vaccine (see Demichelli et al., 2005). Speculation about the possible connection between MMR vaccine and autism was kindled by the fact that approximately 20%–30% of children develop regressive autism. These children appear to be developing typically until around 2 years of age when they lose skills and ultimately show signs and symptoms of an ASD. Because regression begins around the age the child usually receives the series of MMR shots, it has been speculated that the vaccines must have caused the regression, suggesting that the residual measles virus persists after the vaccination and causes autism. Some parent organizations and professionals (e.g., Greier &

Greier, 2003a) have suggested that the presence of Thimerosal as a preservative in vaccines may be the culprit.

Several researchers have proposed such a connection, although there is limited evidence to support the connection. Greier and Greier (2004) have argued that there is biological plausibility and epidemiological evidence showing a relationship between increasing doses of mercury from Thimerosal-containing vaccines and neurodevelopmental disorders and between measles-containing vaccines and serious neurological disorders. They recommend that Thimerosal be removed from all vaccines and additional research be undertaken to produce an MMR vaccine with an improved safety profile. Epidemiologists evaluating the Greier and Greier (2003a; 2003b) studies for the Institute of Medicine's Immunization Safety Review Committee were critical of their conclusions, arguing that they were seriously flawed methodologically (Immunization Safety Review Committee, 2004).

Compelling evidence of a connection between MMR vaccines with or without Thimerosal and autism remains to be presented. Klein and Diehl (2003) conducted a literature search using the National Institutes of Health MEDLINE database (1966–November 2003), with the key terms *measles, mumps, rubella,* and *autism.* They found 10 articles that specifically evaluated the possible relationship between the MMR vaccine and autism. Based upon the evidence presented in those studies, Klein and Diehl concluded that it appears that there is no relationship between MMR vaccination and the development of autism.

Subsequent to 2003, several other noteworthy studies have revealed similar findings. Afzal and colleagues (2006) used highly sensitive assays to determine whether the measles virus was present in white blood cells of children diagnosed with regressive autism, as has been suggested. They failed to find any evidence of persistence of the measles virus in children with ASDs in any of several different assays they used. Honda, Shimizu, and Rutter (2005) studied incidence of ASD diagnoses in Yokohama, Japan, before and after MMR vaccine administration was discontinued. They found that cumulative incidence of ASD up to age 7 increased significantly in the birth cohorts regardless of whether MMR vaccination was done. They concluded that MMR vaccination cannot explain the rise over time in the incidence of ASD, and that withdrawal of MMR in countries where it is still being used cannot be expected to lead to a reduction in the incidence of ASD. Smeeth and colleagues (2004) used the U.K. General Practice Research Database to study children born in 1973 or later who had first recorded diagnosis of PDD between 1987 and 2001. Controls were matched on age, sex, and general practice. They found no differences in MMR vaccination rates among those who were later diagnosed with autism as compared with controls. Having been vaccinated did not increase their risk of developing autism. Their findings suggest that MMR vaccination was not associated with an increased risk of PDDs.

The possibility of a link between Thimerosal and autism continues to persist among some parent advocates. Parker and colleagues (2005) reviewed evidence from all epidemiological studies through 2004. Of particular interest were studies in which Thimerosal had been used in a country and then was discontinued. They found twelve publications that met the selection criteria, although they were concerned because the design and quality of several of the studies showed significant problems. The two epidemiological studies that supported an association were of poor quality and could not be interpreted (e.g., Greier and Greier studies). Parker et al. concluded that evidence from available studies did not demonstrate a link between Thimerosal-containing vaccines and ASD.

Although there may be no final word on the topic that will fully satisfy some members of the public, perhaps the most credible evaluation of available evidence was conducted by the Institute of Medicine (IOM) of the National Academy of Sciences in 2004. In the eighth and final report of the Immunization Safety Review Committee, the IOM examined the hypothesis that vaccines, specifically the MMR vaccine and Thimerosal-containing vaccines, are causally associated with autism. The committee reviewed the published and unpublished epidemiological studies regarding causality and studies of potential biological mechanisms by which these immunizations might cause autism. The committee concluded that the body of epidemiological evidence does not support a causal relationship between the MMR vaccine or between Thimerosal-containing vaccines and autism.

Michael Rutter, one of the world's most respected authorities on autism, concluded after thoroughly reviewing the evidence that the true incidence of ASDs is likely to be within the range of 30–60 cases per 10,000, a ten-fold increase over the original estimate 20 years ago of 4 per 10,000 (Rutter, 2005). He suggested that the increase is largely a consequence of improved identification of cases and broadening of the diagnostic concept. Moreover, Rutter concluded that there is no credible support for the hypothesis for a role of either MMR or Thimerosal in causation. He suggested that a risk of autism due to some as yet to be identified environmental factor cannot be ruled out.

3

Early Intervention
Preventing and Overcoming Acquired Brain Dysfunction in Autism

Some policy makers seem to view early intervention for children with disabilities as a way of giving mothers a break from parenting a difficult child. Although that may be a side benefit, early behavioral intervention for children with autism spectrum disorders (ASDs) is a means of promoting brain development and preventing loss of brain function that would otherwise occur. In this chapter, we will discuss early intervention as a means of preventing and overcoming brain dysfunction that is common in ASDs, early intervention approaches and evidence for their efficacy, and finally choosing an early intervention program for a child.

BRAIN DYSFUNCTION IN AUTISM SPECTRUM DISORDERS

Brain dysfunction in autism involves abnormalities in interpreting facial expressions and organizing sequences and planning (executive function) and compulsivity and problems in language areas.

Face Processing in Autism Spectrum Disorders

A Yiddish proverb states that the eyes are the mirrors of the soul. Parents of children with autism often express concern because their child seldom looks at them. Even when the child looks in an adult's direction, there is minimal eye contact and little is revealed about what he or she is feeling or thinking. When looking at people's faces, we first look at their eyes, for that is where we believe we will discover important information about them—whether they are anxious or happy, whether we should trust them, and so forth. We assess the depth of a person's affection for us by looking into his or her eyes. In *The Merchant of Venice,* Bassanio says, "In Belmont is a lady richly left/ And she is fair, and fairer than that word/ Of wondrous virtues. Sometimes from her eyes/ I did receive fair speechless messages." After looking into another's eyes, even if fleetingly, we look at their mouth, but we usually return to their eyes. Throughout this process several parts of our brain are busily at work, first registering the image (in the occipital visual cortex), and then interpreting what is being seen (see Figure 3.1):

1. The fusiform face area on the underside of the brain determines whether we recognize the person.

2. The almond-shaped amygdala on the inside of the temporal lobe tells us what emotion the person is displaying.

3. The orbitofrontal cortex on the underside of the brain's frontal lobe above a person's eyes places their emotional expression into context—what does it mean, and what is likely to happen next?

Looking at faces is one of the most basic social processes, so much so that even very young infants are interested in looking at people's eyes. From birth, human infants prefer to look at faces that engage them in mutual gaze, with enhanced neural processing of direct gaze. By contrast, in a study of infants who were siblings of a child who had been diagnosed with autism, Zwaigenbaum et al. (2005) found that by 12 months of age, siblings exhibited lack of eye contact or very atypical eye contact. This early sensitivity to mutual gaze among typical newborns appears to be a major foundation for the later development of social relatedness, which seems to be lacking among children who will later be diagnosed with an ASD. In other words, in ASDs there is a significant deficit on the ground floor of social development.

When they studied older children with ASDs, Klin et al. (2002) and Schultz et al. (2000) found that they paid a disproportionate amount of attention to the mouth versus the eyes, as compared with matched controls. When presented with facial expressions of various degrees of fear, youth with high-functioning ASDs showed little activation in the amygdala or orbitofrontal cortex, as compared with typical controls whose amygdala's were highly responsive to images of fearful faces (Ashwin et al., 2006). If the only visual information comes from images of eyes (without the remainder of facial expression), people with ASDs show virtually no activation of the amygdala, orbitofrontal cortex, or cingulate, which are very active in matched controls (Baron-Cohen et al., 1999).

The brain's fusiform face area has also been called the area of visual expertise. The fusiform gyrus becomes most active when visual stimuli, which are important to us and with which we have a great deal of experience, are presented (e.g., when leaves are shown to a forestry expert, or images of birds are

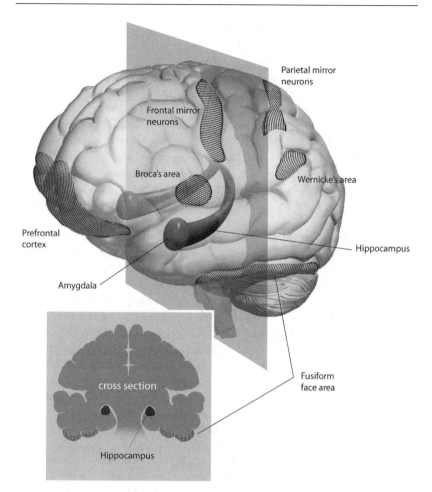

Figure 3.1.   Schematic diagram of the human brain from the left side. The main structures that have been shown to be dysfunctional in brain imaging and anatomical studies are indicated in darker gray. The lower left inset shows a cross section indicating the location of the hippocampus and fusiform face area within the temporal lobe. (*Source:* Scott Andre, Minneapolis, Minnesota; used by permission.)

presented to an ornithologist). Since faces are important to people and we have a great deal of experience looking at them, one would expect the fusiform gyrus to become highly active when looking at someone's face. But since a child with autism seldom looks at faces, their fusiform gyrus isn't experienced in interpreting facial information, and it is inactive when presented with a person's face. Individuals with ASDs appear to obtain very little useful information from looking at faces, so it shouldn't be surprising that they seldom look directly at us when we talk to them.

Executive Function and Compulsivity
in Autism Spectrum Disorders

Children with ASDs are typically preoccupied with concerns about what is going to happen next and when specific future events are going to occur. Brain structures involved in planning, sequencing ideas, and related executive functions are dysfunctional among individuals with ASDs. Among typical children, areas of the frontal lobe are usually active when given tasks to perform that require thinking through several steps and anticipating what will occur next in a sequence. While problems with executive function are not unique to individuals with ASDs, the dysfunction is usually more pronounced, and, combined with other limitations, creates significant problems for them.

People with obsessive-compulsive disorder (OCD) who do not have an ASD exhibit differences in activity of the basal ganglia, the structures at the base of the brain involved in Parkinson's disease. Whiteside, Port, and Abramowitz (2004) found consistent impairments in the head of the caudate nucleus, within the basal ganglia, among individuals with OCD. Van den Heuvel et al. (2005) found impaired prefrontal-striatal responsiveness during an activity that required planning in OCD patients, again implicating the basal ganglia in OCD symptoms. Studying individuals with ASDs, Hollander and colleagues (2005) found that the right caudate nucleus and putamen (components of the basal ganglia) volume were increased, and the increased size was correlated with repetitive behaviors. Specialized channels that regulate the concentration of two neurochemical transmitters (dopamine and serotonin) inside and outside nerve cells in the *corpus striatum* (part of the basal ganglia) appear to be dysfunctional. Collectively, evidence points to a brain chemical impairment within the basal ganglia of individuals with autism, as well as connectivity among these structures and the frontal cortex, which is involved in planning. These impairments among individuals with ASDs appear to be shared with psychiatric patients with OCD. The basal ganglia defect appears to play a major role in all of the "oughts" exhibited by people with autism. The fixed, repetitive routines, difficulty tolerating changes, and obsessive recurring thoughts and verbalizations seen in ASDs are very likely related to these OCD-like brain impairments in the basal ganglia.

Language Processing and Brain Function
in Autism Spectrum Disorders

Several reports have revealed anatomical and functional differences in brain areas important to language in ASDs. There is growing evidence that early language and social development are dependent on typical functioning of the "mirror neuron" system in the forebrain. This is a group of cells in the frontal and parietal motor cortex that are necessary for understanding people's gestures. In other primates (e.g., monkeys) these visuomotor neurons discharge both when a monkey does a particular action and when it observes another individual (monkey or human) doing a similar action (Gizzolati & Craighero, 2004). Evidence from human-brain imaging studies indicates that the human mirror neuron system functions similarly. There is also strong evidence that children's language development typically depends on a scaffolding relationship with gesture (e.g., pointing, beckoning; Bates & Dick, 2002). Children with ASDs are generally unable to respond to others' gestures or, without explicit training, to use gestures communicatively. Several studies suggest that there are deficiencies in responsiveness of mirror neurons in high-functioning individuals with ASDs when observing other people's movements, as compared with age and IQ-score-matched comparison individuals (Fecteau, Lepage, & Theoret, 2006; Oberman et al., 2005).

Herbert and colleagues (2002) found that boys with ASDs had significant asymmetry reversal in the size of frontal language-related cortex: 27% larger on the right in ASDs and 17% larger on the left in controls. DeFosse et al. (2004) studied brain volumes using MRI in boys with specific language impairments (SLIs) alone and boys with ASDs with and without language impairment. They found language-impaired boys with autism and SLI both had significant reversal of asymmetry in frontal language-related cortex: larger on the right side in both groups of language-impaired boys and larger on the left in both unimpaired language groups. In another report, Just, Cherkassky et al. (2004) compared brain activation of a group of participants with high-functioning autism and a verbal IQ-score-matched control group, using functional brain imaging during sentence comprehension. The autism group reliably produced more activation than the control group in Wernicke's area and less activation than the control group in Broca's area. Furthermore, the degree of synchronization of the activation among the language cortical areas was lower for the participants with ASD than the control participants. This suggests a lower degree of information integration and synchronization across the language cortical network.

Brain Dysfunction and Features of Autism Spectrum Disorders

Collectively, the available evidence suggests that the symptoms of ASDs can be traced to dysfunctions in specific brain areas, primarily the amygdala, prefrontal and parietal motor areas (mirror neurons), orbitofrontal cortex, fusiform face area, cingulate, basal ganglia, and the two primary speech areas. It appears that there may be primary neurodevelopmental dysfunctions in ASDs that are genetically programmed before birth. Other brain areas appear to become dysfunctional secondary to failure in the primary areas. The fact that very young children (months old) who are later diagnosed with an ASD show little interest in faces, and eyes in particular, suggests a fundamental amygdala defect. Failure of the child to orient toward and engage in early deictic communication via facial expression and orientation is thought to lead to acquired fusiform gyral dysfunction—failure in the brain's visual expertise area. Similarly, developmental dysfunction of the mirror neuron system appears to lead to delayed or absent deictic gesture and, perhaps indirectly, spoken language. The fact that very young children (under 1 year of age) with ASDs exhibit very limited or lack of gesture suggests that this defect may be genetically programmed before birth and is not experience-dependent. The consequence would be significant impairment in language and other forms of communication. Given that these structures tend to be dysfunctional among individuals with ASDs, what can be done to overcome these disadvantages?

DEVELOPMENTAL NEUROPLASTICITY

Since the 1970s, a growing body of evidence has indicated that early experience affects brain development. Early laboratory studies with animals showed that when young rats were reared in an "enriched" environment, with many opportunities to engage in a wide array of activities with a panoply of sensory input, brain cortical volumes were larger compared with animals reared in standard metal cages in relatively impoverished environments (Rosenzweig, Bennett, & Diamond, 1972). In 1987, Huttenlocher and de Courten published a series of landmark studies that demonstrated very rapid growth of new connections in brains of young children between 6 and 18 months of age, after which the formation of new connections declined. By 4–5 years of age, the rate of forming new connections, called synaptogenesis, had fallen by 50%–60% from its peak around 10–12 months of age. It is during this same period that typical infants spend a great deal of time looking at faces, eyes in particular, and begin developing language.

The developing brain operates on the "use it or lose it" principle. All young children have far more brain cells than they will need in later life. Cells that become synaptically connected are spared and those that are not connected are lost through a process called *cell pruning*. Bauman and Kemper (1985, 1994, 2005) studied brain tissue from young children with ASDs who had died from a cause unrelated to their brains. They discovered that in the brain areas we now know are usually dysfunctional in children with ASDs, there were far too many tightly packed immature brain cells, but very few synapses (e.g., hippocampus, amygdala, entorhinal cortex). In similar studies with brain tissue from young adults with autism, there were fewer neurons in those same structures. It appears that the lack of sufficient synaptic connectivity in those structures early in life may have led to excessive cell pruning (i.e., loss of too many neurons). It is also possible that the typical process of neuronal cell loss (i.e., pruning) that naturally occurs in all brain development could have malfunctioned. It follows that prevention of neuronal loss requires either finding a way to promote synapse formation in those structures early in life, ideally corresponding to the period of most rapid synapse formation, or preventing excessive cell pruning.

NEURODEVELOPMENTAL RATIONALE
FOR EARLY INTERVENTION IN ASDS

At present, we have no definitive proof that early intervention in autism creates new synapses, consolidates old ones, or prevents neuronal loss through cell pruning. There is no obvious way to conduct such a study, although many researchers are trying to find a way to do so. However, the foregoing evidence suggests that early intervention that requires the developing child's brain to repeatedly use the structures that have insufficient synaptic connectivity may promote synapse formation and consolidation within those structures. Two main rationales underlie the assumption that early intervention promotes synaptogensis and brain development: 1) laboratory animal studies on neuroplasticity and 2) research indicating that synapse formation is activity- or experience-dependent.

Laboratory Research on Synapse Formation

Work with laboratory animals indicates that specific types of experiences promote synaptogenesis in structures that were involved in gaining that experience (Greenough & Black, 1992), making this a plausible strategy. This would serve two intertwined purposes; that is, it would prevent the acquired loss of brain cells (and associated skills) due to lack of experiential activation of those structures requiring that input (e.g., an amygdala defect leads to lack of looking at faces, which leads indirectly to lack of fusiform response to faces). Secondly, it would lead to new synapses that are needed for later learning and behavior.

Experience-Dependent Synapse Formation

In brain structures that are developmentally synaptically deficient (e.g., the prefrontal mirror neuron system), carefully crafted early intervention experiences could promote synapse formation and consolidation in some of those primary dysfunctional areas that lead indirectly to acquired brain dysfunction. In this case, intense training of gesture, motor, and oral imitation in very young children with ASDs could overcome some mirror neuronal dysfunction and promote development of early language skills.

EARLY INTERVENTION HISTORY

Maria Montessori was the first person to suggest early intervention as a means of overcoming limitations of children with developmental disabilities. Susan Gray and Rupert Klaus conducted their Early Training Project in Murfeesboro, Tennessee, which led to improvements in intellectual and school readiness skills of children growing up in poverty. Head Start, intended for youngsters with economic and social disadvantages, was one of the more successful early intervention programs for young children.

Early Behavior Therapy Attempts

Among the first systematic attempts to apply early intervention strategies to overcoming deficits and resolving challenging behavior of children with autism was the research of Ivar Lovaas (Lovaas, Berberich, Perloff, & Schaffer, 1966) and Montrose Wolfe (Wolfe, Risley, & Mees, 1964). Lovaas and Wolfe began applying behavioral learning principles to teach language and other basic skills to individual children with autism in the 1960s. Lovaas worked several times a week with 7–9-year-old children who had severe autism. The children were nonverbal, noncompliant, had tantrums, and some engaged in self-injury. Lovaas's goals were limited (e.g., task compliance, speaking single words and phrases), and although there were improvements among the children treated, the outcomes lacked practical significance. The children continued to display rigidity and tantrums and occasionally self-injured and engaged in rocking and hand flapping. They were minimally verbal and lacked social appropriateness at the end of intervention. Lovaas concluded that his efforts had been too limited and had begun too late in the children's development.

The UCLA Young Autism Project that emerged dramatically changed our understanding of what is possible with behavioral treatment of children with autism.

Intensive Early Behavior Therapy

Lovaas's work at UCLA and Eric Schopler's work at the University of North Carolina's TEACCH (Treatment and Education of Autistic and related Communication-handicapped Children) spawned a new generation of early intervention procedures for children with ASDs.

Ivar Lovaas's widely cited 1987 study (Lovaas, 1987) of the results of intensive individual home-based early behavior therapy, as compared with much less intensive center-based therapy, was controversial. He reported that when the children entered elementary school, roughly half of the children who had received intensive home-based behavior therapy were mainstreamed into regular education elementary school classrooms and had intellectual functioning in the typical range. None of the children in the less intensive center-based therapy program achieved these performance levels after 3 years of treatment.

Critics found many reasons to question Lovaas's findings; however, none of them could point to an instance in the psychology, psychiatry, or education literature in which any treatment had produced similar outcomes for children with autism, regardless of cognitive ability at baseline. While there were shortcomings in Lovaas's participant matching and assessment procedures, the magnitude of effects obtained were so unprecedented, the critics appeared to be quibbling. Even if there were methodological weaknesses, the results were striking.

Autism Early Intervention Evidence—
National Research Council Review

Some parents and practitioners who have used Lovaas's behavioral treatment approach said that their children had recovered from autism, while others were equally adamant that claims concerning the effectiveness of his approach were exaggerated. Because of the controversy surrounding Lovaas's work, and disagreements among early education professionals, the National Academy of Sciences National Research Council (NAS-NRC) convened an expert panel to review all of the evidence concerning early intervention and autism. The panel was composed of researchers experienced in early intervention but largely eclectic in outlook. In 2001, the NAS-NRC issued a report, *Educating Young Children with Autism,* that reviewed evidence regarding the effectiveness of various approaches and techniques, and outlined characteristics of effective programs. The panel emphasized that the most effective approaches, regardless of their theoretical basis, share common characteristics. The panel concluded that effective programs include the following features:

- Starting early yields better results than beginning later. "Early" means beginning intervention by 2–3 years of age. The panel recommended that a child be entered into early intervention as soon as he or she is suspected of having autism.

- Twenty-five hours per week, 5 days per week, 12 months per year of intervention is recommended until the child enters kindergarten or first grade.

- A therapist- or teacher-to-child ratio of 1:1 or 1:2 (at most) is more effective than group instruction. Each child should receive sufficient individualized adult attention on a daily basis so that interventions designed to meet objectives can be carried out effectively.

- Carefully planned structured intervention yields better results than unstructured or discovery-based programs.

- Quiet, non-distracting environments are more effective than overly stimulating environments.

- Emphasis should be placed on communication and social skills, while also including cognitive development and play.

- Programming should be designed to prevent emergence of challenging behavior.

- Parents should be actively involved in the intervention.

- Participation with typical peers is more effective than being in a segregated setting in which all children have ASD, or with no other children.

- The largest and most enduring results have been obtained with various behavior therapy approaches.

PLANNING AND IMPLEMENTING EARLY INTERVENTION

The first steps in an early intervention program involve assessment and planning the overall strategy as well as the individual steps.

Assessment and Intervention

The core component of effective early intervention, whether home-based or center-based, is a structured curriculum or treatment plan based on a careful assessment of the child's beginning skills within each domain. Therapists or teachers and other personnel should be thoroughly versed in evidence-based practices.

The individualized education program (IEP), the individualized family service plan (IFSP), or the individual treatment plan (ITP) should be designed jointly by an experienced professional (Ph.D., PsyD, or M.S./M.A.) expert in autism in young children, the child's parents, and a lead teacher or therapist. If the school or therapy program employs a speech therapist and/or an occupational therapist, they should be involved as well. All children with ASDs have communication problems (e.g., pragmatics), but some also have speech problems (e.g., apraxia, of speech). An experienced speech therapist can be invaluable in developing effective treatment methods that should be used by all therapists and teachers as well as the child's parents. Speech therapy once or twice a week for a half hour is generally much less effective than having the speech therapist train other personnel and the child's parents in using appropriate interventions throughout all aspects of the child's experiences. Communication therapy should be part of the functional curriculum planned in consultation with a licensed SLP, regarding the most effective communication strategy (e.g., spoken, iconic, or gestural). Many children with ASDs have subtle perceptual-motor coordination problems, which can be addressed by an occupational therapist (e.g., holding a spoon, printing with a crayon). Systematic desensitization to textures, tastes, or specific types of tactile sensations (e.g., water) can be conducted to improve tolerance. In general, sensory integration procedures that involve weighted garments, deep pressure, brushing the skin, and related techniques have not proven effective (see Lord & McGee, 2001). As a child progresses through therapy or special education early intervention, it may be useful to incorporate the child's physical education, art, and music teachers into IEP/ITP planning. Adapted physical education activities can provide opportunities to teach turn-taking and to improve gross perceptual-motor skills. Children with ASDs are often especially interested in, and some are talented in, art or music, which have the advantage of being nonverbal activities that are often inherently rewarding. With home-based therapy, including staff at a community recreation center or the public library can also be helpful.

COMPREHENSIVE EARLY INTERVENTION APPROACHES

A wide variety of approaches to early intervention services for children with ASDs have been developed. Some are focused on specific skills, such as dyadic communication, while others are comprehensive attempts to address all of the core deficits in ASDs as well as other functional skills that will assist in promoting a child's development. In many cases, individual components of comprehensive interventions have been studied systematically (e.g., a specific aspect of language intervention) but the entire treatment package has not. These treatment component studies have often been limited to a small samples. In other instances, comprehensive approaches have undergone evaluation using research designs that provide strong evidence of their effectiveness, which are considered *evidence-based practices*.

Some comprehensive approaches are widely used clinically and educationally but have not been rigorously evaluated. The absence of evidence from well-designed studies does not necessarily indicate that they are ineffective, but indicates more information is needed to evaluate their effectiveness.

Finally, in some cases, focused or comprehensive interventions have been evaluated and found to be ineffective. The following sections are divided into evidence-based early intervention programs and other programs for which strong evidence of their effectiveness remains to be presented.

Evidence-Based Programs

The following comprehensive programs are supported by research studies that demonstrate their efficacy. Few of them have involved random assignment of children to experimental and control conditions; however, in most cases, adequate care was taken to assure that children receiving model interventions were similar in characteristics to those in standard community service comparison groups.

Intensive Early Behavior Therapy

Ivar Lovaas's UCLA Young Autism Project created the stage for much of what would follow in the field of autism early intervention. He conducted a 4-year intervention project and then followed the children into school on completing early intervention. Using an intensive behavioral treatment regimen (40 hours per week of one-to-one contact), emphasizing language development and social skills, he reported that 47% of the experimental group (9 of 19 children) achieved "normal functioning" after 2 to 3 years of treatment, compared with 2% of the comparison group that had received 10 hours per week of intervention in a preschool setting (Lovaas, 1987). In 1993, he and his co-workers published a follow-up study of those children at age 12 and found that of the nine children with the best outcomes, eight functioned relatively normally (McEachin, Smith, & Lovaas, 1993). Lovaas has followed up these same children as young adults and their gains continue to be maintained without specific intervening treatment (Smith, Groen, & Wynn, 2000). Over the next decade, numerous replications of basic components of Lovaas's intervention generally yielded similar results (e.g., Harris & Handleman, 2000; Sallows & Graupner, 2005; Smith, Groen, & Wynn, 2000).

Numerous other treatment programs sprang up around the United States that were also based on principles of Applied Behavior Analysis (ABA); for example:

1. *The Children's Unit at the State University of New York at Binghamton* primarily uses ABA techniques, although more naturalistic procedures may be implemented as the children progress. An elaborate individualized goal selection curriculum has been developed, and there is an extensive computerized assessment and monitoring system (Romanczyk et al., 2000).

2. The *Douglass Developmental Center at Rutgers University* opened in 1972 to serve older children with autism; the preschool programs were added in 1987. The curriculum is developmentally sequenced and uses ABA techniques, beginning with discrete-trial formats and shifting across the continuum to more naturalistic procedures. A small-group classroom emphasizes communication, cognitive skills, and self-help skills; social intervention begins in the form of interactive play with teachers. The emphasis in the inclusive classroom is on communication, socialization, and preacademic skills (Harris et al., 2000).

3. The *Pivotal Response Model at the University of California at Santa Barbara* began in 1979 and has undergone evolution with children of varied ages. Using a parent education approach, the goal of the Pivotal Response

Model is to provide individuals with autism with the social and educational proficiency to participate in inclusive settings. The fundamental strategy is to aim at change in certain pivotal areas (e.g., responsiveness to multiple cues, motivation, self-management, and self-initiations). Intervention consists of in-clinic and one-on-one home teaching, and children concurrently participate in special education services in the schools. Specific curriculum goals are targeted in areas of communication, self-help, academic, social, and recreational skills (Koegel, Koegel, & Carter, 1998).

4. *Walden Early Childhood Programs at the Emory University School of Medicine* was developed in 1985 at the University of Massachusetts at Amherst, where the primary function was as a laboratory preschool to accommodate research in incidental teaching. Following relocation to Emory University in Atlanta, toddler and prekindergarten programs were added to complete an early intervention continuum. The classrooms include children with autism with a majority of typical peers. The incidental teaching approach is based on behavioral research, although there are developmental influences on goal selection. There is a toddler program with both center- and home-based components, and initial goals include establishment of sustained engagement, functional verbal language, responsiveness to adults, tolerance, participation with typical peers, and independence in daily living. The preschool is aimed at language expansions and beginning peer interaction training. The prekindergarten emphasizes elaborated peer interactions, academic skills, and conventional school behaviors (Emory University Autism Center).

5. The *Princeton Developmental Institute* in Princeton, New Jersey, provides a behaviorally based early intervention program for children who are 24 months of age or younger at the time of referral. Toddlers and their parents regularly visit the Institute, and Institute personnel make regular home visits. The program is based on a strong parent–professional partnership, and children receive no less than 30 hours of intervention per week. Individualized programs focus on learning readiness, language, play, family participation, and other daily routines. Core activities focus on language acquisition and social interaction. They promote decision-making skills and independence from caregivers employing incidental learning strategies (McClannahan & Krantz, 1994.)

6. *Individualized Support Program at the University of South Florida at Tampa* is primarily a parent-training program that is implemented in children's homes and community settings during a relatively short period of intensive assistance and ongoing follow-up. The program is intended to be adjunctive to ongoing, daily, special educational services delivered in preschool and by other service providers. Specifically, it is oriented toward

helping families gain the knowledge and skills needed to solve problems, as well as the competence and confidence needed to continue effective intervention and advocacy over the course of their children's educational history. Essential elements of the model include

- Development of functional communication skills

- Facilitation of the child's participation in socially inclusive environments

- Multifaceted family support (Dunlap & Fox, 1999)

7. *Learning Experiences, an Alternative Program for Preschoolers and Their Parents (LEAP) Preschool at the University of Colorado School of Education* opened in 1982 as a federally funded demonstration program and soon after was incorporated into the *Early Childhood Intervention Program at Western Psychiatric Institute and Clinic, University of Pittsburgh.* The original classrooms continue to operate in Pittsburgh, but new LEAP classrooms have been developed in the Denver public school system and have been replicated in other sites. LEAP includes both a preschool program and a behavioral skill training program for parents. LEAP was one of the first programs in the country to include children with autism with typical children, and the curriculum is well-known for its peer-mediated social skill interventions. The curriculum blends a behavioral approach with developmentally appropriate practices (Strain & Cordisco, 1994; Strain & Hoyson, 2000).

Cognitive/Developmental Skills Programs

Two comprehensive approaches to early intervention based on cognitive and social skill development have been widely used and undergone sufficient evaluation to warrant including them among evidence-based early intervention programs: 1) Treatment and Education of Autistic and Related Communication-Handicapped Children (TEACCH) and 2) the Denver Developmental Model.

Treatment and Education of Autistic and Related Communication-Handicapped Children

Treatment and Education of Autistic and Related Communication-Handicapped Children (TEACCH) was one of the early programs developed for teaching children with autism. Developed by Eric Schopler (1964), the basic principles grew out of cognitive developmental psychology theory. Structured teaching within an organized physical environment, developing schedules and work systems, making expectations clear and explicit, and using visual materials have been effective ways of developing skills and allowing people with autism to use these skills independently of direct adult prompting and cueing. While TEACCH is widely used with school-age children with ASDs throughout the United States and Europe, it has also been adapted, with positive results, for home-based preschool age teaching as well (Ozonoff & Cathcart, 1998). Two matched groups of children were compared, a TEACCH treatment group and a comparison group, each consisting of 11 subjects. The treatment group was provided with approximately 4 months of programming and was tested before and after the intervention. The comparison group did not receive the TEACCH treatment but was tested at the same 4-month interval. The groups were matched on age, pretest scores, severity of autism, and time to follow up. Children in the TEACCH treatment group improved significantly on imitation, fine motor, gross motor, and nonverbal conceptual skills, as well as in overall score. Progress in the treatment group was three to four times greater than that of the control group on all outcome tests.

Denver Developmental Model

Rogers and Lewis (1989) provided therapy in a day treatment program for 31 2–6-year-old children with ASD diagnoses employing the Denver Developmental Model. Though there was emphasis on relationship building, these researchers also employed specific teaching strategies for strengthening communication and social skills drawing on cognitive and developmental psychology theory. They used an intervention strategy designed to promote the development of close interpersonal relationships; use of play in all of its interpersonal, cognitive, and structural variety; and a pragmatics-based language therapy model delivered within a highly predictable and carefully structured milieu. Over a 6-month period, children demonstrated significant treatment effects in cognition, perceptual/fine motor, socioemotional, and language skills, which were maintained or increased over a 12- to 18-month treatment period. Play skills increased complexity and generalization. Core autism symptoms were reduced as well.

Other Early Intervention Approaches

Several early intervention programs have been widely used clinically and in educational settings and show promise but have not yet undergone rigorous testing. In several instances, components of comprehensive programs have been evaluated and results published in credible journals, while in others what little research has been done has failed to provide empirical support for their effectiveness.

The SCERTS™ Model

The Social Communication, Emotional Regulation, and Transactional Support (SCERTS™) Model was developed out of 25 years of research and clinical/educational practice by Barry Prizant, Amy Wetherby, and colleagues. It employs a multidisciplinary team approach incorporating concepts from communication disorders, special education, occupational therapy, and developmental and behavior analysis. The approach draws on intervention methods for teaching intentional communication drawn from speech and communication disorders literature. Components of the SCERTS™ model have been studied empirically by members of the team that developed this intervention strategy. However, there have been no controlled investigations of outcomes for children with autism who have received the entire SCERTS™ package, in comparison with standard early childhood special education (ECSE) preschool intervention or other treatment approaches (Prizant, Wetherby, Rubin, & Laurent, 2003).

Verbal Behavior

Vincent Carbone developed an incidental learning approach to teaching social language skills to young children with ASDs based on behavior analytic principles, primarily growing out of Skinner's analysis of verbal behavior (Skinner, 1957). Carbone's approach is widely used throughout the United States, and he and his colleagues have published several empirical papers illustrating the effectiveness of specific aspects of his approach (Carbone, Lewis, Sweeney-Kerwin et al., 2006). In addition, he has provided a detailed theoretical discussion of the rationale for his approach (Carbone, Morgenstern, & Zecchin-Tirri, 2006). However, there are no comprehensive studies of the approach with significant samples of children with ASDs and matched comparison children demonstrating long-term efficacy. It seems likely that the approach should be as effective as other intensive early behavior therapy (IEBT) approaches, but it remains to be demonstrated whether it is more or less effective with children who have specific characteristics than another intervention strategy.

"Mind-Reading"

Simon Baron-Cohen at University of Cambridge (United Kingdom) has developed a neurocognitive theory of autism in which he posits the core impairment being a lack of ability to take another person's perspective. He calls this "mind blindness." Accordingly, Howlin, Baron-Cohen, and Hadwin (1998) have developed a curriculum titled *Teaching Children with Autism to Mind-Read: A Practical Guide for Teachers and Parents* that provides guidelines for helping children with autism spectrum conditions to improve their understanding of beliefs, emotions, and pretence. The curriculum teaches how to interpret facial expressions; how to recognize feelings of anger, sadness, fear, and happiness; how feelings are affected by what happens and what is expected to happen; how to see things from another person's perspective; and how to understand another person's knowledge and beliefs. It does not specifically address language impairments or compulsive repetitive routines. There have been no well-controlled clinical trials of the curriculum, although components have been tested and produced changes as long as instruction is taking place. There have been no longer term studies to date. As a result, little is known about whether gains generalize to new situations or are sustained after intervention.

Motor Programming

Although some professionals have claimed that children with autism suffer from generalized motor dyspraxia, that does not appear to be the case. Teitelbaum and co-workers (1998, 2004) studied infants who were later diagnosed with an ASD and reported that some of the infants' reflexes were not inhibited at the appropriate age in development, whereas others fail to appear when they should. Other specific impairments have been reported among older children with autism, including in-motor imitation, balance, coordination, finger-to-thumb opposition, speech articulation, and the presence of hypotonia. No significant differences have been found in tactile perception or gait, beyond that accounted for by cognitive level (Jones & Prior, 1985; Rapin, 1996; Stone et al., 1990). Adolescents with Asperger syndrome and high-functioning autism have average to above average performance in simple motor tasks, but impairments in skilled motor tasks (Minshew et al., 1997) as well as incoordination (Ghaziuddin et al., 1994) Sensory-motor integration therapy (see below) techniques have been widely used, but there is no evidence that they produce significant improvements or lasting behavioral effects.

Sensory Integration

Sensory integration is a term coined by Jean Ayres (1972). She hypothesized that because intact, efficient sensory processing leads to a child's adaptations across changing environments, dysfunction in one or more senses can lead to deficient or maladaptive adjustment. Ayres assumed that specific sensory-motor interventions would correct the sensory processing dysfunction. Numerous studies have demonstrated that there are differences in processing language, auditory, and to a lesser extent, visual information entering the brains of children with autism. Dunn (1997) developed an assessment for possible sensory integrative impairments (*The Sensory Profile*) that she has used to assess a large sample of children, including typical children and those with ASDs and ADHD. She conducted factor analytic and discriminant function analytic studies of responses to items within *The Sensory Profile* and reported significant

differences among groups of children. A variety of sensory integration therapy techniques have been employed by occupational therapists based on Ayres'
theory and Dunn's *The Sensory Profile*, but there are no well-controlled clinical
trials among children with autism.

In its 2001 report, the NAS-NRC committee (Lord & McGee, 2001)
found that there was a paucity of research concerning sensory integration
treatments in autism. Approaches based on sensory integration therapy include
the "sensory diet," in which the environment is filled with sensory-based activities that are hypothesized to satisfy a child's sensory needs. The "alert program" (usually with higher functioning individuals) combines sensory
integration with a cognitive-behavioral approach to give a child additional
strategies to improve arousal modulation. Few, if any, empirical studies of these
techniques have been published. Sensory stimulation techniques vary but usually involve passive sensory stimulation; they are incorporated within the
broader sensory integration programs or used in isolation. Examples include
"deep pressure" to provide calming input by massage or joint compression or
using an apparatus such as a weighted vest. Vestibular stimulation, another
example, is often used to modulate arousal, facilitate postural tone, or increase
vocalizations. These interventions have also not yet been supported by empirical studies.

Auditory integration therapy is a type of sensory integration for autism that
has received considerable media attention. Proponents of auditory integration
therapy suggest that music can "massage" the middle ear (hair cells in the
cochlea), reduce hypersensitivities, and improve overall auditory processing
ability. From a review of available studies, it appears that there is no empirical evidence from controlled investigations that auditory integration therapy
has any effect on children with autism. The underlying assumptions behind
the method have been considered questionable on scientific grounds (Lord &
McGee, 2001).

There is no consistent evidence that sensory-based treatments have
specific lasting effects on the behavior of children with ASDs (Dawson &
Watling, 2000; Goldstein, 1999). Although a lack of empirical data does not
necessarily prove that a treatment is ineffective, it does indicate that there is
no evidence to date demonstrating that such treatments have significant practical benefit for children with ASDs.

Affective/Relationship Development Programs

Affective or relationship therapies are based on the premise that overcoming
core autism features depends on developing a strong emotional bond between
the teacher/therapist or parent and the child. Therapies vary in the degree to
which they attempt to teach specific skills. Some reject the notion that it is
appropriate to attempt to change the child's behavior, while others incorporate skills development into their approach.

Floor Time

Floor time, developed by psychiatrist Stanley Greenspan, is described as a developmental-individual difference-relationship-based strategy. During spontaneous floor time play sessions, adults follow the child's lead using positive affect interactions through gestures and words by first establishing a foundation of shared attention, engagement, simple and complex gestures, and problem solving to guide the child into ideas and abstract thinking. It provides an opportunity to transform preservative play into more meaningful and developmentally beneficial behavior, and to expand the child's play themes, which are typically restricted. At the same time, it is designed to help the child develop relationships with others. Greenspan emphasizes that the goal is not to teach specific skills but to indirectly promote skill development (Greenspan & Wieder, 2006). There have been no prospective studies evaluating the effectiveness of floor time for improving core autism symptoms in young children. One chart review suggested that floor time was capable of producing substantial improvements; however, there were significant methodological problems with that report. Floor time was not among the approaches found by the NAS-NRC committee to be among credible evidence-based interventions for young children with ASDs.

Relationship Development Intervention

Relationship development intervention (RDI) was developed by Steven Gutstein, a clinical psychologist whose background was in helping typical children cope with stress and in crisis intervention for neurotypical adolescents with emotional and mental health problems. In 2001, he published a book titled *Autism/Asperger's: Solving the Relationship Puzzle,* which was followed in 2002 by *Relationship Development Intervention Activities for Young Children.* The two books and Gutstein's workshops provide examples of play activities that promote social relatedness as well as other skills relevant to core autism symptoms. However, it appears that, as with other affective/relationship-based therapies, relatively less emphasis is on developing specific skills; rather it focuses on the quality of the relationship between the therapist or parents and the child.

Gutstein (2004) compared outcomes for 17 children (ages 2–10) undergoing RDI with 14 similar children who averaged more than twice the amount of intensive intervention services. Gutstein reported that 70% of children in the RDI group improved their diagnostic category on the ADOS. More than 50% of the RDI group scored in the non-autism category 18 months later. Though only 12% of the children were in regular education classrooms at the outset of treatment, at its conclusion 82% were in regular education placements. Without knowing more about the two groups of children, the nature of the comparison intervention, and exactly what was done, it is difficult to evaluate these claims. Although some aspects of RDIs are appealing, in the absence of evidence from well-controlled studies of children with comparable disabilities, it is difficult to determine whether these approaches assist young children with ASDs in overcoming core symptoms.

Quasi-Neuroscience-Based Methods

Several approaches have been developed that use concepts and language from neuroscience research; however, the degree to which the interventions actually employ neuroscience principles and methods may be unclear.

Biofeedback

Various forms of biofeedback (called neurofeedback or neurotherapy) have been used in an attempt to improve cognitive and behavioral functioning of children with ASD. In a pilot study (Scolnick, 2005), electroencephalogram (EEG) biofeedback was used to improve focusing and to decrease anxiety in 10 adolescent boys diagnosed with Asperger syndrome attending a therapeutic day school. Five of the boys dropped out of the study before 12 sessions were completed. The analysis of pre- and post-intervention quantitative EEGs for the five students who completed the study showed a trend to "normalization" but did not reach statistical significance. All five boys who completed 24 sessions were rated by parents and teachers as having improved behavior, but since the raters were not blind to treatment and there was no placebo treatment group, it is difficult to interpret the results. Sichel, Fehmi, and Goldstein (1995) reported positive effects of electromyographic neurofeedback treatment in a case of a youth with mild autism. Only subjective clinical impressions were reported.

FastForWord

FastForWord is a commercially available computer learning system that is claimed to improve speech in children with SLIs. Its development was occasioned by basic neuroscience research by Benaisch and Tallal (2002) suggesting that difficulty processing rapid sequences of sounds (as in speech) was predictive of later dyslexia and language problems. There have also been claims that it promotes language among children with ASDs. Cohen et al. (2005) studied 77 children between the ages of 6 and 10 years with severe mixed receptive-expressive SLI, who participated in a randomized clinical trial of FastForWord (Scientific Learning Corporation, 1997, 2001). The program uses acoustically enhanced stimuli that are modified to exaggerate their time and intensity properties as part of an adaptive training process. Three groups were compared: a FastForWord group, a control computer-training group, and a no-additional-therapy group. Each group made gains in language scores, but there was no additional effect for either computer intervention. Their findings do not support the efficacy of FastForWord as an intervention for children with severe mixed receptive-expressive SLI, including those with ASDs. No studies have been published employing FastForWord for children with ASD diagnoses who do not have a language disability, although numerous clinics and special schools offer FastForWord on a fee-for-service basis. Experts in speech, language, and hearing science have been critical of claims by proponents of FastForWord (see Studdert-Kennedy, 1998).

Summary: Early Intervention Alternatives

The NAS-NRC committee (Lord & McGee, 2001) concluded that the only early intervention methods that had evaluated the long-term outcomes of children receiving treatment were variations on Lovaas's original UCLA Young Autism Project. Developmentally based programs such as the Denver Developmental Model and TEACCH have provided evidence of their effectiveness for shorter periods, suggesting that they may have longer-term efficacy as well. Various intervention models employing aspects of intensive early behavior therapy are all based on similar behavioral principles but have different emphases (e.g., incidental teaching versus discrete trial teaching, inclusion of developmental concepts in sequencing therapy). Strategies by Vincent Carbone, called Verbal Behavior and by Partington (the STARS School) are also outgrowths of ABA. Sundberg and Partington have published numerous reports on aspects of their approach to teaching language in autism, but not outcome studies of comprehensive intervention programs (see Sundberg & Partington, 1998). There have been no comparisons of the various behavior therapy approaches, so it is impossible to know whether one yields better results than another. In all probability, differences in outcomes will depend on child characteristics and intervention intensity. Table 3.1 presents most of the major comprehensive early intervention programs and many more focused programs for young children with ASDs along with the strength of the evidence indicating their effectiveness.

SELECTING AN EARLY INTERVENTION PROGRAM

Several factors enter into selecting the most appropriate setting for a child's early intervention program, including setting, theoretical approach, degree of integration with typical peers, and approach to behavioral challenges.

Setting

The first decision parents make in selecting an appropriate early intervention program for their child involves deciding whether a center-based or home-

Table 3.1. Summary of major forms of early intervention, empirical support for each, and types of gains demonstrated or claimed. (See legend at bottom of table for explanation of numbers and letters in the two right-hand columns.)

Comprehensive programs	Program type/ emphasis	Evidence of effectiveness	Possible effects on core autism symptoms
Denver (Rogers)	Developmental-cognitive model	3	S & L
Floor Time (DIR)	Relationship development	1	S
Mind Reading (Baron-Cohen)	Cognitive social skills development	1-2	S
Pivotal Response Training (Koegel & Schriebman)	Comprehensive communication, social, and cognitive model	4	L, S, & R
RDI (Gutstein)	Relationship Development	2	S & L
SCERTS™ (Prizant & Wetherby)	Comprehensive communication, social, and cognitive model	1-2	L, S, & R
TEACCH (Schopler)	Comprehensive developmental, cognitive, and communication model	3	L, S, & R
UCLA (Lovaas)	Comprehensive behavior analytic intervention; emphasis on discrete trial methods	4	L, S, & R
Verbal Behavior (Sundberg & Partington)	Comprehensive behavior analytic intervention; emphasis on language development	3	L, S, & R
Verbal Behavior (Carbone)	Comprehensive behavior analytic intervention; incidental teaching emphasis on language	1-2	L, S, & R
Walden (McGee)	Comprehensive behavior analytic intervention; incidental teaching emphasis	4	L, S, & R
Focused Interventions			
Auditory Integration	OT integration of auditory input	1	0
CompuThera	Computerized reading instruction	0	L
Facilitated Communication		1	0
FastForWord	Computerized reading program	0	L
Gentle Teaching	Philosophy of relationships	0	S

(continued)

Table 3.1. (continued)

Comprehensive programs	Program type/ emphasis	Evidence of effectiveness	Possible effects on core autism symptoms
Kindermusik	Music therapy	0	S
Miller Umwelt Method	Cognitive developmental systems approach similar to OT	1	0
Motor programming	OT technique to improve coordinated movements	0	0
Neural Feedback	Biofeedback (usually EEG)	0	0
Picture Exchange System (PECS)	Augmentative communication system	4	L & S
Red and Green Choices	Teaches choice-making	1	S
Sensory Integration	OT multisensory input coordination	1	0
Social Stories	Teaches social responses in various scenarios	1	S & L
Son-Rise	Relationship based intervention program	1	S

Evidence of Effectiveness:

0 = No published reports

1 = Case reports of immediate/short-term effects

2 = Studies with selected samples, no or unmatched comparison groups; Limited outcome measures; no long-term measures

3 = Studies with appropriate comparable samples and comparison groups; Reasonable outcome measures; no replications; medium-term outcomes

4 = Studies with appropriately characterized study groups; comprehensive measures and long-term treatment effects; replications

Possible Beneficial Effects on Core Autism Symptoms:

S = Social; L = Language; R = Repetitive behavior and fixed interests

based education or therapy program fits best with their family. School districts and private for-profit and nonprofit organizations provide center-based programs in many communities. Some are half-day and others are full-day programs. Center-based programs have two advantages. First, they are not as disruptive of the family's day-to-day lives. Second, the child with an ASD is in a group setting that may provide opportunities for developing social skills that might be more limited in a home-based program. Home-based programs are nearly always more intensive since they involve 1:1 therapy during most of the scheduled session. Nearly the entire therapy time is spent performing skill development activities, while in many center-based programs other activities are interpolated. Home-based programs also have the advantage that parents are inherently more involved in the therapy because they observe it occurring each day in their own home, and staff intermittently incorporates them into therapy activities throughout the day. They have the disadvantage of limiting the child's opportunities for socialization with peers. Moreover, some parents find the presence of therapists in their homes 15–30 hours per week very disruptive, while others readily adjust to the change in their daily lives and look forward to the therapist arriving to work with their child.

Intervention Approach and Supervision

Once parents decide which setting fits best, they need to consider the educational or therapeutic approach. Parents should visit the center where educational or therapy services are being provided to similar children, or they should seek permission to conduct home visits in at least two homes in which 1:1 therapy is occurring. They should ask what type of training and experience therapists or instruction staff must have to be employed by the program and how often supervision is provided. Programs that describe their approach as very eclectic are usually less structured, with a good deal of time devoted to ancillary interventions (e.g., occupational therapy, recreational activities, other therapies). According to national panels that have reviewed the evidence concerning programs that are most effective, most of the child's time should be structured or semistructured, with the majority in 1:1 or 1:2 teacher/therapist-to-child ratios. Large-group instruction is generally much less effective in teaching young children with ASDs.

Integration with Typical Peers

Therapy staff should be asked how often and to what degree children with ASDs have an opportunity to interact with typical peers. Even in home-based programs, an effort should be made to incorporate siblings, neighbor children, or other peers into therapy on a regular schedule. Parents should ask to see examples of measures of student performance over weeks and months of program participation. If program staff members are reluctant to share such information, the parents should be wary. If the parents witness anything going on during therapy or instruction in the program they find troubling, they should ask a program staff member to explain what is going on and why the particular procedures are being used.

Approach to Behavioral Challenges

The manner in which program staff members deal with behavioral challenges and outbursts is very important. Parents should ask specifically if intrusive or restrictive procedures are used, such as placing a child who is aggressive or disruptive alone in an enclosed room (sometimes called time-out) or in some form of restraint. High-quality programs seldom employ such methods. Finally, parents should ask to speak with the person who directs the program and ask that person to explain his or her approach to serving children with ASDs. By listening carefully to the way a program director describes his or her perspective, parents can often obtain insights into the director's philosophy of working with children with ASDs. Excessive emphasis on compliance and reducing problem behavior, such as repetitive stereotyped movements, should be a red flag. Although it is important to promote appropriate responsiveness to adult requests and to discourage fixed, repetitive routines, those goals should be by-products of teaching appropriate skills. Conversely, a program director who speaks in vague generalities about promoting self-efficacy and a sense of psychological well-being, without indicating how that is achieved, should be a warning signal. An effective program director should have an unambiguous vision, with clear measurable goals for children with ASDs, and a strategy for achieving those goals. The director should be able to explain his or her approach with minimal use of jargon and in concrete language anyone can understand.

SUMMARY

Early behavioral intervention can be thought of as a form of early brain intervention; that is, a means of promoting synapse formation and preventing neuronal loss in brain areas that would otherwise be dysfunctional. It is one of the more important things that parents, teachers, and therapists can do to improve the likelihood of a child with an ASD leading a full and productive life.

Chapter 4 will discuss ways in which developmental neuroscience can help inform intensive early behavior therapy principles and strategies, incorporating concepts from many of the foregoing programs.

4

Families
The Foundation
of Child Development

———————————————————

Family life bears more resemblance to a jazz quartet improvising *Love Me or Leave Me* than the Academy of Ancient Music's performance of the *Second Brandenburg Concerto*. Like jazz improvisation, family life is unpredictable, with one person playing off the other, sometimes reacting a bit behind the beat, but somehow it all hangs together. Each member of a family has a part to play: the bread-winner, the nurturer, the needy one, or the mediator. Crises test the mettle of families. Substance abuse, mental health problems, or the death of a family member can abruptly change the homeostatic balance upon which families thrive. The discovery that one of the children within a family has an ASD challenges that stability, shifting priorities and often changing roles. Families with a solid foundation list and yaw like a sailboat encountering a sudden squall, but they tack into the wind to ride out the rough waters ahead. Families that were tenuously struggling prior to diagnosis of their child with autism may be headed for the rocky shoreline.

MAKING SENSE OF YOUR CHILD WITH AN ASD

Doctors, teachers, therapists, and various other professionals provide special insights into children with ASDs, each from his or her own perspective. But in the last analysis, parents are the ones who often know their child best.

Parents Usually Know Their Child Best

Parents strive to understand the perplexing child that has emerged in their midst. They love him as much as their other children but often feel no affection in return. With time, parents who live with a child with an ASD come to know their child far better than anyone else. Like any other parent, they see nuances in their child's behavior others miss, the glimmer in the child's eye, the fleeting facial expressions, the subtle signs of pleasure—little things that may take therapists or teachers weeks or months to recognize. Parents learn through painful experience all of the "oughts" and "ought nots" and what triggers a "meltdown" and how to avoid it, at least most of the time. A child's family is the primary vehicle for promoting his or her development. They serve as the conduit through which teachers' and therapists' efforts are realized. Teachers and therapists play very important roles, but in the last analysis, limited progress can be made without full family participation.

Coming to Terms with a Child's Diagnosis

Every parent hopes and expects that their newborn will be healthy, mentally capable, and able-bodied. Because children with autism seldom appear very different for the first 6 to 12 months of life, it comes as a shock when their child's pediatrician informs them a year or more later that their child has an ASD. Many parents simply cannot accept an ASD diagnosis, especially after having been told by previous doctors that their child appears to have a mild developmental delay, or a speech problem, or perhaps is just displaying "the terrible 2s" and that he will grow out of it. Matters are much worse for parents of children with regressive autism. They recall that months before their child seemed normal, and then the child they knew began disappearing, one skill at a time. Replacing those vanishing skills were rocking, hand flapping, and tantrums. "Is there nothing you can do to stop this from happening?" parents plead with their child's doctor. The answer is incomprehensible and unacceptable to them. "Despite all the research that has been done, we are not able to stop autism's regression," their doctor replies.

Much has been written about the grieving process that follows diagnosis. For some parents, each time they look at their 4-year-old with autism, they see a distorted image of what their aspiration had been. In the beginning, treatment and therapies are, for them, attempts to recover their lost child, the child that should have been, but isn't. They consult other doctors and generally receive the same response. They ask other parents of children with ASDs for advice. Some suggest trying Secretin, a pancreatic hormone that was claimed to cure autism, but doesn't. Others recommend special diets, free of gluten and casein or high in omega-3 fatty acids. They search the Internet for clues and attend parent conferences and workshops in which new, and often questionable, remedies are discussed. They hear claims about a computer program that is alleged to reprogram the child's brain, about the benefits of removal of all heavy metals from the body by giving the child a chemical chelating agent, and about hyperbaric oxygen therapy in which oxygen is administered at greater than normal pressure to a patient—a treatment normally used for healing problem wounds, chronic bone infections, and radiation injury. Over the next year, they may spend many thousands of dollars trying out various remedies.

Eventually, parents become resigned to the fact that none of those remedies is going to create a child like the one they had initially hoped and prayed for during pregnancy. Coinciding with this process, parents often alternate between anger, because doctors and other professionals have no cure for their child's autism, and depression over their loss. One mother told me that when she looked at her son with autism, a deep ache welled up in her chest, a pain that would not go away; then she was overcome with shame for feeling that way. It is an extremely difficult and heavy burden for any parent. As they work through this process, parents often begin looking for other therapeutic or educational approaches to help their child develop.

INITIAL PARENT INTERVIEW

The time when most children are diagnosed with an ASD (2–4 years of age) corresponds with the period in which it is most important to begin early intervention. Parents who are struggling to accept their child's disability often find it difficult to become emotionally invested in early intervention activities. Other parents view participating in their child's early intervention as a concrete action they can take to improve their child's life, relieving the sense of helplessness. A structured parent interview is a valuable initial step in this process.

Opening the Door Slowly

Parent interviews typically begin with concrete topics that are easier to discuss, such as the mother's pregnancy (or if adopted, age of adoption), the child's medical history, and early developmental milestones. In addition to providing specific facts that can be useful in planning assessments and specific interventions, it is very helpful to hear from the child's parents how they perceive him or her (i.e., "She's always been a problem"; "He's had lots of illnesses"; "We suspected something might be wrong, but he was never really a problem"). Better understanding of parental perceptions and attitudes helps in communicating with them about expectations, participation in an individualized education program (IEP) or individual treatment plan (ITP) development, and helping them accept their role in therapy. It is also helpful to discuss daily routines, roles, and responsibilities of various family members and the ecology of the home environment. That can begin to provide a better understanding of how the child with ASD fits into the family and how each person interacts with the child.

As the interview progresses, it is helpful to ask parents to share something about their child they enjoy most. After they have done so, it is time to explore their primary concerns. Parents who find it difficult to think of anything enjoyable about their child tend to overlook their child's accomplishments and overreact to minor problems. Such parents usually require a great deal more support and coaching in carrying out interventions. During the initial interview, most parents express immediate and longer-term concerns. Their immediate concerns usually revolve around behavior problems (i.e., "melt-downs"), noncompliance, and their child's lack of social interest and communication. Their longer-term concerns are expressed in various ways. Among the most common are "What do you think she will be like at the end of therapy?" "How far do you think he can go?" "Is she going to be able to go to school like other kids?" "When she is an adult, will she be able to live on her own, or will we need to care for her?"

Addressing Parental Concerns and Expectations

Parents' short-term concerns can usually be addressed expeditiously, because they are usually greatly improved in a matter of weeks or months. With careful planning, availability of qualified staff, and parent support, most behavior problems can be overcome. Most children with autism begin communicating and, with assistance, develop enjoyable social interactions with their family. Answers to the parents' longer-term questions are much more difficult. One never knows with any degree of certainty what a child of 2 or 3 with an ASD will look like when he or she is 5 or 6 years old, let alone when he or she is in junior or senior high school. We can usually tell within 30–60 days, by how rapidly a child is progressing, the general trajectory toward longer-term achievement. However, it is important to avoid making specific predictions such as "She's likely to graduate from high school" or "He'll probably live in a group home as an adult." It is impossible to accurately make such predictions. By keeping parents involved and informed as intervention proceeds, they begin to develop a more realistic appraisal of their child's abilities and a range of possible outcomes on their own.

"WHY DOES HE DO THOSE THINGS?"

Parents are perplexed, frustrated, and sometimes alarmed by their child's unusual behavior. Couples ask each other, "Why does he do those things?" Their child's failure to comply with simple requests, their tantrums, repetitive routines, and inability to relate to other members of the family are unsettling and create distress. Suddenly parents find that daily routines take twice as long as they did before their child with an ASD entered their family. They wonder if their daughter with an ASD is ever going to be like other kids. "What will she be like when she grows up?" they ask. They struggle with accepting their child for what he or she is, and experience self-reproach for thinking that way. Navigating this emotional minefield requires arriving at a new understanding of this unusual child in their midst who seems so unlike their other children. It demands rethinking their parental roles and priorities. It is a turbulent period most parents experience. Support of professionals, friends, and relatives is important in helping parents navigate this alien territory.

Noncompliance

At times, parents interpret their child's actions incorrectly, especially non-compliance. In frustration, the mother of a 3-year-old said, "He refuses to eat with his spoon. He knows perfectly well how to use his spoon, but he uses his fingers instead." But when I watched Brian closely at mealtime, it was apparent that it was difficult for him to manage larger pieces of food with his spoon; it was easier for him to use his fingers. I suggested that we cut his green beans and piece of chicken breast into small pieces that would easily fit on his spoon, but he continued to use his fingers to pick up his food. Then we spooned some applesauce into another small bowl and placed it on the table out of his reach, but where he could clearly see it. His mother said, "Brian, eat with your spoon, then you can have some applesauce," pointing to the applesauce. He looked at the applesauce, then at his green beans and chicken, and picked up his spoon and proceeded to eat with it. Brian wasn't being obstinate, or refusing to do what his mother was asking him to do out of spite, he was doing what was easier, and he needed a little motivation to "prime the pump."

At other times, children resist performing tasks the way their parents or teachers prefer because that involves a change in their routine. Another "ought" has reared its head. One child with whom I worked preferred to put on his pullover shirts inside out. His mother, understandably from her vantage point, wanted him to put the shirts on correctly. The child refused, and when his mother insisted, he screamed, cried, and tried to hit her. We never knew why it was so important to him to wear his shirt inside out, but it simply was. Negotiation is a wise strategy in those circumstances. I suggested that the mother say, "Mickey, this time you can wear it inside out, but next time you wear it the other way" and show him what she means. When the next dressing occasion arises she could say, "Remember, this time you're going wear it this way (showing him)," and give the child a minute or so to ponder what she said. Then she could ask him to put on his shirt, using manual guidance if necessary. He will probably fuss and may resist, but he will do as requested. Of course, heap praise on him and give him a hug "for being such a big boy."

Time Is the Enemy

The brain of a child with an ASD processes verbal information much more slowly than a typical child. Making matters worse, the child has great difficulty organizing sequences of steps that are part of a single goal-directed activity (e.g., putting on shoes and socks). If it should take 5–10 minutes for a child to put on his socks and shoes, plan for 15–20 minutes. A teacher who says, "Hurry up, Michael, you're going to miss the bus. You know how to put on your socks, get a move on" is overloading the child's verbal processing system by using too many words stated rapidly. Think of your child with autism like an old PC with a 128K processor. If you try to open a large document, it will take forever to open, and when you become impatient and click on the document again, and the computer tries to open it, the computer freezes halfway through the process. That is what occurs if you try to rush children with autism: They figuratively "freeze" halfway through the sequence. The result is likely to be an emotional outburst.

"Her Rituals Are Driving Us Crazy"

Nearly all children with an ASD have fixed routines they follow as they maneuver through the day. While everyone follows similar sequences when they get ready for work in the morning or pack for a business trip, the sequence of events children with autism feel they must follow are far more rigid. This is their way of organizing their world so that it is predictable and makes sense to them. If those sequences are disrupted, the children become confused and alarmed. They don't know what to expect next, which for a child with autism is a fate worse than death.

A father remarked, "She has to be the first one to get in the car in the morning when we drive her to school. One morning I decided to start the car and let it warm up so the windows wouldn't fog up on the way to school. When I went out to open the car door and get in, she started screaming, threw herself on the floor, and tried to kick her mother." This is a predictable response of a child with autism to an unexpected change in her routine. Parents sometimes say, "She has to have things her way," with the implication that the child is spoiled. The child isn't spoiled, she just has no idea what additional chaos is going to be foisted on her. There are simple steps parents can take to reduce this type of reaction. The first is to provide information several minutes in advance that today things will be done differently. "Daddy is going to get into the car, and then Becky can get in the car." Assist with the transition by telling her that she can hold her favorite doll when she walks to the car and that as soon as she gets into the car she can listen to her favorite song on the car's CD player. As her father walks out the door to the car, give her the doll and repeat, "As soon as Daddy is in the car, Becky can get in the car." After the car has been running a couple of minutes, walk the child to the car and repeat, "What a good girl! Dora's going to ride with Becky in the car." It is likely that the child will object and may pucker up with tears in her eyes, but she will probably accept the change in routine. After she has experienced the changed routine for several mornings and nothing bad has happened, she will accept it on subsequent mornings.

"Is She Ever Going to Be Like Other Kids?"

Every parent of a child with an ASD wonders whether their child will ever be like his or her siblings. Or will their child always twirl objects aimlessly, speak in short staccato phrases, and have meltdowns when an unexpected situation arises. Occasionally, amidst their child's "otherness," parents see glimpses of other family members' features and quirks that remind them that this child, who seems so unlike them in some ways, is very much a member of their family.

She's Like the Rest of Us

During a home visit, the father of a child with whom we were working remarked that his daughter Olivia was beginning to establish more eye contact. "Every once in a while, Olivia looks at me with that quizzical, sort of amused expression of hers. I'd swear I was looking at Martha (his wife)." This touching moment was especially important because he recognized that his daughter with autism was very much like the woman he fell in love with and married. When a parent says, "Eric's got his father's ears," or "Joleen's laugh is just like her grandma's," they are taking giant steps toward accepting their child, who at times seems very odd and unlike others in the family. During home-based therapy, staff can encourage recognition of specific features or qualities of a child with autism that resemble those of other family members. One of the therapists remarks, "Did you notice, Kenny uses one of his blocks to pretend he's shaving like his dad?" The more parents and siblings see the "us-ness" in their child, the easier it becomes to incorporate the child with ASD into family activities and routines. It changes the focus of attention from "How can we make him stop flapping his hands?" to "How can we include him when we go camping?"

A Child with ASD Is Not a "Special Project"

More than one father of a child with autism has told me that they view their son or daughter as their "special project," conjuring up images of putting a new roof on the garage or making a quilt. A project has a beginning, middle, and it usually has a clear endpoint. It involves a series of steps that must be completed in a specific order to get the job done right. When it's complete, you can stand back and, with your arms folded across your chest, survey your handiwork and conclude, "I did a pretty darned good job, didn't I?" Rearing any child, including one with autism, isn't a project. There are few well-defined steps to be followed in parenting a child with autism: It's all middle and there is no end in sight.

Parenting as Being "Case Managers"

Some couples define good parenting as being terrific case managers for their son or daughter. They create concrete activities for themselves that appear similar to the steps involved in building that garage roof or piecing, layering, and binding a quilt. They spend countless hours finding a doctor who will prescribe dietary supplements for their child, jousting with the school district for increased services, threatening litigation to obtain additional insurance coverage for their child's various therapies, driving their child to three or four therapies each week, and in other ways advocating for and escorting their child through an incredibly complex array of services. But at the end of the day when they tuck their child into bed at night, they are frustrated and saddened because despite their best efforts to assure their daughter the best possible services, she still hasn't recovered from autism.

"What will you do," I asked one couple, "if he always has symptoms of autism to some degree?" Their eyes were engulfed in pain. After an awkward delay, the husband replied with intensity, "We're *not* going to give up on Randy!" I replied, "I'm not talking about giving up, but just suppose, despite all of the heroic efforts you and Kris have made, Randy still has language and social limitations when he's 18 years old. Are you saying you will feel differently toward him than his sister Ginny?" Randy's father silently looked down at his hands tightly clasped in his lap, and tears rolled down his wife's cheeks and she sobbed. "You'll love Randy just like you love Ginny, of course you will," I said. "He doesn't need to be any special way for you to accept and love him," I added. This was a new way for this couple to begin to think about how they chose to parent their son Randy. It became much easier for them to include Randy in their family and for them to more fully participate in his therapy programs when they saw him as their cute, quirky son rather than as a project to be completed: a project they could appraise with satisfaction for the job they had done. It is important for parents to stop thinking of their child as their son or daughter with autism, and to simply enjoy him or her as their child who needs special assistance.

PARENTAL COPING

Parents' emotional health and well-being are critically important to their child's development. Recognizing emotional distress and developing coping strategies to deal with the stress of parenting a child with an ASD are important steps for all parents.

Depression and Anxiety in Parents of Children with ASDs

While the primary focus of this book is on the child's needs, it is often impossible to do so without helping couples resolve some of their differences. Toward the conclusion of my first interview with parents, I explore their degree of emotional distress and problems the child's disability is creating for their relationship. Stress is commonplace among parents of children with ASDs, especially mothers (Bromley et al., 2004; Duarte et al., 2005; Eisenhower, Baker, & Blacher, 2005). There is considerable evidence that mothers of children with autism suffer from depression far more frequently than mothers of children with other disabilities or of children without a disability (Hastings et al., 2005; Koegel, Schreibman, & Loos, 1992; Olsson & Hwang, 2001). Mothers experience the most distress, anxiety, and sometimes depression surrounding their child's behavior problems. They frequently feel that they are lacking support, and have difficulties with the way their husband copes with their child's problems (Freeman, Perry, & Factor, 1991; Hastings, 2003). However, there is also evidence that depression and anxiety disorder run in families of children with ASDs above and beyond the stresses and strains involved in parenting a child with autism (Micali, Chakrabarti, & Fombonne, 2004; Piven & Palmer, 2001; Piven et al., 1992). Mothers, in particular may be more prone to depression independent of their child's behavior problems. Indeed, the frequency of major depression among close relatives of children with autism is 37.5% compared with 11.1% found among relatives of control children. The frequency of social phobia, 20.2%, is nearly 10 times more common than that found among the relatives of the control children (2.4%). Single mothers of children with disabilities were found to be more vulnerable to severe depression than mothers living with a partner (Olsson & Hwang, 2001; Smalley, McCracken, & Tanguay, 1995).

Differences in Coping Strategies

Each partner in a marriage copes with his or her child's disability differently. One is the eternal optimist, the other the pessimist. One is the disciplinarian, the other likely to excuse the child's outbursts. One parent wants to do battle with the school over the child's services, the other prefers to work with the school rather than develop an adversarial relationship. These differences in coping strategies can lead to enormous tension within marriages, which is amplified during behavior problem flare-ups. Fishman, Wolf, and Noh (1989) studied marital stress in parents of children with autism and Down syndrome and found that mothers but not fathers were more depressed, and that marital intimacy was much lower for parents of children with ASDs as compared with parents of children with Down syndrome.

The stress of parenting a child with an ASD can drive an emotional wedge between the parents. Reminding parents of two things can help. First, they're in this together, and life will be a great deal better for everyone if they can play ball on the same team. Second, if they allow their differences and emotional distress to make them dysfunctional as individuals and as a couple, there will be no one to parent their children, including their child with autism. I encourage parents to sign a metaphorical pact to set aside their differences, to look for ways to compromise with their spouse, and to find common ground. That is the best way to help their child and themselves.

A couple with whom I worked had a clash of emotional styles. The husband lost his temper easily, raising his voice, and becoming verbally angry with his son with autism. He occasionally resorted to punitive measures. That is a risky parenting strategy that often backfires. (As James Baldwin remarked, "Children have never been very good at listening to their elders, but they have never failed to imitate them.") Shouting and corporal punishment are the last things one wants to encourage. His wife was not easily ruffled, but she was disturbed by her husband's angry outbursts, which she found unacceptable. Instead of arguing and trying to convince him that he had to stop expressing his anger, she suggested that if he felt himself beginning to lose his temper, he should go upstairs to his study, close the door, and listen to a his favorite Keith Jarrett recording, or else leave the house and go for a walk. She agreed to deal with their son's difficult behavior to give her husband a break and time to cool down. At other times when she had been caring for their son much of the day and needed a break of her own, her husband agreed to take over for an hour or so while she had coffee with one of her friends. Instead of insisting that the other person change his or her emotional style, both found a way of helping each other cope with situations they both found nearly intolerable at times.

Over time, most couples become more understanding, forgiving, and tolerant of each other's differences and foibles. "Don't sweat the little stuff" becomes their mantra. But sometimes couples find themselves at an impasse and are unable to back away from growing conflict. It is important that they seek outside help such as a marriage counselor or couples therapist.

Information Resources for Parents

Several books for parents provide helpful reading. *Keys to Parenting the Child with Autism* by Marlene Targ Brill (Brill, 2001) is an excellent starting place. Most parents are concerned about the impact caring for a child with autism has on their other children. Gold (1993) studied the relationship between sibling gender, age, birth order, qualities of the boy with autism, family characteristics, and siblings' depression. Siblings of autistic boys scored significantly higher on depression than the comparison group, but not on other problems of social adjustment. For parents who are especially concerned about impact on siblings, Sandra Harris and Beth Glasberg's *Siblings of Children with Autism: A Guide for Families* (Harris & Glasberg, 2003) is very helpful.

Include the child with autism in family activities, but don't ask siblings to routinely care for their brother or sister with autism. That will lead to resentment and later guilt over feeling resentment toward their brother or sister with an ASD. When a sibling has friends over to play, encourage them to include the child with an ASD but don't insist that they include him or her. That may lead the siblings' friends to leave and decline to return on another occasion when invited. They become annoyed about having to tolerate the child's problem behavior, which can lead to loss of friends for brothers or sisters of the child with autism. Siblings often feel they are being treated unfairly because their own minor behavior problems (e.g., arguing with their parents) are often punished, although those of the child with autism are not. By setting up an individualized point or "star" system for both children, both youngsters earn tangible recognition for helping out and either child's negative behavior has consequences as well. A chart can be placed in a prominent place like the refrigerator door listing tasks each child is to complete each day. Whenever they complete a task, they receive a star or a point on their respective charts. At the end of the day they exchange their stars for a preferred reward. Some parents take away points for behavioral outbursts, but that can backfire at times.

One of the most important ways of reducing family stress is to obtain help overcoming the behavioral challenges of the child with an ASD. Nearly all studies indicate that behavioral challenges are the major source of maternal stress and depression. The father's negative reaction to the child's behavior and the resulting discord about how to deal with the problem exacerbates the mother's emotional distress. As a result, as soon as possible following diagnosis, parents are encouraged to begin down the pathway of procuring appropriate behavioral, educational, and medical services for their child.

GETTING HELP

Assisting parents in identifying sources of support from family, community, doctors, and other professionals is an important part of preparing families to begin any form of intervention.

Obtaining Support from Other Parents

At the conclusion of the initial interview with the parents, it is important to provide them with a road map for how to access the resources they will need. The name, telephone number, and e-mail address of an individual in the local autism society is essential. When I have suggested that they contact the local autism society, some parents have replied: "We're not joiners," or "My husband hates going to meetings." Parent advocacy organizations are one of the most useful contacts any parent will make. Parents who already have had to deal with the same issues have learned how to find solutions to problems that new parents haven't even anticipated. Parents whose child has been recently diagnosed will have a host of practical concerns, such as how to find a doctor and dentist who specialize in autism and how to obtain help from county social service agencies. Parents need to plan for in-home support services such as personal care attendants, respite, or other Waivered Services support. All parents of children with ASDs should develop a plan for respite services. It is inevitable that times will arise when parents will need respite care for their child, due to illness, a death in the family, or another unforeseen event. Planning ahead pays off when the need arises. Most public school districts have an autism specialist who will gladly meet with parents whose child has been recently diagnosed to discuss possible special educational service options.

Working with Doctors and Nurses

Every family of a child with an ASD should search for a pediatrician who specializes in treating such children. Working effectively with physicians also involves learning to work with their nurses regarding common health and dietary issues. Taking the time to establish positive relationships with these key health care providers will pay off when problems arise later.

Finding a Doctor

According to the American Academy of Pediatrics (2001), pediatricians are usually the first professionals to determine that a child with a developmental delay has an ASD. Although some children with autism are seen and treated by family practitioners, it is generally agreed that they should receive their health care from a pediatrician, if possible. While general pediatricians (who are internists for children) see children with autism in their practices, they commonly refer them to a developmental behavioral pediatrician who has specific training and experience with autism. There are approximately 800 developmental behavioral pediatricians in the United States, most of whom work in medical schools, with the next largest percentage being in specialized pediatric group practices. It is often difficult to identify a pediatrician who is knowledgeable and experienced in caring for children with ASDs. When one is identified, it is common for parents to face a 3–6 month wait for a first office appointment.

Getting to Know the Nurse

It is useful for parents to get to know the nurse in their pediatrician's office. When parents call the doctor's office with a concern or question, they will talk with the nurse, not the doctor. The more specific they can be about their concern the better. "His outbursts have escalated from once per week to two or three times per day over the past week" is much better than "His outbursts are out of control." If parents are worried about a side effect of a drug, they should take their child's temperature, blood pressure, and pulse, and they should keep a record of how much urine is being produced. If the child has vomited, they should record the time and how much the child threw up. If the child's speech is unusual or he or she looks glassy-eyed and muscle tone seems atypical, parents should note that. These pieces of information will be useful in deciding whether the child needs to be seen and how soon.

Addressing Common Health Problems

There are no medical treatments for autism, but there are treatments for health and psychobehavioral disorders that coexist with autism. Autism is associated with other health problems, so one of the first issues a pediatrician faces is identifying other conditions that may be present with autism that require treatment. The most common condition is epilepsy. If a child is suspected of having a seizure disorder, the youngster will be referred for an EEG. Approximately 60% of children with ASDs will have atypical EEGs, but not all of those children will have a clear seizure disorder. Unless a child has more obvious motor, cognitive, and/or behavioral components to suspected seizures, the EEG alone will not necessarily prove that the child has a seizure disorder. EEG abnormalities are more common among children diagnosed with ASDs who also have subtle dysmorphic physical features and a lower IQ score. Treatment of seizure and mental health disorders will be discussed in Chapter 9. There is some evidence of autoimmune disorder among some children with ASDs, especially thyroid disease among family members (Molloy et al., 2006). Fragile X syndrome overlaps with autism in about 20%–25% cases, and, less commonly, children with autism also have tuberous sclerosis (see Chapter 9). Children with autism are more likely to experience obsessive-compulsive disorder (OCD) or depression than other children with developmental delays as well as coexistent attention-deficit/hyperactivity disorder (ADHD; Hattori et al., 2006).

Pursuing Dietary Treatments and Alternative Medicines

Many families wish to pursue dietary or other alternative medicine treatments for their children with ASDs, but they generally find an unsympathetic ear when they approach their child's pediatrician about the idea. Physicians are constrained by ethical and legal standards of medical practice, which include the proviso that they may only recommend or prescribe treatments that have been demonstrated in controlled clinical studies to be safe and have demonstrated efficacy. There are few if any controlled clinical studies with most herbal or other nonprescription medications for individuals with ASDs. Most controlled studies with elimination diets (e.g., gluten–casein-free diets) have failed to demonstrate efficacy in changing children's behavior or functioning. It is very important that families tell their child's doctor about any dietary conditions or any over-the-counter medicines their child is using. High doses of some minerals and vitamins can cause diarrhea, nausea, and vomiting. Some extreme dietary restrictions can cause mineral or vitamin deficiencies, and some herbal over-the-counter medications can interact with prescription medicines the doctor may be considering for a child. For example, tryptophan and St. John's wort interact with antidepressant medications such as Prozac or Paxil, which are used to treat anxiety and OCD in people with ASDs. The combination can cause a dangerous toxic condition called central serotonin syndrome. Some doctors may seem dismissive when parents suggest alternative therapies, but increasingly pediatricians are good listeners who explain to parents what they know about the proposed treatments and give their recommendations.

Getting Help with Behavior Problems

Tantrums, aggressive outbursts, compulsive routines, and self-injury are major sources of stress for families of children with ASDs. Understanding the reasons for such disturbed and disturbing behavior is at the root of finding a solution, whether medical or behavioral.

Medical Solutions

If parents are concerned about behavior problems, it is a good idea to keep a record of the number of outbursts per day and bring that to the appointment with the child's doctor. If outbursts occur daily, two weeks of observations should be sufficient. If outbursts occur less often, a month's worth of data is necessary. If parents have access to a camcorder, a short video sample of what the child looks like in the midst of an outburst gives the doctor a concrete idea of the severity and nature of the behavioral outburst. Video samples of suspected seizures can also be extremely helpful to the physician in deciding whether to order an EEG or MRI.

A frantic mother calls her doctor's office because her child with autism has started striking his head and she can't make him stop. She calls the doctor's office and speaks with the nurse. "This is Elizabeth Jones, Billy's mother," she says. "Billy has autism and is one of Dr. Carlson's patients. He is out of control. He's been hitting his head since this morning and I can't make him stop." The nurse realizes that Mrs. Jones is alarmed and that Billy is hurting himself, but she needs specific information to recommend a course of action. It would be more helpful if Mrs. Jones had said, "This is Elizabeth Jones, Billy Jones's mother. Billy has autism and will be 9 in August. He's nonverbal and has had tantrums in the past, but not this bad. Dr. Carlson gave him Tenormin to calm him down, but it isn't doing any good. After breakfast this morning he started hitting his head with his fists. I tried to restrain his arms but he bit me and then started hitting his head on the kitchen table, on the door-frame, and on the floor. He has a big bruise on his cheek where he hit himself and a cut on his forehead from hitting the corner of the table. He has been doing that on and off now for the last 6 hours. Nothing we do seems to calm him down. I took his temperature and it was 101. I think he might be constipated. The last time he had a BM was 2 or 3 days ago." Based on this information, it is possible that the nurse will tell Mrs. Jones to find another adult to restrain Billy and transport him to an emergency room so that he can be seen. The important point is that for medical staff to help parents, doctors and nurses need specific information rather than general expressions of alarm or concern.

Behavioral Interventions

Often the most effective solutions for behavioral challenges of children with ASDs can be obtained from psychologists or special educators who are specifically trained to analyze and treat such problems. Some pediatric practices and mental health clinics employ psychologists trained in behavior analysis who have experience analyzing the social causes of problem behavior and developing practical treatments. School districts often employ special education teachers or school psychologists who are authorized to make home visits to assist parents with difficult behavior problems. In other cases, psychologists in private practice may be available to consult with parents. They are often able to provide practical methods parents can employ that are highly effective in overcoming behavioral challenges. These approaches will be discussed in detail in Chapter 7.

5

Principles of Early
Behavioral Intervention

Early intervention provides a child who has an ASD with the skills necessary to adapt to school, to interact effectively with his or her family and friends, and to take part in community activities. Ideally, children should begin receiving early intervention between 2 and 3 years of age, but in some regions children don't begin early intervention programs until they make the transition into kindergarten. The most important early intervention priorities are

1. Developing functional spontaneous communication

2. Developing social instruction/therapy in various settings

3. Obtaining experience with parents, multiple adult teachers, and therapists

4. Developing cognitive and play skills

5. Learning to interact with typical peers

6. Developing proactive approaches to preventing behavior problems (Lord & McGee, 2001)

Many 2-year-olds with ASDs are nonverbal or echolalic, follow few if any adult directions, and show limited interest in others. Most have behavior problems, usually crying and becoming upset when expected routines are disrupted, and a minority are aggressive with a small percentage engaging in self-injury. Their lack of social interest makes it difficult for them to communicate with others. They ward off social overtures from parents, teachers, and peers by ignoring the speaker, looking away when spoken to, or leaving the area. They seldom look at people's faces or establish eye contact, which makes nonverbal communication difficult. While they view their mothers as a source of safety and comfort, they tend to be wary of other adults, which is the first barrier to early intervention.

FAMILY SUPPORT AND STRENGTHENING PARENTING SKILLS

Most parents of children with ASDs want to actively participate in their children's learning and development. When the child with an ASD is a second or third child in the family, parents may be understandably resistant to the idea that they need help learning to parent a child with ASD, since they have been successful parenting their previous children. But they usually do need assistance and, after struggling for months or longer with the care of their child, parents come to that realization. While they may initially feel at a loss about how to cope with their very different child, most parents can acquire the necessary skills to effectively promote their child's development.

Helping parents involves providing information, opportunities for observation, and specific skill-building strategies. Many parents are initially unable to absorb specific intervention information because they are still trying to cope with the idea that their child has an ASD. Once they have come to terms with that reality, providing them with reading materials and videos can be a valuable next step. Although some parents react negatively to attending a meeting of an ASD parents group, it can often be extremely helpful. Hearing other parents discussing challenges with their own children that mirror those of the parents whose child was recently diagnosed can be beneficial. Realizing that they are not alone and learning from others can be liberating for many parents. Many state and local chapters of the Autism Society of America offer parent-training activities.

Information, Referral, and Resource Recommendations

Family circumstances and parental characteristics determine the goals, approach, and the degree to which parents can be involved in parent-training activities. Intensive home-based family skills collaboration is not a viable option for some families. For a variety of mental health reasons, personality characteristics, belief systems, and other health reasons, some parents are unable to effectively participate in in-home family skills training services. For those families, more reasonable goals involve providing information, recommending various support services, and helping the families connect with school or other center-based services for their child.

Family Mental Health and Personality Traits

A family with whom I worked included a father who had characteristics of the broader ASD phenotype and a mother who was clinically depressed. The father did not appear to enjoy interacting with his children and the mother often found it difficult to get out bed. After several months of attempting home-based therapy services, the parents acknowledged that they found it nearly impossible to regularly implement the recommended therapy procedures on their own. They were encouraged to enroll their son in a center-based program, which removed the pressure from them to carry out parenting activities that were beyond their current capabilities and they were referred to an agency for mental health services for themselves.

The mother of a 4-year-old with a severe ASD had been an artist before her son was born. She was a creative, intelligent, very funny woman, and had an unorthodox approach to life. She acknowledged that she was disorganized and would have great difficulty keeping track of her child's intervention programs. She often appeared distracted and confused. While she understood the rationale behind her son's proposed early intervention program, she found the implicit structure inconsistent with her own lifestyle, which was spontaneous. She longed to be able to return to her creative work, but found it nearly impossible while parenting the child with an ASD and a younger sibling. While she was a loving and dedicated mother, she was not a good candidate for home-based family skills collaboration.

Another couple had both been previously married. A 5-year-old girl from the wife's first marriage with a high-functioning ASD was adopted by her new father. The stepfather was a warm, loving man who led a busy professional life, with a great deal of travel and long hours at work. He acknowledged that when he was at home with his family he tended to be impatient and often "had a short fuse." In addition, it was extremely difficult for him to accept and implement recommended intervention strategies, and the child's mother found it difficult to do so entirely on her own.

Family Beliefs and Financial Stressors

Another couple experienced financially distressed circumstances. They had three children less than 5 years of age with ASD diagnoses. Their belief system included very strong notions of personal responsibility that appeared to emanate from their upbringing. Their notions of personal conduct that they considered right and wrong extended to their preschool children with ASDs. Although the parents said they were aware that their oldest child with Asperger syndrome did not fully understand what right, wrong, and "ought" meant, when the child shoved his younger brother and took away his sibling's toy, his father firmly scolded the older child and told him he "ought to know better." Such strongly held beliefs, together with the numerous financial stressors impinging on their lives, made it extremely difficult for this couple to actively participate in family skills training activities.

Physical Illnesses of Family Members

The mother of an 8-year-old son with a high-functioning ASD was divorced. After several months of home-based services, the child's mother was diagnosed with a serious illness and underwent a series of treatments that made her weak, very tired, and at times nauseous. Although she wanted to continue home-based services for her son, she was not physically capable of participating. The treatment team made arrangements for her son to receive intervention at a nearby community center with assistance from experienced therapy staff. The boy's mother was encouraged to remain involved in the services provided by staff at the community center to the degree it was physically possible.

For parents with limitations such as those described above, it is often most helpful to provide information, assist with accessing other support resources (e.g., physician, personal care attendant, respite providers, crisis assistance), and help identify center-based services for the child with an ASD.

COLLABORATIVE HOME-BASED FAMILY SKILLS TRAINING

For many parents who are well organized with high-achievement motivation, a more hands-on approach to parent collaboration and training can be effective. These parents are more likely to find the recommended procedures in Table 5.1 consistent with their general approach to life. They are often people who attend classes on refinishing furniture, learning how to use Photoshop software, or preparing low-cholesterol meals. For them, family skills training makes sense. Home-based collaborative services usually begin with a parent-orientation meeting followed by several informational sessions.

Observing and Assessing Ecology

The next step typically involves observing experienced teachers or therapists working with other children with ASDs in a school-based or home-based program. Parents are given reading materials describing the intervention they are about to observe and explaining the rationale behind the methods being used. After a short observation period, an experienced staff member meets with the parents and encourages them to ask questions and explore their concerns.

Parent collaboration is often more effective than a purely didactic approach to parent training. In the past, many programs presented a series of lectures and demonstrations of intervention principles and techniques, and then encouraged parents to attempt to use the same principles and techniques on their own. There are two problems with this approach. First, the amount of information is often overwhelming, contains numerous unfamiliar abstract

Table 5.1. A multi-session orientation plan for parents and other caregivers embarking on home-based therapy services (*Note: Presenters and discussion leaders include other parents, experienced therapists and teachers, and social service agency staff and professionals such as psychologists who supervise services.*)

I. Being the Parent of a Child with an ASD
   A. Introductions: Tell Us About You and Your Family
   B. What Are Your Main Concerns?
   C. What Are Your Hopes and Aspirations?
   D. Living with Your Special Child
II. Main Features of ASDs: Why Does He Act That Way?
   A. Diagnostic Features
   B. Types of ASDs
III. Understanding Your Child
   A. Compulsivity in ASDs
   B. Coping with Behavior Challenges
   C. The World Is a Confusing and Scary Place for Children with ASDs
   D. The Child's Need for Control
      1. Many Children with ASD Have Obsessive-Compulsive Disorder
      2. Gain Control by Relinquishing Control
IV. Resources
   A. Schools
      1. Referral Process
      2. School Identification
      3. Early Childhood Special Education
      4. Individualized Family Service Plans (IFSPs) and Individualized Education Programs (IEPs)
      5. Working Collaboratively with School Personnel
   B. Doctors
      1. Identifying an Appropriate Doctor
      2. Medical Diagnosis
      3. Common Diagnostic Tests
      4. Common Health Problems
      5. Medications
   C. County Social Services
      1. Respite
      2. Personal Care Attendants
      3. Waiver Services
      4. Crisis Support
   D. Parent and Advocacy Organizations
V. Home-Based Early Intervention
   A. What Is Intensive Early Behavior Therapy?
   B. Individual Treatment Plan (ITP)
   C. Discrete Trial and Incidental Learning
   D. Parents as Team Members
   E. Team Members' Responsibilities
   G. Components of Therapy
   H. How Many Hours Per Week for How Long?
   I. Monitoring Progress

concepts, and is difficult to assimilate. Second, parents will likely have difficulty understanding how to apply the principles and techniques to the daily routines and demands of their own lives.

An alternative strategy is to begin with the reality of a family's day-to-day life, or the typical classroom routines, and demonstrate how the principles and techniques can fit into those routines. By doing so, parents and school personnel begin to immediately grasp how to apply a principle or concept to their daily lives. This circumvents the problem of translating an abstract concept (e.g., generalization) into a practical daily situation (e.g., responding appropriately to both mother and father). This approach makes it unnecessary for parents to create a contrived situation within which to practice a given skill (e.g., fading prompts) because they will be employing that technique in the course of their typical daily home life. This approach also is especially effective if parents are actively involved in selecting priorities and targets for intervention. When introducing a new concept or technique to parents, it is possible to interrupt a typical daily routine (e.g., setting the dinner table) to teach a discrimination (e.g., how to tell forks from knives and spoons), which may require a series of repeated trials. After a block of discrete trial instruction to maximize opportunities to learn a new discrimination, the typical daily routine can be resumed.

Preparing for Therapy

Children with ASDs receive various assessments, primarily *norm-referenced tests,* designed to determine how a child is functioning in various domains relative to other children. Intellectual, cognitive, language, neuropsychological, and diagnostic assessments are used to evaluate a child's ability levels related to thinking, reasoning, use of language, and possible brain-functioning differences affecting learning. These assessments are not designed to determine which specific skills a child does or does not have, nor do they prescribe what interventions should be employed to overcome skill impairments. Assessments to serve the latter purpose are called *prescriptive* or *criterion-referenced assessments.*

Two primary prescriptive assessment tools have been used to assist teachers and other therapists in devising intervention strategies to develop needed skills: *Psychoeducational Profile-Revised (PEP-R;* Schopler, Reichler, Bashford, Lansing, & Marcus [1979]; *Assessment of Basic Language and Learning Scale-Revised (ABLLS-R;* Partington [2006]). The PEP-R, developed by Eric Schopler at TEACCH at the University of North Carolina, was originally published in 1980 and updated in 1990. The PEP-R is an inventory of behaviors and skills designed to identify uneven and idiosyncratic learning patterns. The PEP-R is most appropriately used with children functioning at or below the preschool range and within the chronological age range of 6 months to

7 years. It provides information on developmental functioning in imitation, perception, fine motor, gross motor, eye/hand coordination, cognitive performance, and cognitive verbal areas. PEP-R is used in conjunction with two volumes that provide specific suggestions for translating assessment data into an individualized education program (IEP). These accompanying programs consist of a collection of more than 250 teaching activities, and each activity states the goal, immediate objective, materials, and procedures for teaching. Activities are arranged by function and developmental areas.

The ABLLS-R, developed by James Partington, is a prescriptive assessment and curriculum intervention guide as well as a skills tracking instrument (Partington, 2006). The ABLLS-R Protocol contains a task analysis of the many skills necessary to communicate effectively and to learn from everyday experiences. It consists of a protocol for administering the assessment and the *ABLLS-R Guide*, which includes strategies to assist parents, teachers, and therapists in developing effective IEP and ITP (individual treatment plan) programs. In the following example, the ABLLS-R was used to evaluate a 2-year-old child who was just beginning services.

1. Translating Theory into Practice

When the doorbell rang, Sarah didn't know what to expect. Sarah is the mother of three children; the youngest, Aaron, is a 2½-year-old who has been diagnosed with autistic disorder. When she opened the door, Brenda, Aaron's clinical director, and Tom, a senior behavior therapist, introduced themselves and were welcomed into Sarah's home. Sarah's husband Michael was at work, where he was employed as a computer programmer. Brenda, who is in her early 30s, has a master's degree in applied behavior analysis (ABA) and is a board-certified behavior analyst. Tom, who is several years younger than Brenda, is working on his master's degree in psychology and is helping Brenda prepare for Aaron's therapy. The three sat at the kitchen table drinking coffee and discussing Aaron and the next steps in his intensive early behavior therapy (IEBT) program. Although Sarah had read about IEBT, it is one thing to read about it and another to see it in action.

Brenda began by exploring the family's daily routines, i.e., which person performed which activities and when. She discussed the likes and dislikes of each family member with Sarah to create an inventory of typical daily routines (see McWilliam & Bailey, 1992). Evidence from numerous sources indicate that optimal effects of home-based early intervention depend on integrating interventions within typical daily routines as much as possible (e.g., Albin et al., 1996; Bambara et al., 1995; Moes & Frea, 2002), especially after initiating procedures within more controlled situations. Brenda explained what was involved in conducting a baseline assessment and how important that was in developing an ITP. She gave Sarah a blank ITP form to begin filling out and then reviewed the components with her. As their conversation evolved, Sarah realized that Brenda had a great deal of experience, and Tom had a wonderful, relaxed way with children. Tom picked up Aaron's 4-year-old sister Esther and held her on his lap as he participated in the conversation. Brenda explained that a baseline assessment was conducted to determine which skills to begin teaching. She mentioned that standardized norm-referenced tests, such as those used during the diagnostic assessment, aren't intended for this purpose. Instead, they would use a prescriptive instrument—the ABLLS-R (Partington, 2006)—developed for this purpose (see Figure 5.1).

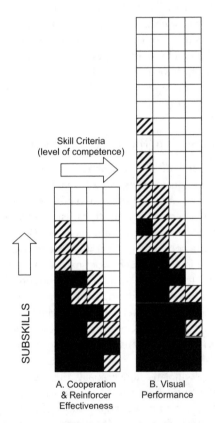

Figure 5.1. Truncated examples of the first two ABLLS-R skills tracking scales (of 25 scales). *Note:* Each vertical box for each scale represents a teachable skill. Horizontal boxes represent degrees of competence in executing skills. Baseline performance is assessed prior to beginning IEBT (black boxes) and repeated at 6-month intervals (diagonal stripe). Progress can be assessed qualitatively and quantitatively by tabulating percentage of new skills acquired per 6-month interval and at specified competence levels. In practice, boxes are usually filled with a felt-tip pen using a different color for successive 6-month periods. (Based on the ABLLS-R by permission of Behavior Analysts, Inc.)

Tom offered Sarah a copy of the short form of the ABLLS-R, which is made up of 25 scales, with each scale divided into specific component skills (from 6 to 52 skills, depending on the scale). Component skills are scored according to the percentage of time they are done correctly or the amount and type of prompting necessary to evoke a correct response. The first few scales emphasize accepting rewards or reinforcers from the therapist, complying with simple motor requests ("come sit"), matching familiar objects, and imitating motor actions such as clapping hands. The assessment is conducted in 2-hour blocks of time, typically on two successive days, and provides a good starting point for planning intervention. The vertical boxes for each scale represent new skills, and the horizontal boxes represent percentage correct or prompting necessary to produce correct responding. As each scale and item is tested, boxes are filled with a colored felt-tip pen producing a profile of all skills the child exhibits at baseline. Brenda explained that some scales for the most advanced skills or that take place in other settings such as school won't be evaluated at baseline. Tom indicated that every 6 months, they will re-administer the ABLLS-R to update Aaron's progress and to aid in setting goals for the next 6 months. Each subsequent assessment is indicated by a different color to make it easy to track progress over time. Although the sub-skills within the ABLLS-R are roughly developmentally sequenced, some therapy and instructional programs have re-sequenced items to more closely follow typical skill development (see Figure 5.2).

Brenda encouraged Sarah to observe the baseline assessment. Brenda has learned that the more aware parents are of the difficulty their child has with skills the parents had assumed he or she was capable of performing, the better they understand the child's concerns. Parents begin to realize that the reason their child appeared to be noncompliant or was having tantrums when asked to put away his or her shoes or get ready for bed was because these were requests the child didn't understand and also didn't have the ability to comply with. Moreover, it is useful for parents to understand the meticulous process of skill development by breaking complex tasks into minute component skills, each of which must be taught individually. This helps parents interpret their child's progress through the painstaking intervention process.

INDIVIDUALIZED TREATMENT AND FAMILY SERVICE PLANS

Determining the most appropriate location in which to begin intervention, and becoming accustomed to having therapists in their home, are the next steps families face in initiating IEBT for their child.

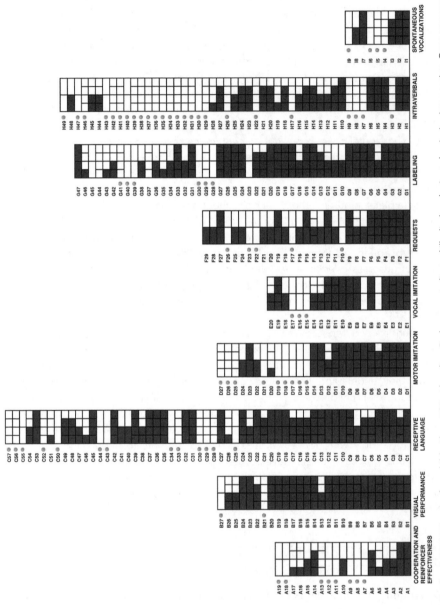

Figure 5.2. The first 9 ABLLS-R scales for a child with an ASD at baseline. Dark squares indicate skills displayed prior to beginning intervention. Open squares indicate skills that remain to be acquired. (Source: Behavior Analysts, Inc.; reproduced by permission.)

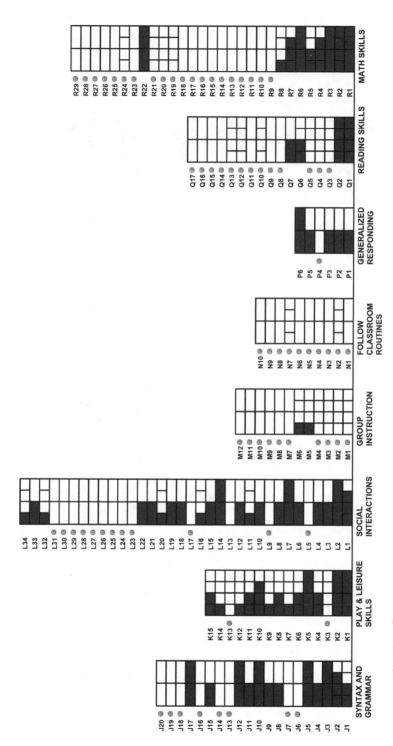

Figure 5.2. (continued)

(continued)

85

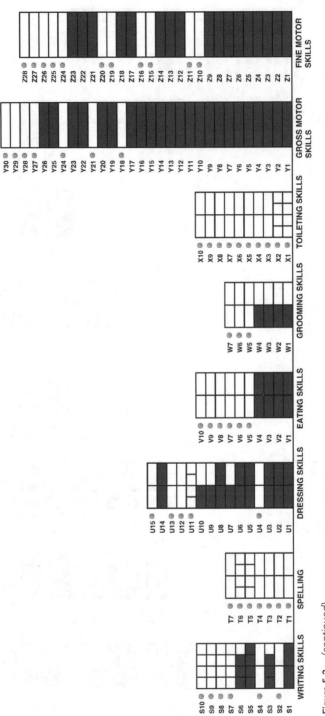

Figure 5.2. (continued)

86

1. The Therapy/Instructional Setting

Brenda had already explained to Sarah on the telephone that they would need a designated "therapy area" with a small table and two chairs, preferably in a recreation room, extra bedroom, or another room used infrequently by the family. They would need a place to store therapy supplies and a lockable cabinet for therapy records and staff member time sheets. Brenda and Tom stood in the recreation room surveying the layout Sarah had rearranged for Aaron's therapy. "It looks perfect!" Brenda said. Sarah led Aaron by the hand into the room, and Brenda squatted down to his level facing him and said, "Hi, Aaron." Aaron turned his head away from Brenda and made an odd sound, with a rising inflection that sounded as though he were asking a question. Tom explained that before they could obtain a valid measure of Aaron's abilities, they needed to spend several days establishing rapport with him. Brenda remarked, "It will probably look as though we aren't doing anything special, but actually it is an important step in getting to know Aaron and making him feel comfortable with us." Sarah began to feel more at ease with these two young people in her house and realized that they had a real knack with Aaron, with whom most people found it difficult to relate.

Adjusting to Home-Based IEBT

Brenda's experience is typical of the first interaction of therapy staff with a parent during the first home visit. Parents are initially anxious and somewhat doubtful about the depth of knowledge and skills of the staff members who will work with their son or daughter. It takes time for parents such as Sarah and her husband to feel confident of Brenda's and Tom's skills and knowledge. Most parents are concerned that perhaps their house will look too messy or that the therapy staff would disapprove of how they parent their other children. Sarah and her husband initially felt that they had to be on guard, but that feeling diminished over several weeks as they got to know all members of the therapy team. Effective team leaders like Brenda dispel concerns very quickly with a comment such as, "You should have seen my house this morning. What a mess. I didn't have time to straighten up before dropping my daughter off at school." Staff members are trained to exercise the utmost confidentiality regarding what they see or hear when in a family's home. They are also trained not to be judgmental about the way families lead their lives. One family is highly organized and the house always meticulous, and the next seems a bit chaotic with an extemporaneous quality about it. Some parents are clearly on the same page with one another regarding their child's concerns while others seem to frequently disagree. But all parents who seek IEBT services love their children and are committed to doing whatever is necessary to help their child with an ASD prosper. That is what matters. The staff members' only concern is to enlist parental cooperation and support for their child's therapy plan, and to help the parents in whatever way possible through a demanding experience (Larsson, 2002).

Establishing Rapport with the Child

It is difficult to begin to work effectively with others, including a child with an ASD, without first establishing a mutually positive relationship (Maag, 2001). The approach most commonly employed to do this, called The Child's Game, resembles Greenspan's "floor time." The therapist sits on the floor with the child and very gradually engages the child by following his or her lead. For example, the therapist might gently roll a ball toward the child. Many children will ignore the ball and continue a repetitive action (e.g., moving a toy car back and forth, twirling an object). To familiarize the child with the therapist's voice and to help the child feel comfortable, the therapist gently comments on his or her actions (e.g., "Bobby push car"). When Bobby stops pushing the car and reaches for the ball, the therapist says in an animated voice, "Bobby push ball" and holds out his or her hands as if to receive the ball. Sometimes the child will push the ball toward the therapist and other times he or she will not. As the child moves about the room engaging in various activities, the therapist accompanies him or her, commenting on the child's actions but making no requests. If the child whines or seems annoyed, the therapist turns away and appears to be busy with something else, resuming undivided attention as soon as the child stops fussing.

Each session lasts approximately 2 hours. The goal is to assure the child that the therapist isn't going to ask him or her to do something disturbing and to begin to develop a positive relationship. By the third session, the therapist begins intruding on the child gently but more directly by rolling the ball toward the child and then holding out his or her hands to the child saying, "Bobby push ball." By this point, most young children with ASD are beginning to physically interact with the therapist, handing the therapist toys or sitting on his or her lap. If the child doesn't seem to understand what "push ball" means, the therapist manually (and gently) guides the child through the motion of pushing the ball. When the child responds affirmatively to the therapist's prompt, the therapist claps her hands and says, "Great! What a smart boy" or makes a similar positive comment. By the end of the fifth session, the child is comfortable with the therapist and has begun to actively solicit interactions. When the therapist arrives at the child's home, the child often runs up and tugs at the therapist's skirt or jeans, or takes the therapist's hand and attempts to lead him or her to the room in which they have been playing for the past week. Now it is time to begin therapy in earnest.

On the last day of rapport building, Brenda and Tom met with Sarah to prepare her for structured therapy. They told her that there were practical considerations. "It will take time to become accustomed to having several therapists, each working 3-hour shifts in your home for 30 hours per week," Brenda said. "We'll do our best to stay out of your way, but for a while it is going to seem as though there is always someone coming or going," Tom added. Brenda suggested that Sarah inform the neighbors on either side of her house and across the street that therapists' cars will be parked in the street in front of her house and occasionally in front of their houses, and that on Thursdays, when the team meets at 3:30 PM, there may be additional cars when the supervising psychologist and others participate in the meeting.

2. Therapy Begins in Earnest

"Aaron may fuss off and on during the first week, as he is becoming accustomed to therapists asking him to do things that he isn't used to doing," Brenda said to Sarah. "But try to avoid entering the therapy area as much as possible during the first week. That will make it emotionally easier for you and will prevent Aaron's running to you to avoid therapy activities." Tom chimed in, "He should stop fussing after a few days once he becomes accustomed to the new routine and to us." Brenda added, "At the end of each shift, please raise any questions you might have with the staff member on duty, or give me a call. I'm always glad to hear from you."

Over the next 2 weeks, Sarah called Brenda every day or two with a question, but over succeeding weeks and months, as she and her husband grew more comfortable with the staff and Aaron's program, the calls dwindled to a trickle.

SCHOOL-BASED ASSESSMENT AND INTERVENTION

Sarah asks whether it is a good idea to enroll Aaron in early childhood special education (ECSE) as well. Brenda replies that it would be a very good idea because it could help promote Aaron's social skills and encourage generalization of things he learns at home to school. When Sarah calls the nearby public school ECSE program, she is put in touch with Germaine Johnson, the teacher who serves as multidisciplinary team (MDT) coordinator and who assists in individualized family service plan (IFSP) team assessments. Ten days later, Sarah and Aaron visit Maryville Elementary School, where one wing is devoted to ECSE classrooms. Ms. Johnson welcomes them and introduces Sarah to other members of the MDT (usually a lead special educator, an occupational and speech therapist, a vision specialist, and, if there are medical issues, a school nurse).

Multidisciplinary Team School Assessment

After Aaron begins playing with the toys provided by Ms. Johnson, the speech therapist takes his hand and leads him into an adjacent room with a one-way window so that Sarah can watch the assessment. Over the next 2 hours, various members of the MDT evaluate Aaron and review the recommendations from the nearby Children's Hospital at which a full battery of tests have already been done. Ms. Johnson says it appears that Aaron qualifies for ECSE services based on the test information and her initial observations, but she will need to wait for the MDT assessment results before making recommendations. At the conclusion of the session, Ms. Johnson explains that it will take 2 weeks to score the test and determine Aaron's eligibility for ECSE services. Once that is done, the entire team will participate in developing the individualized family service plan (IFSP), including Aaron's parents. As she is about to leave with Aaron, Sarah asks if it would all right if Brenda, as director of Aaron's home behavior therapy team, participates in the IFSP planning meeting. Ms. Johnson says she would welcome Brenda's input.

The Individualized Family Service Plan

Ten days later, Sarah receives a telephone call from Ms. Johnson who says that most of the assessments have been scored and the team has tentatively agreed that Aaron is eligible for ECSE services. She suggests that a date be established for planning an interim IFSP for Aaron and his family. She indicates that the purpose of this meeting will be to determine the specific services Aaron and his family will receive. She explains that the school district uses the PEP-R as a criterion-referenced assessment for curriculum planning. Sarah and her husband Michael, Brenda, Ms. Johnson, the director of ECSE for the district, the speech therapist, and the occupational therapist are present at the meeting. During the meeting, Aaron's abilities across various domains are discussed. Sarah and Brenda describe Aaron's home-based therapy routines and how they can be coordinated with his participation in the ECSE program. Sarah and Michael describe challenges they have been experiencing with Aaron's behavior at home, although they report that his behavior has begun improving over recent weeks. The team discusses home and community activities in which Aaron participates (e.g., attending the Jewish Community Center for swimming lessons). Each member of the team is encouraged to propose strategies that may be useful for improving Aaron's skills and preventing his occasional outbursts. The family strengths and the unique traits that Aaron brings to the situation are examined to see if there are ways to build on them. A major purpose of the meeting is to explore the family's concerns for Aaron and to determine the best way to construct a plan to address those concerns.

Over the course of the IFSP meeting, the PEP-R as well as additional language assessments and a sensory-motor assessment are being administered in a nearby room. The PEP-R uses a standardized kit of toys, test materials, and instructions for scoring the child's performance in each skill and sub-skill. Because Aaron is already somewhat familiar with the teacher administering the assessment, the initial process of familiarizing Aaron with the teacher is shortened. Over the next 2 weeks, Ms. Johnson and Aaron's new special education teacher, Caroline Cohen, prepare a draft of an interim IFSP to review with his parents.

Brenda and Sarah meet with Ms. Johnson and Ms. Cohen to discuss the details. They decide as a group that Aaron will receive ECSE services three mornings a week to begin with, focusing on social skills, communication with peers, and cognitive school-readiness skills. As the school year progresses, the school will consider increasing the number of hours of ECSE services. Brenda indicates that for the first week either she or Tom will spend an hour each day (Monday, Wednesday, and Friday mornings) while Aaron is in school observing and making suggestions for intervention strategies that might be useful. They will also glean ideas for ways of promoting generalization of skills being worked on at school to the home setting. Ms. Cohen indicates that she plans to make a home visit during therapy time to compare notes sometime in the next 2 weeks. The team agrees that every 2 weeks there will be an exchange of data and observations by staff across the two settings.

Once the ECSE program begins, similar principles guide the beginning of instruction, with short periods of intervention alternating with periods in which no adult demands are made. Higher-functioning children may attempt to imitate peers (e.g., taking their seats, sitting down at circle time), while children with greater challenges may require interpolated one-to-one skills practice in a discrete trial format. Because the staff-to-student ratio is less favorable in most classrooms, instructional staff typically rotate from one student to the next with a change of activity approximately every 15 minutes (the time varying from school to school), with a proportion of the students being involved in less-structured activities without one-to-one intervention at any one moment in time (e.g., sandbox, swing, trampoline).

DISCRETE TRIAL TEACHING/THERAPY

Lois, the mother of 4-year-old Christopher, expressed concern that she had heard from the mother of another child with an ASD that "ABA," as she referred to IEBT, would turn her son into a robot. Many people who only know about IEBT secondhand are not aware that there are numerous variations on the use of behavior analysis principles within ASD services, varying from largely discrete trial methods to entirely naturalistic, incidental teaching approaches. Nor are they aware of the value good programs place on developing a positive relationship between therapist and child. Most people who make such comments have never seen IEBT being conducted nor are they aware of the progression from simple to very complex and naturalistic situations and skills that are basic elements in effective IEBT programs.

In acquiring many of the basic skills, there are often insufficient numbers of spontaneous occasions on which a teaching opportunity arises during typical daily routines. The therapist arranges the situation so that the child has more opportunities to practice new skills. Discrete trial therapy involves teaching the child in a specific location devoid of distractions in series of nearly identical recurring trials. The therapist presents a specific cue (discriminative stimulus) and rewards the child following an appropriate response to the cue. Trials are usually repeated with the intention of providing the child with practice sufficient enough to enable them to begin learning a single skill, such as pointing to a shape or imitating a movement (e.g., clapping hands). Unlike incidental teaching, the therapist makes the relevant cues very clear to the child and teaches the child that a specific consequence will reliably follow his or her action. This capitalizes on the child's preference for predictable routines. In incidental teaching, the child must learn to ignore numerous other events occurring around him or her and focus only on the cue presented by the therapist and the forthcoming consequence, which is often extremely difficult for a child at the beginning of therapy. The child doesn't know whether to attend to the therapist's voice, the object the therapist is holding, the pet dog running through the room, or his or her mother seated at a nearby table (Anderson, 1987; Harris, 1986; Lovaas, 1987).

Prizant and Weatherby (1998) examined the role of incidental learning versus discrete trial methods in enhancing spontaneous language and related social-communicative abilities of young children with an ASD or a PDD. The approaches are described as existing along a continuum from massed, traditional behavior analytic methods to social-pragmatic, developmental methods. They correctly noted that this is not usually an either/or decision, but represents instead a continuum of methods. Discrete trial teaching is useful at the beginning of therapy or instruction, especially with children who have more cognitive delays and serious attention problems. It is also useful when working with children who are easily distracted by sounds coming from outdoors or other rooms in the house or school. A 6-year-old boy with whom I worked commented each time the refrigerator compressor turned on in an adjacent room, although most people found the muffled sound barely audible. It is also helpful when beginning a new and more difficult task. In discrete trial therapy, the child and therapist are seated at a child-sized table with the child's chair opposite the therapist's. During the "child's game," discussed previously as a tool in rapport-building, the therapist learns which things are captivating to the child, which snacks he or she prefers, and which activities he or she will choose without prompting. The therapist says, "Karen, come sit" and points to the chair at the table. Often the child will appear to ignore the therapist. The request is repeated, and if the child does not approach the table, the therapist gently guides the child to the table manually and, as soon as he or she is sitting, offers a small portion of the child's most preferred snack and says, "Good job!" The same basic approach is used in a classroom setting. If possible, it is wise to wait until a child is no longer engaged in a self-stimulatory activity (rocking, finger flicking) before trying to attract their attention and invite them to "come sit" for instruction. Manual guidance is usually necessary because the child is unfamiliar with the request and he or she may be distracted by other activities in the classroom. It is often useful to begin instruction by seating the child and teacher or instructional aide behind screens that reduce visual distraction.

Once seated, the teacher or therapist places a desirable piece of fruit in his or her hand and holds it out to the child. Which items are voluntarily selected and eaten are recorded, and those the child does not choose are noted and removed from the list of potential reinforcers. After 5–10 minutes, the therapist returns to the area in which they had been together during the child's game and says, "Karin play ball" (or "push car"). The next 10–15 minutes is a free-play period, followed by the request to "Come sit," using a pointing gesture. In a classroom, teachers usually have less flexibility regarding length of each brief instructional activity because it is necessary to begin working with another child. Usually by the end of the first or second 3-hour session, the child is sitting when requested without a gestural prompt. Over the course of the session, the child is offered two items—one a known reinforcer and the other something the child often doesn't accept. The child usually accepts the preferred reinforcer and may look away from the nonpreferred item. Over the next several sessions, the child is given objects that are not edible, asked with a gesture to place them in a box, and rewarded if he or she does so with a tangible reinforcer. Reinforcement becomes intermittent, and various edible reinforcers are substituted for one another so that the child won't always expect the same consequence. At this point, the therapist begins substituting preferred activities for edibles (e.g., spinning a top, "tickles"). By the end of this teaching sequence, the child performs a range of single-step responses following a request, and reinforcers vary from edibles to activities to sensory stimulation.

Once a child is responding appropriately to single-step requests made by an experienced teacher or therapist, the child's mother or father is encouraged to participate by using the same methods within the context of discrete trial therapy. Sometimes when a parent is substituted for the therapist, the child relapses into old habits, whining or resisting, but in most instances if parents patiently employ the same methods as the therapist, the child quickly adjusts to parents playing a different role. Subsequent skill sets, such as matching objects and beginning receptive language, are usually introduced next. The speed with which new skills are introduced varies greatly from one child to the next. Some more capable children acquire early skills very quickly and reach intermediate levels of difficulty in several weeks. When children begin spontaneously displaying skills they have learned outside the teaching or therapy situation, often an incidental teaching approach is intermixed with discrete trial teaching.

In the example discussed above, Aaron's teacher, Mrs. Cohen, indicates that she usually employs incidental teaching strategies for children with ASDs in her classroom. In Aaron's case, that may be especially appropriate because he has already developed basic attending skills and is able to follow simple directions at home.

DESENSITIZATION TO UNFAMILIAR OR NON-PREFERRED STIMULI

Many children with ASDs have strong preferences for certain tastes, textures of foods, fabrics touching their skin, and sounds. There are two approaches to this potential problem. First, it must be decided whether it is important at this time that the child changes his aversion to a stimulus he or she avoids. In many instances, it isn't essential. If the child doesn't like raw fruit at snack time, then don't insist he eat raw fruit. In other cases it may not be essential, but it would be helpful, if a child would learn to accept different foods. Many children with ASDs will eat chicken but no other meat. A 2-month collaborative home–school desensitization process will usually overcome this problem. The child's parent prepares baked "chicken fingers" that the child can bring to school for snacks. After a week of consuming chicken fingers composed completely of finely chopped chicken, the child's parent gradually introduces a little ground beef into the mixture. The first day the child may balk at the new taste, but in most instances children will accept it. Each week the proportion of ground beef is increased and the proportion of chicken decreases. At the end of approximately 2 months, most of the children who previously had rejected the flavor of beef will now accept ground beef.

A child who dislikes rough textures on her skin, such as coarsely woven wool fabric, can be similarly desensitized so that she or he tolerates a wider range of fabrics. Begin by helping the child on with a sweater made from a smooth but coarsely woven synthetic fabric. The child may resist at first but will very likely accept the new feeling if it is smooth and not at all scratchy. After several weeks, the child will likely accept another sweater made of 15% wool or cotton and 85% smooth synthetic fabric. Over several months, by gradually exposing the child to slightly more wool and less synthetic fabric, it is likely that he or she will accept it. An occupational therapist who is experienced working with children with ASDs can help develop such a desensitization sequence. Attempting to achieve the same goal by encouraging the child to handle or touch small swatches of fabric usually does not generalize because that experience has no relevance to the child's day-to-day life.

At times, it is more practical to help the child avoid the aversive source of stimulation than to attempt desensitization. Robbie, a 7-year-old boy with an ASD, was reported by his teacher to frequently insert his fingers into his ear canals or cover his ears with his hands. His parents took him to a specialty clinic in another state for extensive auditory assessments. It was found that he had a somewhat greater evoked auditory potential response to sounds in the 4500–6000 cycle per second range than surrounding sound frequencies. Unfortunately, those frequencies of sound are needed for typical speech perception, which meant that there was no practical way to prevent this student from exposure to sounds in this frequency range. As Robbie moved around his classroom during various activities, I noticed that he tended to more often put his fingers into his ears when he was on the left side of the room near the front. When I approached that area of the room, I noticed a distinct humming sound emanating from the ballast of an overhead fluorescent light fixture. Apparently, Robbie found the humming sound unpleasant. The solution to the student's sensitivity to the humming sound was to change his seat in the classroom.

INCIDENTAL TEACHING/THERAPY

When components of skills that have been previously taught can be imbedded into typical daily routines (e.g., meals, bathing, bedtime activities), it makes sense to incorporate *incidental teaching.* In incidental teaching, instruction or therapy is conducted in the context of other routine ongoing activities such as eating lunch or toy play. The primary challenge encountered in conducting incidental teaching is that the therapist, teacher, or parent must recognize teachable opportunities in the midst of ongoing activities. Incidental teaching is like riding a bicycle. One can't stop to think about which pedal should be pushed as the bicycle is going down the sidewalk. The therapist or teacher's skills must be so ingrained that the teacher uses them almost without thinking when opportunities arise spontaneously. Incidental teaching works most effectively using naturally occurring materials such as dishes, forks, and spoons at the dinner table or soap and a washcloth when bathing. The reinforcing consequences are more effective if they are natural and logically related to the situation. One would not reinforce tooth brushing with an M&M candy or bathing with rambunctious tickles and hugs. When a child is beginning to make spoken requests, one does not reinforce talking with consequences unrelated to the requests such as tokens or extraneous edibles. If a child says, "More milk," the reinforcer should be a drink of milk (Ingersoll & Schreibman, 2006; Smith & Dillenbeck, 2006).

After 3 months of IEBT with her son Christopher, Lois, the mother who was concerned that our therapy might turn her child into a robot, sat in her kitchen with tears in her eyes and said, "Your therapy team has saved our family." Before therapy had begun, Christopher had been hurting his 18-month-old little brother several times a day, including trying to push him down a flight of stairs. From observing Christopher, it was obvious that he was utterly frustrated, climbing on top of furniture trying to reach things he wanted, falling down, and hurting himself. He was constantly demanding his mother's attention. When Christopher wasn't pushing and hitting his little brother, he made irritating noises (e.g., repeatedly banging a tablespoon on the kitchen table). Lois told Christopher to stop making noise. She explained to Christopher that she couldn't talk with the therapist while he was making noise, but she didn't realize that in doing so, she was differentially rewarding Christopher for interrupting her when she was talking with an adult.

After several months of therapy, Lois reported, "We were at our wits end. We were coming apart at the seams." The initial focus of therapy was on language development, which proceeded rapidly. The second focus was on helping Lois learn to selectively pay attention to Christopher when he was playing nicely with his little brother. After several weeks, when the therapists arrived at his home in the afternoon to work with Christopher and his mother, Christopher ran to them to be hugged, given horseback rides, and tossed in the air and caught. Christopher's mom realized that her apprehension about IEBT based on secondhand information had been unwarranted. There were, of course, other elements to the intervention plan, but after only 3 months, Christopher's aggression had stopped and he was asking for things that he wanted and speaking in 3- and 4-word sentences. It was obvious that he was a very capable child. Two years later, Christopher is in an inclusive kindergarten class, and while he has some limitations in using abstract language, he functions very well.

EARLY INTERVENTION PRINCIPLES

In conducing an IEBT, it is more important to understand the principles of early intervention than specific techniques. In the next section, intervention strategies are explored based on a few basic principles.

Establishing Stimulus Control

With 2–4-year-olds, a structured routine with minimal changes is most effective in the beginning. Therapy is much more effective if distractions such as TV, music, siblings, or peers and pets are not present for the first few weeks. By removing mirrors or other shiny, eye-catching objects that will distract many children with ASDs, it will be easier to solicit their attention to relevant cues. Activities that incorporate self-stimulatory elements such as video games and television are often problematic. The same wording of instructions should be used during each instructional or therapy period until the child's behavior is under good instructional control. Only then should wording be systematically changed in small steps. For example, "Point to the dog" may not seem the same thing as "Point to the doggy" to a young child with an ASD until taught that they are equivalent.

In the beginning, it is often most effective if therapy or instruction is conducted in a single distinctive setting. Settings can be made more distinctive by placing a brightly colored rug on the floor beneath the table in which therapy is conducted, and erecting folding screens around the therapy or instructional area to reduce distractions. Ideally, the therapy or instructional setting shouldn't be used for any other purpose (e.g., free play, watching television). Sometimes that can be difficult in classrooms in which areas must serve multiple purposes. Reinforcers used in therapy are most effective if they are not available at any other time throughout the day. Later, they will be transferred across settings and adults.

Establishing Session Length

Therapy periods for the youngest children are divided into 5–10 minutes of teaching followed by 5–10 minutes of free play during the first week or two. As the child progresses through therapy, teaching-time duration is gradually increased and free-play periods remain constant. By the end of 1–2 months of therapy, teaching times are 20–30 minutes long, alternating with child-directed play. Therapy cannot be started and stopped purely based on elapsed time—it must be adjusted for task difficulty, the child's mood, and behavior. Some days, the child may feel tired or not well, or otherwise may have a lower tolerance for the demands of therapy, in which case each teaching period should be shortened. It is important that parents participate in therapy intermittently throughout the period that a trained therapist has been working with the child to promote generalization. After a teacher or therapist has conducted a series of trials, it is a good idea to suggest that the child's father or mother conduct the next block of trials.

Structuring the Session

Each session begins with an activity the child prefers, has previously self-selected, and can perform well. It is important that the child not be asked to perform a task he or she has strongly resisted until later in therapy. Follow the same sequence to therapy activities each session and across sessions. Once the child is actively participating, small changes in sequences of activities can be introduced.

Avoiding Power Struggles

The child must fully cooperate with and trust the teacher before non-preferred activities are gradually introduced. Avoid power struggles. Once a therapist gets off on the wrong foot with a child, it is often difficult to undo the damage. Sometimes it is possible to repair a damaged relationship by temporarily

reducing demands and repeatedly pairing a variety of highly preferred reinforcers with the staff member who had a power struggle with the child.

Capitalizing on Behavioral Momentum

Laboratory and clinical studies have demonstrated that it is possible to promote actively participating in a non-preferred activity if it is briefly embedded in a highly preferred activity. This is called *behavioral momentum* (Mace
et al., 1988). When introducing a new, more difficult skill, interpolate it
within an ongoing easier activity. For example, if a child is being asked to
point to letters or numbers, insert several trials of that activity in the middle
of a larger block of trials of pointing to familiar objects the child usually
answers correctly (e.g., ball, car, and dog). When the child succeeds at the
more difficult task, increase the amount of reinforcement for that task, and use
abundant praise and positive comments such as, "Great job! That was fun!"

Introducing Complex Skills Gradually

More advanced therapy activities involving sequencing pictures of events that
occur in a particular order (e.g., the steps in making a sandwich), identifying
pictures by the functions of objects in pictures (e.g., "What do you fly in?"
with a choice of a car and an airplane) or by properties of the objects (e.g.,
"Tell me the name of three things that are blue"), pictures of faces showing
different emotions (e.g., happy, sad, afraid) and social situations that require
interpretation (e.g., people arguing), and answering who, what, and where
questions must be introduced one at a time. Advance to a more complex
skill only after the child is performing the simpler skill correctly 80%–85%
of the time.

More complex discriminations may involve identifying what is wrong
with a picture. For example, a group of people is seated at a picnic table but
there is no food present, and the child is asked what is missing from the picture (e.g., "hot dogs," "soda"). These increasingly complex tasks prepare the
child for what will be expected of him or her in the school or community.
Pretend play is typically absent or minimal among most very young children
with ASD. Toward the end of the first year or the beginning of the second year
of therapy, increasing attention is given to imaginary play activities. That
helps children learn to think about what another person would do in a given
situation. Especially capable children are taught to use hand puppets to act out
a vignette with several characters, which provides practice with perspective-
taking and helps prepare the children for appropriate interactions with peers.
Developing appropriate social interactions, including how to initiate and
maintain an interaction and recognizing social signals, comes toward the conclusion of therapy or ECSE.

Promoting Generalization

Once basic skills have been mastered in the first 2–3 ABLLS-R scales, therapy activities can be replicated in one other setting (e.g. at the dinner table, in the living room). Use the same instructions and the same reinforcers in the new setting. After the child is responding appropriately to one adult in the new setting (e.g., the mother) a second adult can begin playing the therapist role (e.g., the father). Once the skills are being maintained in the second setting, add a third setting (e.g., deck, backyard), employing the same procedures (Koegel et al., 1989). If the child begins to balk or resist when a new setting is introduced, back up one step and provide more practice in the previous setting, and then attempt to promote generalization in a new setting. It is common for children to initially resist when encountering a new situation, so patience and tolerance for minor resistance is required.

Depending on the speed of progress, it is useful to begin introducing siblings or neighborhood children to therapy activities after a month or so. Often, older brothers or sisters are effective at conducting therapy activities and take pride in being recognized as helpers. Siblings or neighborhood children who participate in therapy can be given an award or certificate of appreciation that they can display in their room. Therapists should routinely set aside time to talk with brothers or sisters about their activities and show special interest in siblings' achievements to prevent them from feeling excluded. Depending on the season and climate, once the child's behavior is under reasonably good control, therapy can be conducted outdoors in the family's backyard or in a nearby park. Most of this teaching is done incidentally, but it uses the same format as the home teaching. This promotes generalization across situations and makes it more likely that the child will display appropriate skills when he or she and the therapists begin visiting a nearby recreation center, the library, or a shopping mall (Jahr, Eldevik, & Eikeseth, 2000; Kamps et al., 1992).

Preparing for School

Over the course of the last year of early intervention, children with ASD are taught preacademic skills including naming and printing letters and numbers, recognizing common safety words such as *stop* and *go,* recognizing the words *boys* and *girls* on restroom doors, and beginning phonemic awareness with 2–3-syllable words. Phonemic awareness refers to the ability to segment and manipulate sounds of spoken language. Common examples are rhyming words (e.g., *fat, cat*) and segmenting (e.g., *cat, cuh/aa/tuh*). By using game formats, the repetitiveness of routine instruction can be reduced (e.g., playing "War" with sight words on flashcards, identifying words that have specific sounds). Similarly, board games can be used in which a child must read a word, solve a math problem, or segment a word phonemically when the child's game piece lands on a square with the word or math problem. Many children with ASDs have fine perceptual-motor skill impairments, so time is spent tracing, copying, coloring, and cutting out shapes. Neighborhood and recreation center children are enlisted to help with small-group art and music activities.

As the time approaches for discharge from early intervention, most therapy and instructional activities simulate typical daily routines. Family conversations incorporate the child with an ASD. Parents can encourage the child to respond appropriately to the context of the conversation that has gone on previously (Ingersol & Schreibman, 2006). The therapist or parent will start a story about adventures of an animal or an imaginary person, and the child will be asked to tell the rest of the story, remaining on topic and logically relating it to earlier events in the story. Among the final activities will be appropriately participating in group instruction, taking part in community outings such as going swimming at the recreation center with a friend, going to the library and selecting a book, or having lunch at a restaurant with a friend and the friend's mother or father.

INDIVIDUALIZING EARLY INTERVENTION

Before Corina started therapy, when her mother looked out the window and pointed at a bird and said, "Look at that bird!," Corina's gaze shifted and she looked out the window to see to what her mother was referring. That is called *joint attention* and is predictive of a better outcome in intensive early behavior therapy. Trent, a 3-year-old with no speech, didn't display joint attention. When his dad clapped his hands in front of Trent and said, "Do this," Trent stood motionless for a few seconds and walked away. It is impossible to predict with precision how Corina and Trent will do at the end of the first year of therapy, but it is likely that within a month or two Corina will be progressing more rapidly than Trent. Studies have indicated that approximately half of the children with an ASD who have participated in IEBT are similar to Corina and they progress rapidly. The other half progresses slower and they are often placed in special education classrooms at the conclusion of early intervention (Lovaas, 1987; Sallows & Graupner, 2005).

For children who make rapid progress in spoken language (imitation, single words, and phrases), it is appropriate to encourage social and cognitive skills and preacademic activities as long as the child continues to profit from them. For children who are having more difficulty with spoken language and basic cognitive skills, it is important to encourage the development of an alternative communication system and functional skills that will make their life at home and in the community better. If they are not acquiring spoken language after 1 or 2 months of intensive therapy, consideration may be given to implementing an augmentative communication system. In some cases, children with severe language disabilities use both systems, sometimes called *total communication* (Carbone, Lewis, et al., 2006). It is essential that a young child with an ASD have a means of communicating his or her wants and needs, and an iconic system such as the Picture Exchange Communication System (PECS) can be very helpful. That is one of the best ways of preventing the emergence of behavior problems.

Social skills include participation in meals with family members such as helping to set the table, eating appropriately with utensils, and using augmentative communication systems (e.g., PECS) to make requests. Motor imitation and task compliance and task completion activities continue to be part of therapy or instruction. By teaching a child the generalized motor imitation skill after a request by the parent or therapist to "Do this" followed by a demonstration of the desired response, new skills can be more effectively taught through modeling. Familiar stimuli from the child's daily environment are often more effective for teaching discriminations. Instead of teaching colors and matching using abstract shapes, familiar objects are often more effective (e.g., socks, plastic forks and spoons). For example, the child is presented with a pile of intermixed blue and red socks. The therapist or teacher says, "Sort socks, put blue socks here" (pointing) and "Put red socks there" (pointing to another container). Place one sock of each color in the appropriate container as a matching cue and then reinforce correct responses. When the child is performing the task correctly, the matching colored sock cue can be faded out so that the child learns to respond only to the name of the color. It is also useful to incorporate gross and fine motor skill activities into the therapy curriculum for children who are having more difficulty with language and cognitive skills. Improved gross motor skills generalize to dressing, physical education, and recreational activities. Fine motor skills are useful for promoting buttoning clothes, sorting smaller objects, and learning to hold crayons and other smaller manipulatives.

A child who lacks joint attention, verbal and motor imitation, and basic preacademic skills at the outset of early intervention is more likely to be placed in a special education classroom on entering kindergarten or first grade than children possessing those skills. Few special education teachers are troubled by the fact that a student with an ASD doesn't know all the letters of the alphabet or the numbers 1 to 20. They will not be concerned by the fact that the child has difficulty printing his name or coloring inside the lines and cutting out shapes. The skills that lead to better school transition include facility at basic self-help skills (e.g., toileting, eating, dressing), following simple spoken directions (e.g., "take your seat"), remaining seated in school, waiting in line, and avoiding behavior problems. Certain out-of-seat behaviors—pushing into line ahead of other children, frequent self-stimulatory behavior, shoving or hitting other students or the teaching staff, bolting out of the classroom—create problems for children with ASDs, sometimes potentially serious problems. The more a child is prepared for school transition during early intervention therapy, before he or she enters school, the better are the child's chances of fitting in and enjoying the school experience. That is why parents of children who have difficulty acquiring language and basic social and cognitive skills are encouraged to focus on functional skills that will enhance their success in a special education setting.

MONITORING PROGRESS

Monitoring and evaluating progress is essential in determining the appropriateness and value of a given intervention program for a child (Matson, 2006). Parents, teachers, and other staff members who participate in a child's IEBT program monitor progress several ways. Parents develop impressions of how well a child is doing and discuss between themselves whether they think adequate progress is being made or whether there are continuing unresolved problems. Therapists and teachers who work directly with a child maintain records of the percentage of correct responses per session for each goal on which they are working. Those data are regularly summarized graphically for each goal. In home-based programs, staff members are also required to keep daily progress notes (Figure 5.3). Progress notes are brief accounts of the time spent in therapy, the name of the therapist, goals toward which they are working, and an indication of progress for each. Any problems encountered are indicated and suggestions for remedial action by the next therapist who works with the child are noted. Progress notes are signed daily by the therapist and initialed weekly by the therapist's supervisor, who reads each progress note and determines whether they are complete and whether any pending issues should be discussed.

In addition, at weekly team meetings, data from the previous week are summarized and discussed. The focus is on problematic issues that require a solution, usually by group consensus. Parents are full participants in team meetings and make suggestions, share personal observations, and raise objections if they have concerns about specific procedures. Monthly graphs of each child's progress are summarized and presented to the supervising psychologist or special education supervisor, although additional meetings may be convened between the monthly meetings depending on circumstances. The supervising psychologist makes recommendations for changes in procedures or approaches to overcome difficulties that arose over the preceding month. Once every 3 months, the supervising psychologist and clinical director meet with the child and his or her parents in their home to review the child's progress. Following the meeting, the psychologist prepares a summary of major findings and issues that still need to be addressed. The following is an excerpt from a psychologist's quarterly review summary in connection with IEBT services for a 4½-year-old girl with a PDD-NOS diagnosis. The child

Child's Name: <u>John Jones</u>   Date <u>9-9-06</u>

Place of Service: Home <u>x</u>   School _____   Other (Specify) _____

Parent/Adult Present: <u>mother</u>   Others present: <u>Mary (sister)</u>

Start Time: <u>8:15 A.M.</u>   End Time <u>11:15 A.M.</u>

ITP Goals Addressed: Goal 2—Requesting Using Speech; Goal 4—Compliance with Requests; Goal 5—Discriminating Facial Expression

Progress:

Goal 2: John said "cracker," "juice," and "more tickle" to request food or beverage items and preferred activity 60% of the time correctly.

Goal 4: John's compliance with requests began at 64% and reached 80% over the last hour of the session.

Goal 5: John correctly identified angry and happy on 7 of 10 trials; however, he is still unable to discriminate *sad* and *afraid* facial expressions.

Problems Encountered: When Ms. Jones left the room, John became distracted and aggressive. Need to practice alternative responses to mother's absence over the next few sessions.

Staff member name: <u>Jane</u>   <u>Doe</u>
                   (first)   (last)

Supervisor Signature: <u>Patti Johnson</u>

Figure 5.3 Typical progress note from a home-based IEBT program. Progress on each goal area is summarized and problems encountered are noted to alert the next person who works with the child about changes that may be required to address the issue.

(Melanie) had received 17 months of therapy at the time of this meeting and when the summary was written:

Melanie has made remarkable progress overall. She has completed all items on the following ABLLS-R scales: Cooperation, Imitation, Vocal Imitation, and nearly all items on Receptive Language, Visual Performance, Labeling, Spontaneous Vocalization, Play and Leisure, and Social Interactions ABLLS Scales. She has mastered Pronouns, "Wh" Questions, Social Questions, Community Safety, and Potty Training. During this final 6-month period, emphasis will be placed on When, How, and Why Questions, Problem Solving, Conversations with Peers, and Following Complex Instructions. Family Skills Training will focus on Roberta's learning to per-form Functional Assessments and Promoting Independent Play.

Roberta (Melanie's mother) is planning for Melanie's educational future. She is weighing two programs in River Creek, one typical and the other a combination classroom.

✦✧✦

Melanie is clearly ready for school, but she will probably need additional support during the fall semester. Based on staff observations, it seems likely that Melanie would become distracted in a large classroom. I advised Roberta that it would be better to leave Melanie in a smaller classroom if at all possible for at least one more year.

The following is an excerpt from a 6-month review of a child with mild cerebral palsy as well as a high-functioning ASD.

Kyle has made good progress in interacting with peers (ABLLS-R Scale L) and cognitive functioning. He is now able to label emotions (ABLLS-R G39, G40), raises his hand in school (ABLLS-R M5), dresses (ABLLS-R U) and feeds himself (ABLLS-R V), and toilets with reminders (ABLLS-R X). He continues to display repetitive speech and is preoccupied with specific topics. Over the next 6 months, we plan to increase emphasis on his ability to participate in group conversations (ABLLS-R H39) and follow non-verbal social cues (ABLLS-R L3, L4), and on his ability to participate in non-preferred activities, brush his teeth, and increase his independence at school. At home, training in safety rules (e.g., traffic) is a high priority. Kyle's mother is concerned about his difficulty understanding others' emotions and expressing his own emotions. The team's main task is to prepare Kyle for increased independence in school next fall. His mild cerebral palsy limits some of his play/socialization opportunities, which may require a peer–buddy strategy.

Formal 6-month reviews that include which goals have been mastered and quantitative progress on each remaining goal are included with prior authorization requests for continued funding to support services for an additional time period. Six-month reviews are signed by parents, the clinical director, and the supervising psychologist after discussing progress and developing plans for the next 6-month period.

Is Child Making Adequate Progress?

Most parents are pleased that their child is receiving early intervention services and is showing progress. Parents of children who are progressing rapidly usually stick with the program in which their child is prospering. Sometimes parents think that insufficient progress is being made, and they might consider transferring their child to another educational or therapy program.

One strategy to use to decide this is to look at the child's IFSP or ITP and determine whether the stated goals will realistically prepare the child for kindergarten. If they are goals that are meaningful steps toward preparation for school, it is reasonable to ask whether, given the rate of progress over the past 6 or 12 months, how long it will take to reach the stated goals. Most programs plot each child's progress on graphs. If graphs representing progress for the past 6 months are assumed to continue at the current rate of progress, when will the child reach the stated goals? If the answer is 6–9 months, perhaps sufficient progress is being made. However, if it appears that it will require 1 or 2 years based on the current rate of progress, it is unlikely that the child will reach the goal by the time he or she would normally enter kindergarten. This suggests that something may be amiss.

In the progress graph in Figure 5.4, the vertical axis shows percentage correct for each goal achieved and the horizontal axis shows successive quarters participation in the program. Based on the results for the first four quarters (a year), the child in Figure 5.4 has a high likelihood of achieving Goal 2 by the sixth quarter (18 months), but has very little chance of achieving Goal 1 by the time he or she enters kindergarten.

Reasons for Slow Progress

There may be several reasons for slower than expected progress. For example, the program may not be appropriate for the child. Not all children profit

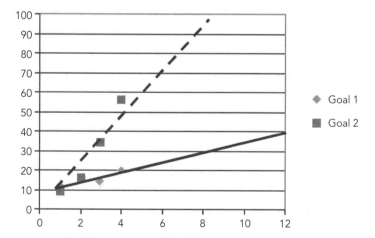

Figure 5.4. This graph shows progress made on two goals for a child with an ASD over the first four quarters and estimates of achievement by projecting progress lines over subsequent quarters. Estimates are best-fit lines based on the first four points.

equally from the same intervention method. Higher-functioning children are more likely to profit from programs based on incidental learning such as Carbone's verbal behavior approach than more cognitively challenged children. Children with more severe disabilities tend to profit more from a discrete trial program that incorporates some incidental teaching methods. If the program doesn't seem to match the child, parents might explore other early intervention programs.

Or, the program may be appropriate but the way the particular staff members are implementing the procedures may be inadequate. Sometimes well-intentioned staff members don't connect well with a given child. They keep trying the same procedures over and over and obtain the same result (i.e., little progress). This represents a failure of supervision. If the staff member's supervisor is not monitoring a program's progress, the child's parents are encouraged to meet with the supervisor and request that a different staff member be assigned to their child. If the supervisor resists that request, parents may wish to consider moving their child to another program.

A third reason might be that something is happening at home that is impeding progress. For example, as noted in Chapter 4, parents may be experiencing mental health or substance abuse problems that could have an impact on their child's progress. Or marital discord or a family member's serious illness may be having an adverse effect on the child or may be limiting the parents' ability to devote time to their child's skills development.

Progress may be impeded because the child is suffering from another disability in addition to an ASD that is limiting his or her progress. Children with ASDs who also have a specific language impairment (SLI) develop language very slowly. Perhaps the child needs supplementary services to overcome the additional disability. Still other children may have neurological problems (e.g., a seizure disorder, frontal lobe syndrome) that require medication. Some children with ASD may have a severe obsessive-compulsive disorder that makes it difficult for them to progress. Treatment with an appropriate psychotropic medication may help resolve the problem.

Finally, a child may actually be progressing as rapidly as he or she is capable of progressing, given the nature of the disability. If that is the case, parents may wish to consider whether continuing with an intensive therapy program is most appropriate for their child. Perhaps he or she would progress equally rapidly in a less demanding center-based or school program that might provide more social opportunities.

The best rule of thumb for parents is that if progress doesn't seem right, maybe it isn't right. To begin to sort out how to proceed:

1. Determine whether your perception of the rate of progress is accurate.

2. Determine whether, given your child's rate of progress, he or she can reach the goal in a timely fashion

3. Determine whether your expectations for your child's progress are consistent with his or her abilities and degree of disability.

SUMMARY

Most children with ASDs profit from IEBT, some making more dramatic gains than others. IEBT is a partnership between teachers or therapists and parents that requires regular open communication and flexibility. In planning and implementing early intervention, it is more important to understand the principles and rationale behind intervention strategies than thinking of them as specific techniques. A specific technique may not be effective for a given child under one set of circumstances, but another technique based on the same principle may prove to be quite adequate. Parents should monitor their child's progress regularly, and when it appears that limited gains are being made, they must first determine whether their expectations are realistic. If they are realistic, then alternative strategies for improving program effectiveness should be explored.

6

School Transition

E stablishing a positive working relationship between parents and schools is important in promoting the language and social development of children with autism. Parents are concerned about the most appropriate educational placement for their child, and school personnel are concerned with providing the most appropriate educational services to meet a child's needs. Achieving parent and school goals requires establishing a relationship before the child enters school and devising ways of maintaining effective communication among the various parties involved in a child's services.

WORKING WITH SCHOOLS

Parents of children who are making the transition from home-based therapy or center-based early childhood special education (ECSE) to kindergarten and then to first grade face a disturbing period. When visiting school programs, parents are either confronted with the substantial discrepancy between their child's functioning and that of their typical peers, or they may be disappointed when they visit a segregated special education classroom for children with autism spectrum disorders (ASDs). On one hand, parents are made keenly aware of how different their child will seem in a classroom of largely typical peers and may be concerned about their child's ability to succeed in that setting. On the other hand, school personnel may recommend placement in a classroom with all autistic children, some of whom may be considerably more disabled than their child and may exhibit more disturbed behavior. Many parents find neither alternative acceptable, preferring that their child receive educational services in an inclusive classroom. Unfortunately, that isn't always possible.

This dilemma leads some parents to pursue a confrontational approach with the school district, which usually produces detrimental results for everyone concerned. Even if the parents succeed in obtaining the placement and the number of hours of services they request, the damaged relationship with school personnel may be difficult to repair. Even if school staff make every effort to behave professionally and are supportive of the child, it is likely that the disagreeable feelings generated during the process will linger. It is preferable for school personnel and parents to develop a collaborative relationship, beginning before a placement decision is necessary.

Collaboration Between Parents and Schools

Complaints by parents about the inappropriateness and inadequacy of educational services for their children with ASDs are rampant. At the same time, school personnel express frustration and consternation about dealing with parents whom they perceive as unrealistic and excessively demanding. The solutions lie in improved teacher training, adequate support from administrators, and an atmosphere of collaboration between parents and schools. Esler, Godber, and Christenson (2002) defined home-school collaboration as "establishing and maintaining productive, working relationships between families and schools to facilitate children's learning."

In reality, parents can influence the degree to which their children are engaged in school, and parental involvement can help teachers view children as learners rather than as problems. The National Educational Goals Panel (1990) stated, "Every school will actively engage parents and families in a partnership which supports the academic work of children at home and shared educational decision-making at school." This requires that a positive relationship be established between the family and the school based on short-term and long-term goals. Teamwork between parents and schools regarding shared responsibility for goal outcomes is a useful step before a referral or placement decision is at hand. For the partnership to be effective, the relationship needs to be flexible and sensitive to diversity among families. There must be a mutual parent and staff commitment. Often, both parents and teachers need additional training to work for the benefit of the child and to eliminate power and control issues.

One of the best ways of reducing these problems is by maintaining regular contact between families and teachers throughout the school year. At times, this may be difficult due to parental feelings of inadequacy, feelings of cultural devaluation, or school suspicion. Moreover, many families find that the lack of child care limits their ability to be involved in their child's school activities (Christenson & Sheridan, 2001). Time and money constraints also create problems for parents. Teachers are wary and apprehensive about conflicts with parents, occasionally stereotyping parents (e.g., "troublemakers"). Frequent negative communications from teachers to parents about a student create additional barriers. Parents conclude, "All they see are his behavior problems; they never say anything about his progress." Many teachers, especially general education teachers serving students with ASDs, lack the necessary training and feel under pressure due to time constraints to serve all the other children (Lord & McGee, 2001).

Home-school collaboration is a preventive, problem-solving approach focused on supporting students based on the belief that both families and educators are critical to a student being socialized. Teachers are encouraged to begin the school year by establishing regular personal contact with each family. It is important that a working home–school relationship is established *before a conflict arises.* When conflicts arise, and they almost always do in programs serving children with ASDs, families should be contacted at the first sign of concern. By building the home–school partnership over time and through different avenues of communication, problems can usually be prevented and the child's learning facilitated (Christenson & Conoley, 1992).

General, Inclusive, or Special Education

According to the Individuals with Disabilities Education Act (IDEA) of 1990,

> *"To the maximum extent appropriate, children with disabilities, including children in public or private institutions or other care facilities, are educated with children who are not disabled, and special classes, separate schooling, or other removal of children with disabilities from the general educational environment occurs only when the nature or severity of the disability of a child is such that education in general classes with the use of supplementary aids and services cannot be achieved satisfactorily."*

This policy is called the least restrictive environment (LRE). Alternative placements vary in the degree to which the student with an ASD participates alongside typically developing peers. A special education setting is one that is primarily composed of students with disabilities. Primary instruction in this setting is presented by a teacher who is licensed in special education. Categorical placement involves grouping special education students together on the basis of their IDEA eligibility category. Alternative models include noncategorical placement and cross-categorical placement.

Students with Asperger syndrome and pervasive developmental disorders not otherwise specified (PDD-NOS) are often included in general education classrooms, sometimes with a part-time paraprofessional aide and other times without supplementary supports. Other students with ASDs may be placed in an inclusive setting composed of students with and without disabilities sharing appropriate educational experiences. Primary instruction may be presented by a special education teacher and general education teacher (i.e., co-teachers) or a dual-certified teacher. Students with more severe disabilities may receive services in a community setting outside of school property in which individualized education program (IEP) goals, objectives, and a functional curriculum are the focus of instruction. These services are more common with older students who have severe disabilities.

Parents wonder which setting is most appropriate for their child with an ASD, and there is seldom a clear answer. Children who can read at or near grade level, are able to remain seated, and pay attention and follow directions within a group setting can often profit from placement in a general education classroom. They may receive one-to-one services with a teacher or therapist in a separate room in reading, math, and speech therapy. Otherwise, they may participate effectively in the general education classroom. This has the advantage of promoting social interactions and learning how to function among typical peers.

Other students gain more from an inclusive setting in which a special education and general education teacher share responsibility for instruction. More adaptations for special needs students are available, as well as the skills of a teacher trained to work with students with ASD. At the same time, students with ASD have the opportunity to interact with typical peers and to develop group social skills. Placement in a segregated special education classroom is usually reserved for students with more severe cognitive limitations and greater behavioral challenges. Typical class size is smaller (6–15 students) with a full-time teacher and several paraprofessional aides to assist with instruction and behavior management. Some students who have the cognitive ability to function in an inclusive setting may be transferred from a special education to an inclusive classroom later in the school year once their behavior challenges have been brought under control (Altman & Kanagawa, 1994).

Individualized Family Service Plan

Preschool children who are participating in ECSE programs may be eligible for services delivered at home as well as in school. A detailed written document that outlines the services to be delivered, who will deliver them, and the number of hours per week the services will be offered is called an individualized family service plan (IFSP). Goals and objectives are established in consultation with parents and often focus on school readiness skills. Unlike an individualized education program (IEP) that is typically more comprehensive with longer-term goals, the IFSP is by its very nature time limited and intended to prepare a toddler for kindergarten. Typical IFSP services include speech and occupational therapy and parent training focusing on managing behavior problems, self-feeding, toileting, dressing, and other activities that will enable the child to function within a school environment.

Individualized Education Program

The individualized education program (IEP) is the heart of a child's special education services once he or she is in kindergarten or elementary school. Under IDEA 1990, IEP describes the educational program that has been designed to meet the unique concerns of a child who is eligible for special education services. Each IEP must be designed for a specific student. The IEP creates an opportunity for teachers, parents, school administrators, related services personnel, and students (when age appropriate) to work together to improve educational results for students with disabilities. An IEP must include the student's disability, a vision statement for the student's long-term goals (1–5 years in future), and describe how the student's disability affects his or her progress in the classroom. It should contain short-term objectives based on the child's own learning strengths and weaknesses, how the child's progress toward these goals will be measured, and how the goals will be evaluated. The IEP also will list all accommodations and modifications. For students who have behavioral or emotional issues that interfere with their learning, the IEP should contain a program designed to teach the student appropriate behavior and social skills and behavior management techniques to be used. Finally, the IEP will include summer services, transport concerns, and type of placement.

PRESCHOOL READINESS

Preparing a child for kindergarten, whether taking place in a center-based preschool program or home-based therapy, involves teaching the child specific skills to promote success in school.

More Direct Instruction, Less Discovery-Based Learning

Many preschool educators assume that a safe, nurturing, and well-organized environment that offers stimulating opportunities for discovery-based learning is optimal for 2–4 year-old children. While there are ample data to support this approach in working with typical or above-average functioning young children, children with special needs often require greater structure, less stimulation, and more direct instruction. This is especially true of children with ASDs. Instruction for preschoolers with ASDs begins with a *classroom ecology* that involves understanding what typically takes place in the classroom, which people are involved, and which activities or materials are employed. It also considers the physical layout of the classroom and other areas of the school in which services are provided. McWilliam (2003) has created a routines-based interview form that can help in this process. The form sets the stage for developing an educational intervention plan that fits within typical daily school routines, rather than imposing a novel routine that may seem alien and unwelcome to the classroom teacher. This is especially true for children with ASDs who will be placed in general education or inclusive classrooms.

Careful planning of the classroom and the types of activities is essential. Reducing extraneous sounds (e.g., loud music) and play materials that create distracting noise (e.g., loud rhythm instruments) will make it easier for the child to focus on relevant educational cues. While a classroom can be made more attractive by placing posters on the wall and decorations around the bulletin board, it is important for children with ASDs to minimize distracting cues. The goal is to help them learn to focus on the cues relevant to specific activities. For each daily routine activity, it is helpful to provide distinctive cues associated with the area in which each activity occurs, such as a colored mat on the floor during circle time, a distinctive tablecloth for snack time, and removal of the sandbox cover during free play.

While typical youngsters will often occupy themselves creatively with a variety of play materials—first in parallel play and later in social play (e.g., pretend play)—if most young children with ASDs are left to their own devices they will engage in repetitive self-stimulatory activities, usually involving a very limited range of materials. They rarely interact with other children, except perhaps to take away a toy from another child. The more they are allowed to lapse into isolated self-stimulatory behavior, the more difficult it becomes to teach them adaptive skills. As a result, it is necessary to design carefully planned learning opportunities that engage the child. Structured instructional activities can often be embedded within routine activities and taught incidentally or by interpolating blocks of teaching trials within a daily routine. It is generally more effective to teach preschool children with disabilities in the presence of a small number of other children or during small-group activities rather than in pullout. It has been demonstrated that the overall percentage of productive time engaged in learning skills leading to IFSP or IEP goals is as much as four times greater when instruction is within the context of a typical daily small group or individual within classroom routines than when the child and a single adult are in a pullout situation (McWilliam, 1996).

Promoting Basic Preschool Cognitive Skills and Play

Most preschool programs employ incidental teaching strategies, which require careful planning and staff training through modeling, making it possible to embed instruction within on-going classroom routines.

Modeling In-Class Teaching

For this strategy to work, a teacher, therapist, or behavior analyst experienced in incidental teaching strategies models ways of incorporating goal-related instruction into other activities for other staff to observe and then practice (Hart & Risley, 1982; Koegel & Koegel, 1995; Quill, 2000). While Edward is playing in the sandbox, the classroom aide might say, "Pour the sand into the *red* cup" [teaching colors]. When he is playing with cars on the floor, she might ask, "*How many* cars are there?" [teaching number sense] When Edward is stacking toys, the aide might say, "Put the blue box *in* the red box" [teaching prepositions]. Staff can be taught to recognize such opportunities through the modeling by an experienced special education teacher or therapist. With careful planning, teachers can create a list of opportunities that typically arise over the course of the school day and post them next to instructional stations within the classroom.

Focusing on Communication

With verbal children, scripts can be used to teach 3–4-part exchanges, again first with a staff member and then with a peer (McClannahan & Krantz, 2005; Sarakoff, Taylor, & Coulson, 2001; Thiemann & Goldstein, 2001). "What day is it today?" the speech therapist asks. "Monday," Kevin replies. "What do we do on Monday?" the therapist asks. "Feed the fish," Kevin replies, after which he is allowed to feed the fish. It is possible to begin teaching spontaneous answers based on general knowledge and vocabulary. "Tell me things that are in the sky," the teacher says. Kevin thinks for a moment and replies, "Bird… clouds … rain," to which the teacher enthusiastically responds, "Right! And a plane and stars!" [an expansion].

Children who have few verbal skills must be taught to communicate their wants and concerns to promote their cognitive and social development and to prevent behavior problems from emerging. If a child says some words, it is usually possible to teach him or her to request desired objects or activities. If the child's verbal skills are weak, it is common to begin with a gesture such as pointing; however, if the child produces some words, instruction moves quickly to teaching him or her to verbally request something (e.g., glass of milk). The word is first modeled, and then the child is taught to hold his or her lips in the correct position and say, "mmm," which is initially reinforced. Over successive repetitions, the child will gradually say, "mk" without the intervening "il." It is important that any reasonable approximation of the word is reinforced in the beginning. After several weeks have passed, the instructor requires a closer approximation to the correct pronunciation of "milk." Later, the teacher will add "please" to the request, and the child will learn to request, "Milk, please." Similarly, children are taught to request a break from a nonpreferred activity, first by holding up a "break" sign, and then combining that with a spoken approximation of the word *break*. By providing young children with the tools to ask for what they want and to request a delay in completion of an activity they dislike, an important step will have been taken toward avoiding serious problems later.

Developing Social Skills

One of the reasons inclusive classrooms are advantageous is that they facilitate social skill development. Beginning reciprocal play can first be taught by a teacher or aide but then transferred to a typical peer. For example, the aide may roll a ball on the floor to Bonnie, and then when she rolls it back, the aide will praise her saying, "Good job, Bonnie!" After this simple exchange has been established, the number of alternations in rolling the ball back and forth is gradually increased until there are 5–8 alternations. At that point, a typical peer replaces the teacher, while the staff member stands behind the peer encouraging and verbally reinforcing the student with an ASD if necessary. Once Bonnie is rolling the ball back and forth with a peer, the teacher fades herself out by standing to one side, and then gradually standing several feet away observing the children engaging in a reciprocal play activity.

Preventing Repetitive Behavior

Repetitive behavior is problematic for several reasons. If steps are not undertaken to reduce hand flapping, rocking, twirling, and so forth, the stereotypes grow, gradually consuming more and more of the child's day. Repetitive behavior is often a way of avoiding activities the child dislikes or doesn't understand. The child will increasingly engage in rocking or finger flicking whenever a new activity is presented that they would prefer to avoid, and repetitive nonfunctional behavior will become a generalized avoidance response. Stereotyped behaviors are also stigmatizing. While very young peers may pay limited attention to rocking or other repetitive movements, by the time the child is in first or second grade, his or her peers may think such activities are funny and may laugh at them, or, alternatively, may avoid the child because of the peculiar behavior. That will preclude the development of social relationships. Finally, for children with more severe ASDs and intellectual disabilities, stereotyped responses can transform into self-injury. The most common emergent forms of self-injury are finger, hand, and wrist biting and head hitting (with fists or against hard surfaces). Once self-injury becomes entrenched, it is often difficult to eliminate.

KINDERGARTEN TRANSITION

The first day of kindergarten is intimidating for all children, typically developing as well as children with disabilities, such as ASDs. For a child with an ASD, entering a school building filled with children who are talking, laughing, and jostling one another on their way to their classroom is a hair-raising experience. There are ways to prepare for the transition from pre-school or home based intervention to kindergarten that will make that process much less alarming, and enable the child with an ASD to adjust to kindergarten.

Preparing for the Transition

A month or more before a child is to spend his first day in kindergarten, the child's teacher and parents should begin to plan the transition. A book consisting of photographs of the new school, classroom, teacher, and any educational assistants that will be in the room can be prepared. It is a good idea to include photos of any other school personnel the child is likely to encounter (e.g., principal, office staff). A photo of the entrance to the school with the door open and the hallway to the child's classroom are often helpful. Each photo is placed in an album with a short caption, "Miss Penny, my new teacher." Seven to fourteen days before the first day of school, the child's parents should begin to read the book to the child and look at the pictures and captions together. Even if the child isn't very verbal, he or she will become acquainted with visual features of the new school setting. Several days before the first day of school, it is a good idea for the child's parents to select several familiar toys the child enjoys and place them in the child's cubby in the new school in anticipation of his arrival. Several days before the first day of school, the child and a parent should visit the school when there are few children present. This could occur after school when the hallways aren't crowded and the school is fairly quiet. The child can stop by the office and meet the staff and principal, and then walk to his classroom and meet the teacher who should show the child some interesting toys, including one of the toys from home. After visiting the classroom, the child is taken to the playground to play on the swings or other equipment before going home and having a treat. This transition preparation will greatly reduce the child's anxiety about the new setting and reduce the likelihood of a tantrum or meltdown during the first hours of his first day in school.

Accepting a Slower Processing Speed—It Takes Longer

When the aide in his classroom asks Mike to pick up his crayon, Mike at first shows no reaction. After several seconds, Mike looks on the top of the table on which the scissors, paper, crayons, and felt-tip markers are located and appears confused. His classroom aide calmly repeats, "Pick up crayon," and Mike immediately picks up the red crayon. This is typical of the auditory processing delay seen in ASDs and also the difficulty retaining an instructional request in auditory memory long enough to act on the request (Boddaert et al., 2004; Keerman, Fan, & Gorman, 2005; Oram Cardy et al., 2005). Mike was not being oppositional; he was having difficulty understanding what was said to him and then acting on it. If the assistant had repeated in an irritated tone of voice, "Mike, I told you to pick up your crayon!" the child would very likely have started crying or retreated from the table. Repeating a request more rapidly or loudly makes matters worse.

Within Classroom Transitions

Judith J. Carta and colleagues (Carta et al., 2000) at the Juniper Gardens Children's Project in Kansas City, Missouri, developed a program to promote classroom transitions for preschool and early elementary school students with special needs. The program, called Skills for Learning Independence in Developmentally Appropriate Environments (SLIDE), is an instructional model that uses assessments and interventions to enhance the independent functioning and success of young children in preschool and early elementary classrooms who are at risk for learning difficulties. The SLIDE assessment strategies can be used for gathering information about teachers' behavioral expectations in the next setting and for determining individual children's current level of performance relative to those expectations. The intervention strategies help prepare children to meet the expectations in both current and future classroom settings and focus on four areas: fostering smoother within-classroom transitions, providing opportunities for practicing independent work, facilitating active engagement during group instruction, and teaching children how to self-assess.

Kindergarten Adaptation versus Shorter Assignments

Some early education teachers may have limited backgrounds in special education. As a result, when an early education teacher first encounters a child with an ASD in the kindergarten classroom and is called on to adapt the curriculum, his or her first attempt at adaptation usually involves reducing the lesson size. If children are learning to trace letters on a sheet of paper, instead of asking Janice to trace eight letter "Ts," the teacher may ask her to trace four. But Janice may not understand what tracing means. She may never have been previously asked to trace a line. Janice may also have some minor fine motor problems and poor eye-hand coordination. As a result, adapting the tracing lesson calls for more than reducing the lesson size. Janice must first develop sufficient hand/eye coordination by working with an occupational therapist and then must be taught what is meant by "tracing a line."

Thorough cognitive and perceptual motor assessment, as well as basic adaptive skills assessment, is an important starting point for instruction with kindergarten transition students. While most classroom instruction, even for very young children, employs numerous abstract concepts (e.g., shapes, colors, sizes), the concepts are generally difficult for children with ASDs to master. It is easier for children with ASDs to learn those concepts by *teaching concretely.* By employing three-dimensional objects with which they are already familiar (e.g., plastics spoons, socks, toy animals) or photographs of objects, rather than line drawings or abstract shapes (e.g., triangle, circle), most children with ASDs learn more rapidly. Since many young children with ASDs have limited imaginary play, the idea that a two-dimensional black-and-white drawing on a piece of paper (e.g., of a school bus) represents, or means the same thing as, an actual object (e.g., the yellow vehicle waiting outside the school) often exceeds children's current cognitive skill levels. Even if an instructor can teach a child to say "bus" when shown the drawing, the child may not understand that the drawing represents the same idea as the actual vehicle. This is called *stimulus equivalence,* and generally must be taught systematically through a series of steps (Sidman, 1977, 1986; Wilkinson & McIlvane, 2001).

Preacademics

In addition to developing functional adaptive skills useful in school and strengthening communication and social skills, kindergarteners begin acquiring preacademic skills, which generally requires adapted lessons. Basic perceptual motor skills such as learning to trace and then copying letters and numbers are essential preparation for later activities. Subsequently, children can be taught to point at and name letters and numbers and later learn to print them. Learning to color within lines and cutting out shapes is useful preparation for subsequent math, science, and social studies projects. Early phonetics and phonemic awareness assignments prepare the child for reading. For example, recognizing matching phonemes and parsing out syllables by clapping hands with each syllable are helpful phonemic awareness activities. Recognizing common printed words such as *boys, girls, stop,* and *go* are steps toward socially appropriate behavior and safety. Most children with ASDs can participate in art, music, and physical education activities with typical peers, although they may need a paraprofessional aide during the initial transition period.

Some of these preacademic activities can be taught using either board game or card game strategies. For example, copies of game boards can be reproduced from lesson plans and letters and numbers can be distributed on the squares. A single number cube or spinner can be used to determine how many squares each child jumps with his or her game piece. When a child's game piece lands on the square, he or she is asked to say the letter or number. The child receives a token following each correct answer and at the end of the game can exchange the tokens for a small toy from a *surprise* bag.

Phonemic Awareness

Phonemic awareness refers to the ability to segment and manipulate the sounds of oral language, while *phonics* refers to knowledge of how printed letters relate to spoken words. Administering a standardized assessment of phonemic awareness provides a baseline for evaluating progress. The teacher reads words and asks the child whether they rhyme. Next, the child is given two words and asked to name another word that rhymes with the first two. This activity is only suitable for children with good verbal skills. Another baseline activity is to pronounce a word such as *box* and ask the child to say the sound that the word begins with. The child should respond "/b/." Several instruments are available to assess these early literacy skills; for example, *Reading and Writing Grade by Grade: New Standards* from the National Center on Education and the Economy (New Standards, 2004). Once a baseline has been established, lessons focusing first on phonemic awareness and later on phonetics instruction are implemented (Lundberg et al., 1988). A phonemics lesson can involve circling objects that all start with the same beginning consonant. Sorting pictures into stacks according to whether they begin or end with a particular sound extends the phonemics concept.

Art Instruction

Many young children with ASDs lack the skills to create their own pictures from scratch, but given the building blocks they can create interesting and informative collages. It is possible to create instructional activities that provide skill-building experiences integrating several curricular areas. For example, a teacher may have children bring photos from home of family members, pets, their house, their room, their tricycle, their favorite toy, and so forth. In addition, the teacher encourages the children to bring 2–3 small personal items (the size of the palm of their hand) from home (e.g., key, feather, souvenir from their vacation). An instructional aide makes a photocopy of the photos and personal items and asks each child to cut out the photocopied photos and objects. The child's cutting doesn't need to be accurate—just sufficient to include the photocopied object. Next, the child is assisted in arranging the cut-out images on a piece of poster paper in a way that tells the story of his or her family. The child uses a glue stick to affix the copied images to the paper. Now, the child is encouraged to decorate the poster with felt-tip markers or by gluing glitter around the edges of the poster. Finally, each child is asked to print his or her name at the top of the page. If necessary, an aide can provide a dotted-line model of the child's name that can be traced. This activity teaches spatial relations, cutting, pasting, and printing and is a way of telling a story about the children through artistic expression. It also serves as a social studies lesson about relationships within a family and can be an opportunity to promote social skills with typical peers by having children work in pairs, each on his or her own poster, but the typical peer provides assistance to the child with ASD as needed. When the child with an ASD is having difficulty with a specific skill such as cutting, he or she is encouraged to ask the typical peer for help by holding up the scissors and saying, "Help, please."

Early Academic Skills

Arranging instruction thematically rather than by curricular subject matter is a good strategy in teaching children with ASDs. For example, it is helpful to teach math, science, and social studies as inclusive activities rather than as unrelated subjects. Because children with ASDs tend to focus on specific details—parsing the world into small components—a thematic instructional strategy assists them in understanding that one thing is related to another. Instruction begins by assessing skill level in each area required for a given activity. By carefully planning activities around themes that address multiple curricular areas, instruction will promote generalization. Where appropriate, typical peer tutors assist the child, which promotes socialization and helps compensate for skill impairments the ASD child may have.

Social Studies and Art

Art can be a great leveler for children with disabilities in educational settings. Kristy Peterson, Curator of Education at the Kemper Museum of Contemporary Art in Kansas City, and this author conducted a series of art workshops for elementary school children, half of whom were typically developing and half of whom had an ASD. One participant, a minimally verbal child named Tim with an ASD, created pictures of his family using tempera paint. Over the course of one 90-minute session, he created six separate pictures, each on its own 10″ × 14″ sheet of colored paper. Each drawing was structured exactly like the previous drawing, but Tim used different colored markers to represent family members, who were represented as stick figures—the father on the far left, the mother next, followed by his older sister, Tim, his dog, and his pet bird on the far right. The figures were arranged in descending order of size. Below each figure Tim had printed who the figure represented: "Daddy," "Mommy," "Tim," and for the last figure on the far right he printed "BIRD." He used striking, vibrant colors, and his art provided a unique window into the way he saw his family and their relationship with one another.

Science and Math

Activities can be created that teach combined skills. The goal of this activity is to teach number sense and natural science. This is a good activity for the beginning of the school year. Children are provided with construction paper in fall colors, four white sheets of copy paper, fall-themed stickers, and red, yellow, green, and brown crayons. Students are taken for a walk around the school and encouraged to collect as many different types of leaves as possible. On returning to the classroom, children are taught how to make crayon rubbings of the leaves. Each of the four white pages can include rubbings of a different number of leaves, each leaf in a different color. This would be a good place to employ peer tutors if a child needs assistance making the rubbing. Once the rubbings are finished, the child is asked to tell the group how many pictures of leaves are on each page. Then the child prints at the top of each page the numeral corresponding to the number of leaves on each page. A cover is made from seasonally colored construction paper with the title "My Leaf

Book." The child can print his or her name on the cover either by tracing dotted-line letters, or, if the child is capable, by copying the letters from a model. Children are encouraged to decorate the cover with fall-related stickers. This activity provides instruction in natural science, math, art, and printing. It also teaches that a project has a beginning, a middle, and an end. In other words, it teaches task completion. Because it is visually based, it is especially suitable for young children with ASDs.

Language Arts

Children who have some receptive language skills are typically read to by their teacher or aide. For beginning kindergarten students, books that promote phonemic awareness and phonetics are especially useful. For example, a teacher may read Dr. Seuss's *One Fish Two Fish Red Fish Blue Fish* to a small group of children. When the teacher comes to a word with a short "a" or "i," he stops and repeats the word. The teacher holds up the book and points to the "i" and says, "All right, girls and boys, who can tell me how the 'i' in *Fish* sounds?"

After the students have responded, the teacher will say, "Right, it sounds like /ih/—it doesn't sound like /eye/." Children in transition from kindergarten to first-grade classrooms who have ASDs will initially have difficulty listening to stories, but if the teacher combines pictures and words, frequently calls on various children (including those with ASDs), and asks questions, he or she will be more likely to maintain the children's interest. Some teachers create a poster with each child's name and picture on it, and whenever a child answers a question correctly the teacher places a checkmark on the poster. Each child who has a checkmark receives a prize, and the child with the most checkmarks is allowed to reach into a grab bag and pull out a special prize. The teacher can make certain that the child with ASD has an opportunity for the special prize at least once a week.

Crises in the Classroom

Most tantrums or meltdowns of young children with ASDs occur because an expected routine was changed. A simple functional assessment of the circumstances surrounding a student's outburst can be helpful in developing a hypothesis regarding the underlying causes. Jamal, a 6-year-old who is very bright and hyperlexic, engages in extensive compulsive routines (e.g., lining up objects, insisting that items he uses be placed in specific orders). His special education teacher had established that he becomes upset if anything is out of order. One day the classroom aide who usually participated in a sandbox activity with him was busy with another student, so a different aide approached him to start the activity. Jamal began sobbing uncontrollably and threw himself on the floor, flailing his arms and feet. The new aide didn't know what to do. The special education teacher in charge of the classroom sat down beside Jamal and began writing a social story on a sheet of lined paper and asked Jamal to read each line as she wrote it. "Jamal is upset," the first line read. The next read, "Ms. Mary usually plays with Jamal in the sandbox, but she is busy today." The next line the teacher wrote was, "Jamal is sad because Ms. Teresa is going to play in the sandbox with him." As Jamal read each line he began calming down. "It's OK if Jamal is upset, but he will have fun with Ms. Teresa." After reading the last line, Jamal got up off the floor and approached Teresa and took her hand, leading her to the sandbox. The social story was a cognitive behavior therapy technique that translated Jamal's overpowering and diffuse thoughts and feelings into a series of concrete, manageable events and actions that made the episode understandable and acceptable to him.

A child with severe behavioral challenges can completely disrupt a classroom, consuming most of a staff member's time for an entire day. This is especially likely to occur if an event that took place prior to the child's coming to school set the stage for the outburst. A child with an earache, who has constipation, or who didn't sleep enough the previous night has a much lower threshold for being triggered for an outburst by an instructional request with which she would usually readily comply. Boys are more likely to engage in aggression or self-injury, and girls more frequently run about frantically, flapping their hands and sobbing following a trigger event. It is important that parents send a note to school with the child if they are aware that he or she isn't feeling well so that the instructional staff can reduce the number of instructional requests, provide more frequent breaks, and increase reinforcement for compliance.

In some cases, a child may be moody and easily upset for several weeks. School staff is encouraged to speak with the child's parents to discover whether any changes at home may be contributing to the child's problem behavior. In one family, the older brother of the child with an ASD went off to college, and for weeks afterward the youngster was sad and irritable. The slightest provocation would set off an outburst. Teaching staff spent more one-to-one time with the child, increased the number of preferred activities that were part of his daily schedule, and scheduled time with his sister—a student at the same school—to visit his classroom. Gradually, his symptoms of depression and sadness diminished and he became his old self again.

Finally, some children with ASDs, and another concurrent condition such as obsessive-compulsive disorder (OCD), profit from receiving appropriate psychotropic medication. School personnel cannot recommend medication to families, but they can provide families with information about how their child is doing in school and give them pamphlets and other information regarding alternative treatments. If families request it, school personnel can provide a list of clinics, pediatricians, or child psychiatrists who may be helpful.

Falling Behind

Most children with ASDs, even those with IQ scores testing in the typical range, have difficulty keeping up as the learning materials become more abstract and complex. They may be able to read at or above grade level, but their abstract reasoning ability holds them back. As the curriculum calls for more inferential reasoning, children with ASDs begin to lag behind. Lessons that involve interpretations of the reasons for people's actions, such as those that occur in social studies and early literature, are often difficult for children with ASDs and take them longer to complete. For example, a teacher might read the story *The Little Red Hen* to a small group of children and ask why the Little Red Hen said she would eat the bread she baked, but wouldn't share it with the Duck, Cat, or Dog. Answering the question requires a reasoning level about fairness that would be challenging for many children with ASDs. Most young children with ASDs, even intellectually capable students, may find the answer elusive. Similarly, a child with an ASD may find it difficult to discuss why Flopsy, Mopsy, and Cottontail, in the story *Peter Rabbit,* had bread, milk, and blackberries for supper, while Peter was put to bed and given a tablespoon of camomile by his mother. It is unlikely that even a bright 6-year-old with an ASD would conclude that Peter's fate was a result of his disobeying his mother about going into Mr. McGregor's garden. Teachers will find it necessary to prepare different questions for children with ASDs and for typical children to prompt productive discussion. While typical children will be comfortable with "why" questions, youngsters with ASDs will perform better in response to "is" questions—that is, to report what is happening in the story.

By the first grade, written assignments begin to involve a combination of inductive and deductive reasoning. Teachers will find it necessary to provide individualized instruction to students with ASDs using adapted lessons. Although a child may be a 6-year-old and reading relatively well, teachers may find it useful to employ curricula designed for kindergarten students. By repeatedly presenting multiple exemplars of similar problems or social examples, some children with ASDs begin to become proficient. Peer tutoring can be highly effective with children with ASDs in basic reading and math. Several programs developed for slow readers and children with learning disabilities can be adapted for use with higher-functioning children with ASDs. Fuchs, Fuchs, and Burish (2000), Fuchs, Fuchs, Kazdan, and Allen (1999), and Fuchs et al. (2001) developed peer-assisted learning strategies for slow readers and students with other disabilities. Similar to the strategies developed in Greenwood et al. (2001), students are provided with systematic direct instruction designed to promote reading skills, receive positive reinforcement and corrective feedback, and strengthen reading fluency. Although these methods were intended to facilitate reading skills for entire classrooms of students, they can also be used with individual students. They are highly effective methods of promoting reading skills in delayed learners.

ADAPTED EXPECTATIONS

There have been no detailed, long-term follow-up studies of individuals diagnosed with ASDs who have received intensive early intervention services as young children and later therapy and social skills services as adolescents. Several lines of evidence suggest that most children with ASDs who do very well in early behavior therapy and function reasonably well in elementary school exhibit residual ASD symptoms. These symptoms may include attention deficits, limited social skills, and some language limitations (Sallows & Graupner, 2005). Moreover, growing research literature indicates that close relatives of children with ASDs are more likely to display features of the Broad ASD Phenotype—that is, subtle signs or symptoms of ASD features. This term is used to describe characteristics of family members who are not diagnosed with an ASD but that include many subclinical features of ASDs. Although they have been totally integrated into the mainstream of society, hold jobs, are married, and have families, adults with ASD are more likely to have problems interpreting and coping with social relationships, have some language processing difficulties, and exhibit fixed interests in less extreme forms than their children (Bishop et al., 2004; Pickles et al., 2000). This suggests that they, like their children, may exhibit some social and psychological characteristics that distinguish them from their neighbors. Children who had more symptoms of autism when they were very young are more likely to retain residual features into junior and senior high school. While parents may desperately hope that their children will develop friendships and have typical social lives, it is likely that many children with ASDs who have done well through kindergarten and into elementary school will have social difficulties and some academic limitations in junior and senior high school. It is incumbent on schools to create a culture of tolerance for differences among students and proactive, positive approaches to including children with disabilities. Many parents of children with ASDs are willing to speak with students in their child's school about ASDs and help the other students understand children like their son or daughter. This is a case in which collaboration between parents and schools can be especially helpful.

There is no reason why most of these developing youngsters cannot lead healthy, productive, and happy lives, but it is important that parents and teachers adjust their expectations according to the abilities and skills their child or student displays. The child may not be the president of the student council or captain of the football team, but he or she can fully participate in school life. The children's friendships are likely to be more limited and will need to be fostered by caring adults. Youngsters with high-functioning

ASDs or Asperger syndrome may excel in math and science and struggle in literature and social studies courses, but so do lots of other students. As caring adults we do not want to communicate our disappointment that the cup is one-quarter empty; instead, we need to celebrate that the cup is three-quarters full.

SUMMARY

Similar to first discovering that their child has an ASD, transitioning from preschool to school life is often extremely difficult for parents. Through developing a collaborative relationship between school and parents with regular, open communication, it is usually possible to work together to provide a child with appropriate educational opportunities. School placement is a major decision for the child, his or her parents, and the school. It is often a time of crisis for families who are struggling to adjust to how their child's disability will play itself out in this new environment. Using specific strategies for the preschool to kindergarten and kindergarten to first-grade transition, most students are able to adjust to new environments with new expectations. Teachers and parents often need additional training to accommodate the new concerns of children with ASDs once they are in school. By employing adapted educational methods based on solid empirical evidence, schools can assist children with ASDs make the most of their educational experience. Many children with ASDs can do well in preacademics and early academics with appropriate accommodations. As they approach first and second grades, however, they often begin to fall behind in areas that require more complex social reasoning. If parents and teachers adjust their expectations according to the reality of a child's abilities and skills, school life can be a positive experience that prepares the child for a productive and fulfilling life.

7

Functional and Cognitive Behavioral Strategies

A child with an autism spectrum disorder (ASD) is like a mistakenly translated sonnet with muddled meter and an imperfectly rhyming final couplet. Most of the 14 lines are present, but they are oddly out of synch. How do we return the sonnet's meter to the one its author had intended without the original as our guide? This is similar to the daunting task faced by therapists, teachers, and parents as they attempt to construct new skills that will make it possible for a child with an ASD to lead a fuller life. How can they induce the dysfunctional components to operate the way they are supposed to function?

When the therapist arrived at Estelle's home, Estelle's mother Janine was embarrassed because her daughter was screaming and running frantically around the dining room clad only in a diaper. Janine explained that Estelle, who was 2½ years old, had torn off her clothing as soon as she had been dressed earlier that morning and since then has refused to wear clothing. When she saw the therapist, Estelle dove under the dining room table and refused to come out when her mother prompted her to do so. To Estelle, the therapist didn't belong there—things weren't the way they ought to be. Janine tried to pull her daughter out from under the table by her legs, but Estelle scratched and kicked her mother and made screeching noises. As the therapist surveyed the scene, she knew that she had her work cut out for her. It would have been difficult for her to imagine then that after 2 years of intensive early intervention, Estelle would resemble most of her peers, would be well groomed, playing with dolls, and talking in sentences.

Nearly all children with ASDs display behavior their parents and teachers find troubling. From repetitive stereotyped behavior, such as flapping their hands and repeatedly opening and closing doors, to tantrums, aggression, and self-injury, children and youth with ASDs engage in disruptive and disturbing behavior. Estelle's behavior was not unusual for a young child with an ASD who had received no previous intervention. Her life was driven by her desire to control the way her world ought to be. Some children exhibit relatively few or minor behavioral challenges while others have "meltdowns" or aggressive outbursts many times a day. These problem behaviors are disruptive to family life and the classroom, are embarrassing in community settings, and may potentially be physically harmful in some cases. If there is not appropriate intervention by the time children are in elementary school, entrenched behavior patterns are established that may be extremely difficult to change later in life. Prevalence studies indicate that nearly half the children and youth with an ASD receive psychotropic medications for behavior problems (Witwer & Lecavalier, 2005). Other parents cope with their children's difficult behavior using behavioral treatments, and some receive no assistance at all. Caregivers acknowledge having great trouble coping with their children's problem behavior. In a study conducted in Pennsylvania, it was found that 18.5% of children with ASDs in the community survey sample had been physically abused by caregivers, most often the abuse was associated with their children's behavior problems (Mandell et al., 2005).

Maladaptive Coping

Children with ASDs are often confused, frightened, and even alarmed by the circumstances in which they find themselves. They don't understand what their parents, teachers, and siblings are saying to them. They don't know what to expect next and find disruptions of their daily routines intolerable. Their world seems chaotic to them, nothing is as it ought to be. For example, when the mother of a young boy with an ASD tells him that it is time to get ready for school that means he must stop what he is doing, repeatedly twirling a string in circles, a highly preferred repetitive activity. The ensuing tantrum temporarily stops his mother from demanding that he stop his compulsive activity. In other words, it is a means of escaping from a very unwelcome demand. The mother of Loren, an adolescent with a severe ASD, told me that Loren sat on the floor at home and banged the back of his head against the wall repeatedly until she figured out what he wanted. There were periods that he struck his head so hard and so often, it caused severe bruising on the back of his head. As soon as she gave him what he wanted, he stopped hurting himself. Banging his head was his very self-destructive means of telling his mother he wanted something, and, unfortunately, it was the only means of communication he had. These maladaptive coping responses become progressively worse, until an analysis of the reasons for them are found and an appropriate intervention is implemented. In most cases, psychotropic medications are not appropriate interventions under these circumstances.

FUNCTIONAL ASSESSMENT AND POSITIVE BEHAVIOR SUPPORT

Most behavioral challenges can be prevented in the course of intensive early intervention. The primary problems revolve around intolerance for changes in routine, thwarting highly preferred repetitive activities, and an inability to communicate needs and wants. Some children who have not had previous intervention develop behavior problems by the time they are in kindergarten or elementary school and present serious difficulties for parents and teachers. Tantrums, meltdowns, compulsively repetitive behavioral routines, aggression, and self-injury are the most common problem behaviors.

In the 1960s and 1970s, perplexed by the severely disturbed behavior of many children with ASDs, many researchers and practitioners focused their attention on how to eliminate the problem behavior. That seemed to make sense because the children, their parents, and teachers were all in anguish as a result of the children's behavior problems. By eliminating the problem behavior, they reasoned, everyone's life would improve. Procedures such as extinction (e.g., not paying attention to the problem behavior), response cost (e.g., taking away points or tokens), or time-out procedures (e.g., sending the child to his room) were used. Other aversive procedures, such as overcorrection or positive practice, were also employed to suppress problem behavior. These methods often reduced the behavior problem, which is important, but they didn't replace the disturbed behavior with more appropriate activities. Moreover, the effects were often transient, with the problem behavior resuming when a different caregiver failed to follow through using exactly the same methods. These approaches also raised quality of life issues for many in the field.

In the 1980s, a group of special education and psychology researchers began looking at children's behavioral challenges a different way. They asked why it was necessary for a child with an ASD or another developmental disability to display problem behavior, and what could be done to replace behavioral challenges with meaningful alternatives. They sought ways of improving the overall quality of the child's life, not merely eliminating the problem behavior. In a prescient article, Carr and Durand (1985) described a strategy for reducing behavior problems through functional communication training. In 1990, Robert Horner and colleagues published a paper titled *Toward a Technology of "Nonaversive" Behavioral Support* in which they outlined the basic tenets of what would become the field of positive behavior support. Several years later, Todd Risley (1996) published a book chapter titled "Get a Life! Positive Behavioral Intervention for Challenging Behavior Through Life Arrangement and Life Coaching." Carr et al. (2002) described the evolution of positive behavior supports into a more refined scientific approach to solving important problems of people with developmental disabilities. Those publications, along with several others, laid the ground-work for a change in the way we approach helping children with ASDs and related developmental disabilities lead fuller lives.

Most children with ASDs are more like their typical peers than may ini-tially be apparent. They want to play with other children but have no idea how. Learning to play with others is hard work for a child with an ASD, but it is a teachable set of skills. Children with ASDs want to be included in activ-ities with other members of their family. They want to participate in meals, play a game with their siblings, go to the library with their father, and go camping over the weekend. Although children with ASDs often express their desires in ways that may seem peculiar to their family members or teachers, they have been found to have strong preferences and very clear interests when they are taught more appropriate communication skills. If they are given the proper tools, children with ASDs will let their wishes be known.

Positive Behavior Support

Positive behavior support (PBS) is an applied science that uses environmental redesign to enhance quality of life and minimize problem behavior. PBS ini-tially evolved within the field of developmental disabilities and emerged from three major sources: applied behavior analysis (ABA), the normalization/inclusion movement, and person-centered values. Although elements of PBS can be found in other approaches, its uniqueness lies in the fact that it inte-grates the following nine critical features into a cohesive whole:

1. Comprehensive lifestyle change

2. Lifespan perspective

3. Ecological validity

4. Stakeholder participation

5. Social validity

6. Systems change/multicomponent intervention

7. Emphasis on prevention

8. Flexibility in scientific practices

9. Multiple theoretical perspectives
   (Horner 1990; Horner, Sugai, Todd, & Lewis-Palmer, 1990)

   Positive behavior refers to those skills that increase the likelihood of suc-cess and personal satisfaction in normative academic, social, recreational, com-munity, and family settings. *Support* refers to therapeutic and educational methods used to teach, strengthen, and expand positive behavior and increase opportunities for the display of positive behavior. The primary goal of support is to develop a strategy that relevant stakeholders (e.g., the child, parents, siblings, teachers, friends of the child) agree will provide the opportunity for an improved quality of life. This goal is achieved in large part by rendering problem behavior irrelevant, inefficient, and ineffective through helping an individual achieve his or her goals in a socially acceptable manner, thus reducing, or eliminating altogether, episodes of problem behavior.

Planning the Intervention

By the time parents and teachers decide it is necessary to intervene, they often feel an urgent need for immediate action to contain, if not stop, a child's extremely disturbing behavior. Crisis management is not the same as a carefully planned, longer-term intervention strategy. When families are in a crisis because of their child's behavior, they often require respite or crisis-intervention support from an agency that provides such services. At times, psychotropic medications may be necessary to bring problem behavior under control temporarily. While the problem is being transiently managed, a positive behavior support plan can be developed and then implemented.

Everyone who has a significant stake in the child's life should participate in setting goals for the child. This includes the target child, his parents, siblings, teachers, speech clinician, behavior therapy staff, nurse or other health care worker, and the child's social worker. Together they develop a comprehensive approach to addressing multiple dimensions that define quality of life. For a child with an ASD, the plan begins with his or her health and family relationships. Many children with ASDs have recurring health problems that cause discomfort and increase the child's tendency to engage in problem behavior. Children with ASDs don't enjoy having tantrums nor do they like fighting with their siblings or other children. They would prefer that their daily lives are more pleasant and fulfilling, but they don't know how to make that happen.

The plan must include ways for the child to strengthen skills in areas that he or she does especially well, increasing confidence and satisfaction. Personal control is of major importance to children with ASDs, such as how their room is arranged, which personal items they put where, or what they will have for dessert. Each child needs a plan that promotes recreational and leisure skills and provides greater opportunities for community adjustment (e.g., following safety rules, learning to go on outings to the library or recreation center). Opportunities for participation with typical peers in the neighborhood and at school are important elements of the plan.

Some professionals may be concerned that planning participants may have unrealistic expectations for a child; however, it is important that all perspectives are considered in reaching a consensus. In most instances, reason prevails when a group of dedicated and knowledgeable people get together to discuss how they can all help a child have a better future. If everyone has had an opportunity for input, it is more likely that they will all be active participants in supporting the child's support plan.

Making Action Plans

A planning approach widely used in education is called Making Action Plans (MAPS). MAPS is a planning process that brings together the key players in a child's life to identify a road map for working toward and achieving goals for the child (Forest & Lusthaus, 1989; Vandercook, York, & Forest, 1989). The MAPS process identifies where the child currently is, what the goals are for the child, and how the team will work together to reach the goals. MAPS has an established framework that addresses the child's history, identity, and strengths and the team's greatest concerns and dreams for the child. The child's needs and action steps for the plan are identified.

Functional Assessment Interview

After the initial planning meeting, a summary of the group's deliberations and conclusions is distributed to those who attended the meeting and the next steps are initiated. Typically, this involves collecting information about the circumstances within which the child's problem behavior is embedded. Parents are asked to complete a functional assessment interview (FAI) form (O'Neill et al., 1997), which is reviewed with parents by a licensed psychologist, lead special educator, or behavior therapist to clarify any comments or questions raised. The FAI includes a list of problem behaviors, how they are performed, how often, for how long, and with what intensity. The form asks parents to report medications their child is taking, any health problems they may have (e.g., allergies), sleep problems, or difficulty with eating routines. After providing an hour-by-hour schedule for the child's typical day, parents are asked to indicate whether that schedule is predictable to the child, and whether the child has any choices in the course of a typical day. Several questions on the FAI pertain directly to the child's problem behavior. Parents report about the time of day, the settings, the ongoing activities, and with whom the behavior problem is most and least likely to occur and indicate the child's preferred play activities and whether they play with someone else or alone. For each problem behavior, parents are asked to indicate what the child receives or what he or she avoids as a consequence of the behavior. The "efficiency" of the problem behavior in obtaining or avoiding a specific consequence is estimated (e.g., how long the child's tantrum lasts until the parental demand is removed). The child's communicative skills are estimated as they pertain to requests, protesting an activity the child dislikes, or indicating discomfort or illness. Previous efforts to change the child's behavior are listed (e.g., medications, diet, "not giving in to tantrums"). Finally, for each problem behavior, parents create a table indicating the immediate trigger event, the nature of the behavior, what happens afterward, and what function they believe it serves (e.g., obtaining parental attention).

Keeping Records

Although parents often feel that a child exhibits problem behavior constantly, that is very rare. Challenging behavior usually occurs most often at a certain time of day or in specific situations. For the week following the FAI, parents are asked to maintain a record of occasions on which specific problem behaviors occur by day and time, usually divided into 30-minute or 1-hour blocks of time. Each behavior is indicated by a letter code (e.g., A= aggression, T=tantrum, and so forth). The result is called a *scatter plot* and is used to determine periods of the day when problems are most common (Touchette, MacDonald, & Langer, 1985). The 1-week scatter plot is reviewed, and the periods when most of the problems occur are identified (e.g., before going to school, before bedtime). An experienced observer visits the child's home during those periods the following week and records what happened immediately prior to each outburst, the type of behavior (e.g., aggression), and what happened to end the behavior (e.g., a parental request was rescinded; Sugai & Tindal, 1993). This is called an ABC (Antecedent–Behavior–Consequences) chart and is used to determine the probability of specific behavior problems given identified antecedent events (e.g., interrupting a preferred routine), what the child does, and how the episode is resolved (i.e., what happens after the child's response). For example, based on the ABC data for a 1-week period, the observer may determine that out of the 21 aggressive episodes, 13 of them (62%) followed a parental request or demand to do something and the remaining eight (38%) occurred when a preferred repetitive behavior was interrupted. This helps the therapist suggest the types of interventions that should be developed to promote replacement skills, making aggression unnecessary.

Setting Events

During the same week, parents are asked to keep a record of approximately how many hours their child sleeps nightly and whether he or she had any health problems such as a headache, stomach ache, or constipation. They are also asked to record events that appeared to be especially disturbing to the child such as nearly missing the van ride to school, losing a favorite sweatshirt in the mall, or witnessing a severe thunderstorm. Health problems (e.g., lack of sleep) and emotionally disturbing events (e.g., the thunderstorm) serve as antecedent *setting events* that make problem behavior more likely (cf., Carr, Reeve, & Magito-McLaughlin, 1995; Kennedy & Itonken, 1993; Kennedy & Thompson, 2000). When the baby sitter arrives to care for the child, she says,

"Cameron sure has a chip on his shoulder today," meaning that whatever happened earlier in the day made him especially prone to behaving aggressively. On days that setting events have made problem behavior more likely, it is important to reduce the number of adult requests and increase the amount of reinforcement for positive behavior. Parents are encouraged to discuss ways of improving their child's sleep with the child's pediatrician. Giving the youngster passion fruit juice before bedtime can help because it contains high levels of L-tryptophan, which encourages sleep; or, alternatively, the doctor may recommend trying melatonin. Bowel irregularity is a common problem in children with an ASD, and many parents routinely give their child a high-fiber diet or prune juice to obviate this problem.

Planning intervention strategies requires substantial forethought and familiarity with intervention options. *A Replication and Dissemination of Model of Inservice Training and Technical Assistance to Prevent Challenging Behavior in Young Children with Disabilities* by McEvoy, Reichle, and Davis (1995) is an excellent starting point.

Environmental, Intervention, and Organizational Arrangements

Organizing aspects of the classroom or home environment, including physical features, schedules, transitions, staffing patterns, and instruction or therapy methods, prevents many behavioral challenges. Environmental arrangements are important because a well-organized environment tends to increase appropriate and decrease problem behavior. Providing distinctive areas for different types of activities encourages relevant behavior in those situations. *Intervention arrangements* refers to parent-, therapist-, or teacher-directed activities, as opposed to child-directed or child-initiated activities. Providing distinct opportunities for each type of activity over the course of the day helps the child achieve greater independence and makes it clear when the child is expected to follow an adult's lead. *Organizational issues* refers to scheduling, planning for transitions, deciding which adult(s) will assume responsibility at various times, and behavioral expectations. The use of visual activity schedules is an especially effective organizational tool in working with children with ASDs (McClannahan & Krantz, 1999). Clearly, planning for cued transitions reduces challenging behavior, and making it clear when various adults are working with a child provides for planned generalization of skills across the adults and reduces problem behavior when a different adult is involved.

Choice Making

Choice making (selecting one of two activities or reinforcers) encourages the child to feel in control (making certain that things are the way they ought to be) while being certain that the choices are reasonable and within appropriate limits. Children who exhibit problem behaviors to escape from adult requests often benefit from opportunities to choose one versus another activity (Sigafoos, 1999). Beginning with only a few choices often reduces problem behavior in children with frequent outbursts. For children who are withdrawn and less responsive, an array of choices may increase their probability of participation. If a child is having difficulty choosing, breaking the two choices into smaller steps may make the process easier. For example, if the choices are to put on shoes or brush teeth, asking the child to choose between putting the shoes down on the floor or wetting a toothbrush may make a choice easier to make.

Sequencing and Embedding Low- and High-Compliance Activities

Charles doesn't like to put away toys when he's finished playing with them. Asking him to put away toys often precipitates an outburst. Charles stopped playing with the hand puppet 5 minutes ago and is now coloring with markers, an activity he greatly enjoys. His mother says, "Charles, let's color with the red marker," which he does immediately. Then she says, "Charles, make a tree," which he also does promptly. Then she says, "Charles put away the puppet, and then we'll color a dog." Charles stops what he's doing, hesitates, and then puts the puppet in a box. "Good job, Charles," his mother says. When she says, "Let's color a dog," he initiates the activity promptly. By capitalizing on *behavioral momentum*—embedding a low-probability of compliance request within a sequence of a high-probability compliance request—the chances that Charles will have an outburst are decreased (Mace et al., 1988).

Reducing Task Difficulty and Teaching Communication

When we examine Cameron's aggressive behavior, it appears to happen most often when he is asked to do a task that is difficult for him or which he especially dislikes, such as putting on his socks in the morning. Several things can be done to address the problem (Vaughn, Fox, & Lentini, 2006). First, make certain his socks are fairly loose fitting and made of stretchy fabric that is easy to slip on. Second, teach Cameron to say "help" when he is having difficulty putting on his socks. Third, have him put on his socks before he sits down for breakfast, so there is an immediate positive consequence for putting on his socks. A week's worth of manual guidance that is gradually faded out over the next week may solve the problem. Having learned to ask for help in this situation is likely to generalize quickly to other tasks in which he needs assistance. For the first week, make certain he receives his favorite food item (e.g., applesauce) as soon as he sits down to eat breakfast.

It is important for children to have ways of requesting attention from adults that will be honored, if not immediately, then after a brief signaled delay. Similarly, there may be items or activities the child wants that are not available to him or her, such as toys or games that are put away in a closet or food items that must be prepared. Teaching the child verbal, iconic, or gestural ways to request items or activities greatly reduces problem behavior.

Requesting the Delay or Rejection of a Non-Preferred Task

Sometimes a child may have a legitimate reason for not wanting to do a task the moment an adult asks them to do it. The child may be in the midst of building a tower with blocks when a therapist says, "Let's do our letters now." It can be helpful if the child is taught to request a delay in starting the less-preferred activity, using a picture symbol (e.g., a clock), a gesture, or a verbal request (e.g., "later"; Sigafoos et al., 2004). The therapist can respond by saying, "I'll set the timer and when it rings we'll do your numbers." Helena may dislike fresh fruit for dessert, greatly preferring pudding, but her parents may think it's important for her to have fresh fruit in her diet. If her parents elect to force Helena to eat fruit, it is nearly certain that she will have a tantrum. If Helena is taught to say, "No fruit," her parents have the option of saying, "One bite, and then pudding." This is a very old but effective strategy that many parents have used.

Requesting a Break from a Non-Preferred Task

Most adults take a break when they are participating in an activity they find boring or unpleasant. The same strategy is effective for children with ASDs. Paul dislikes a matching task that requires him to match colors with their printed names. After completing 8–10 matches, his classroom aide notices Paul fidgeting in his seat and putting his fingers in his ears. She says, "Paul, would you like a break?" When Paul nods his head "yes," the aide responds by saying, "OK, let's take a break, and then we'll finish your colors." She turns over an egg timer in front of him and says, "When all of the sand is at the bottom, we'll finish your colors." The next day, when they are doing colors, Paul's aide says, "Today, if you need a break, show me this card," pointing to a card with a stop sign on it. After 5–10 minutes, Paul places his head down on his desk and looks distraught. "If you need a break, Paul," his aide says, "show me your break card." Paul looks confused at first, and then grabs the card and hands it to the aide. "Good job, Paul," she says and turns over the egg timer. By the third day, Paul uses his stop sign to request a break 1–2 times per lesson, but he is no longer having tantrums.

Reducing Task Aversiveness

Children who resist tooth brushing either dislike the feeling of the brush on their teeth and gums or dislike the taste of the toothpaste. Several companies manufacture soft or ultrasoft toothbrushes. *Amazing Products Store* (http://www.pacwestserv.com/index.htm) sells ultrasoft toothbrushes for children as well as flavored toothpastes and gels. Soft toothbrushes have nylon bristles with a diameter of 0.007 of an inch or less. The Biotene Toothbrush Super Soft with bristles, with a diameter of 0.003 of an inch, is even softer. Some companies advertise their toothbrushes as being soft, but they are not, so consumers must check with the company to make certain that the bristles are under 0.007 of an inch (preferably smaller).

Flavored toothpastes usually overcome the second problem, dislike for the stringent mint taste of most toothpastes. While most toothpastes sold by the *Amazing Products Store* are mint flavored, they also offer strawberry, strawberry-banana, cherry, herbal bubble-gum, and mango flavored toothpastes or gels. *BreathPalette.Com* sells a variety of flavored toothpastes, such as fresh yogurt, monkey banana, kiwi fruit, strawberry, and blueberry, at least one of which is likely to be appealing to your child. The toothpaste is sold in the United States by Bravo Port, Inc., P.O. Box 1712, Sausalito, California. Most children will accept ordinary toothpaste over several weeks.

Collaborating on Tasks

Some children resist an activity if they must do it all themselves, but they more willingly participate if they complete it with another person. When Carla resists setting the dinner table, her mother says, "Carla, you put the forks on the table, and I'll put on the spoons." By reducing the response requirement, Carla puts the forks on the table by each plate with minimal grumbling. This technique, called *collaboration,* often reduces the likelihood of a behavioral outburst. Over time the child can be requested to complete more of the task, and the adult gradually turns over more responsibility to the child (Reichle, McEvoy, & Davis, 1999).

Identifying Triggering Events (Discriminative Stimuli)

It is important to carefully examine events that trigger outbursts. A child may respond negatively to requests by some people but not others. Hea is a 5-year-old in an inclusive kindergarten. She has a diagnosis of PDD-NOS and has been having outbursts at school, and Karin, her teacher, has said that the outbursts are getting worse. A behavior analyst visits Hea's classroom to see if she can discover what causes the crying and screaming episodes. When the behavior analyst arrives, Karin watches Hea closely and waits until she stops twirling the beads she is holding before speaking to her. In an upbeat voice, Karin says, "Hea, when I count to 3, we're going to do your numbers. Then we can have a treat." Karin pauses for several seconds, and then says, "One, two, three!" holding up her fingers in front of Hea as she does so. Hea watches Karin's fingers intently as Karin counts. Karin takes Hea's hand, leads her to a child-sized table, and as soon as Hea sits down, says, "Great job, Hea. Now let's do your numbers, and then we can have a treat."

Later, when the behavior analyst returns to the classroom, Karin's aide Teddy is about to work with Hea. Hea is seated on a chair that swivels back and forth. She twirls repeatedly and swings her head from side to side as she does so. Teddy stops Hea in mid-swing and says, "Hea, we're going to do letters now." Hea looks away and tries to make the swivel chair rotate, but Teddy holds it firmly. He repeats in a louder voice, "Hea, look at me. We're going to do your letters now." Hea looks at him out of the corner of her eye and begins to cry. Then Teddy says in a firm voice, "Hea, come over here [gesturing]" and grasps Hea's arm, pulling her toward the table as she resists. Hea throws herself on the floor and begins screaming.

There are several important differences in the way Karin and Teddy asked Hea to participate in a non-preferred academic activity. Karin was careful to wait until Hea had stopped twirling the beads, a form of self-stimulation, before calling for her attention. Karin also provided a transition signal with an additional brief period for Hea to process what she had been told. Next, Karin told Hea what reward she would receive for participating in the number activity. Finally, Karin spoke in a calm, upbeat tone of voice. On the other hand, Teddy stopped Hea in the midst of a favorite repetitive routine, undoubtedly upsetting her. He gave her no transition signal to help her bridge from one activity to the next. He spoke in a firm, perhaps irritated tone of voice. While Hea is probably not very good at interpreting emotional tone of voice, she probably realizes that when an adult raises his or her voice volume, something bad is about to happen. Also, Teddy did not offer any positive consequence for participating. Finally, he held Hea's arm firmly and began pulling her against her resistance toward the table. The resulting differences in the child's behavior would be puzzling only if one focused on the fact that in both instances the child was being required to participate in a non-preferred activity. Perhaps the reason Hea is having more outbursts is that Teddy is inadvertently provoking screaming and crying.

Overcoming Skill Deficits

Pablo's mother is disconcerted because he strikes her and his younger sister Isabella. At times, he seems to become very angry and hits his head with his fists. Although he is only 7 years old, he is big for his age, and his aggression and self-injury can cause bruising. Pablo's father is at work in the evening when Pablo is home from school, where he attends a self-contained classroom for children with severe disabilities. His parents, who moved from Guatemala to the United States when Pablo was 2 years old, speak Spanish at home. Pablo doesn't have any spoken language. He still eats with his fingers and is bladder trained, although not reliably. Mrs. Morales indicated on the FAI form that Pablo is frequently constipated. She also indicated that she thought his aggression toward his sister might be to get her attention. A behavior therapist visited the Morales's apartment and observed Pablo, his mother, and his sister for an entire evening. He conducted an ABC analysis over the evening and found that Pablo shoved or struck Isabella when his mother was paying attention to her. He also noted that Pablo hit his mother several times when it appeared that he wanted something he couldn't reach in the cupboard or in refrigerator. In both instances, Mrs. Morales asked Pablo in Spanish what he wanted, and Pablo became more agitated, hitting her harder. Pablo's aggression toward his sister was easier to treat because it was precipitated by a lack of attention from his mother. The behavior therapist suggested that whenever Mrs. Morales was going to talk or play with Isabella, she should first briefly hug or otherwise positively interact with Pablo (see Bambara & Kern, 2005).

Pablo's aggression toward his mother was more challenging. The therapist showed Pablo photographs of an apple, a glass of juice, and a peanut butter sandwich. He asked, "Pablo want apple?" and pointed to the apple. As soon as Pablo touched the photo of the apple, the therapist gave him a slice of a fresh apple. This procedure was repeated for the juice and the peanut butter sandwich. The next step was to attach the photos to a poster board and ask Pablo to point to what he wanted. He learned very quickly to do so. Then the therapist encouraged Mrs. Morales to communicate with Pablo using the picture board. Initially, she wanted to do so in Spanish, but to avoid confusing Pablo with the instruction in school, which was in English, the therapist suggested that Mrs. Morales use English to communicate with Pablo at home as well. Pablo's aggression toward his mother was a dysfunctional communicative strategy that was rendered unnecessary by teaching him to use pictures to make requests. Finally, the therapist suggested that Mrs. Morales speak with Pablo's doctor about possible methods of preventing constipation, which makes him more irritable and therefore likely to behave aggressively.

Increasing Tolerance for Delays of Desired Outcomes

Most children with ASDs have a very low tolerance for delayed gratification. They want the time between when they request something, such as a preferred activity, and when it is made available to them to be as short as possible. Sometimes a parent, teacher, or therapist is busy with another child or activity and cannot respond immediately to the child's request. The child must learn to wait to receive the requested item or activity. The child is provided with a *delay cue* signaling that he or she must complete another activity before being given access to what they want (Durand, 2002, p.121). Sometimes with older and higher-functioning children, the delay cue can refer to an amount of time (e.g., when the timer rings). Initially, the delay is short—usually seconds. Over time, the delay is gradually lengthened as the child comes to tolerate it more. A second stimulus, called a *safety signal*, is introduced indicating that the desired activity or commodity is about to be presented. This indicates to the child that he or she has accomplished the requested task and that the desired outcome is forthcoming. This often averts a tantrum that may arise when the child is unclear about whether the adult is going to honor what was promised—that is, that the desired reinforcer would be available after the child has completed a task.

SOCIAL SKILLS TRAINING AND COGNITIVE BEHAVIOR THERAPY

Among the most striking impairments of individuals with ASDs is their limited ability to negotiate social relationships. Leo Kanner believed that the inability of children with ASDs to interact effectively with others reflected a lack of social interest. Many professionals and parents experienced with individuals with Asperger syndrome and high-functioning ASDs believe that such youngsters have social interest but seriously lack the skills necessary to initiate and maintain relationships.

The problems people with ASDs encounter trying to negotiate typical day-to-day situations and emulate complex social interactions are reminiscent of Dan Ackroyd and Steve Martin's portrayal of George and Yortuk Festrunk on a 1970s' broadcast of *Saturday Night Live.* The two recent Czech immigrant brothers tried desperately to be cool, dressing in tight pants and loud barely buttoned polyester shirts, with medallions swinging over their chests. They explained to the young American women they were attempting to attract that they were "two wild and crazy guys." And the more they tried to be "wild and crazy guys," in ways they thought were like the people around them, the more they stood out as not belonging. They didn't understand the nuances of adult interactions and the symbolic meaning of so much of what we say and do.

Social Interactions and Language that Confuse and Mystify

I watched Max, a 7-year-old with an ASD, during recess at a general education elementary school. A group of boys around his age were running and kicking a soccer ball, laughing, teasing, and shouting challenges at one another—pushing and shoving to get at the ball. Max watched the boys intently from a distance, sat down on the ground, and began pulling up blades of grass and twirling them. He occasionally glanced up at the boys, who were continuing their horseplay 10–15 feet away. One of the boys kicked the ball, which careened across the playground, and the cluster of boys ran across the field after it. Max rose and walked slowly across the playground, tentatively approaching the group of boys, who had resumed their rough-housing. He again squatted down on the ground not far from them, found some stones, and began lining them up in a row. It seemed obvious that Max wanted to play with the other boys, but he didn't understand the meaning of their actions, shouts and laughter, shoving and taunting remarks, or how to participate.

Angie, who just turned 11, is a very bright girl with a high-functioning ASD. She approached two other girls her age, Melissa and Alex, who are looking at a "tween" magazine. When Melissa was younger, she and Angie played with dolls together, but now that they are nearly teenagers, things have changed dramatically. "Luke is so cool, and he has such dreamy eyes," Melissa announces pointing to a picture in the magazine. Angie studies the photograph and notices that Luke has blonde hair. Alex says, "Yeah, and he dumped Hillary, so he's up for grabs," and they both laugh. They abruptly change the conversation to discuss a classmate. "Did you see Kelly today?" Melissa asks. "Like, she was so trashy—I wouldn't be seen dead in those jeans." At this point, Angie has no idea what her classmates are talking about, so she turns and walks away.

Evan was 15 when I began working with him. He had received several years of various therapy services, was bright, very verbal, and expressed an interest in interacting with his peers. One afternoon he looked out his living room window and saw four teenage boys playing basketball in a driveway across the street. He asked his mother if he could go over and play with them. She was delighted and encouraged him to do so. She watched as Evan crossed the street and approached the four boys. She couldn't hear their conversation through the closed window, but she could see that Evan was saying something to other boys. They briefly stopped playing ball and one of them said something to Evan. Then the boys resumed their game and Evan stood there for several minutes watching and then came home. His mother could see that Evan was extremely unhappy, because they hadn't asked him to join in their game. His mother had a very heavy heart, realizing that Evan probably had no idea how to ask to join the game and felt rejected when the other boys rebuffed him.

What Max, Angie, and Evan experienced is typical of young people with ASDs. They don't understand the meaning of other's actions or their facial expressions, and, most important, they are confused by other people's words. "Hey, you dork, throw it over here!" one kid shouts, as the first youngster laughs and instead shoots a jump shot from 15 feet. The ball swishes through the net and another boy yells, "Awesome, man, awesome!" The shooter replies, "Like I didn't know." "Now it's my turn to get my groove on," another boy says and begins dribbling around another youth. He accidentally kicks the ball mid-dribble and bursts out laughing, "Oh, I can't believe I did that!" Imagine how utterly impossible it is for Evan to make any sense of what he is seeing and hearing. When Max sees the other boys shoving one another, it looks to him like they are trying to hurt one another to him. "Hey, stupid," one boy shouts to another, "get outta the way," as he kicks the ball, and then a few seconds later runs over and puts his arm around the same boy as they guffaw. Another grabs a boy's hat and runs with it yelling, "Billy, you run like a duck!" laughing as he tosses the hat back to Billy. Max is mystified, wanting to join in, but fearing the boys' confusing horseplay.

Social Skills Training

Although a great deal has been written about social skills training in ASDs, there have been limited empirical studies of the outcomes, especially generalization and maintenance of skills that have been taught. Social skills instruction began in public schools as a means of improving behavior and reducing the problems of children with emotional and behavior disorders and youth with ADHD. Most children in these categories display empathy and are interested in having friendships. They understand what others are feeling, although they often have problems grasping how others view their behavior. Social skills training is designed to help children in these categories be more aware of the impact their actions have on others and to develop strategies for thinking before they act. Children with ASDs often have difficulty understanding others' feelings and thoughts. Even when children learn to discriminate facial expressions and verbalize what others' actions mean within a clinical or home-therapy setting, they seldom generalize outside that setting (Golan & Baron-Cohen, 2006; Ozonoff & Miller, 1995).

When conducting social skills training with individuals with ASDs, concrete language is most effective. Metaphors, similes, and other figures of speech confuse most people with ASDs, leading them to become fixated on the literal meaning of words that they don't believe are apt for the situation. Someone saying that they feel as though they were going to "explode" is likely to cause problems for many people with ASDs because the word conjures up images of fireworks. Referring to the contribution of a social skills group member as being "cool" is similarly likely to be problematic, because they will try to grasp how the temperature is related to the child's behavior.

The mother of an 8-year-old boy with an ASD walked by her son's bedroom and heard him whispering. She stopped and peeked through the open doorway into his room and saw him seated on his bed alone, whispering. She asked, "What are you doing, Bruce?" He replied, "I'm thinking." She asked him why he thought whispering was thinking, and he replied that Ms. Carlson, his teacher, had told him that thinking was like talking so quietly no one else could hear it. Such similes are very difficult for children with ASDs. One of the reasons children and adolescents with ASDs have so much difficulty understanding their peers is that the language of typical children is replete with figures of speech.

Scott Bellini, at the Indiana Resource Center for Autism at Indiana University, has provided an excellent summary and outline of social skills training strategies (see http://www.iidc.indiana.edu/irca/SocialLeisure/social-skillstraining.html). The following section draws on his information and provides supplementary suggestions. Among the more promising approaches have been a combination of identifying specific skill impairments, distinguishing skill acquisition from performance impairments, employing role playing and video-modeling, and monitoring outcomes and making adjustments accordingly. Evaluation of a child's social functioning strengths and weaknesses is based on a combination of observation (both naturalistic and structured), interviews (e.g., parents, teachers, playground supervisors), and standardized measures (e.g., behavioral checklists, social skills measures). Kathleen Quill (2000) has provided a useful social skills checklist for parents and professionals in her book *DO-WATCH-LISTEN-SAY*. After a thorough assessment of social functioning is complete, the team determines whether the skill limitations identified are the result of skill acquisition problems or performance deficits.

A *skill acquisition deficit* refers to the lack of a particular skill or behavior, such as how to effectively initiate a conversation with another person. A *performance deficit* refers to a skill or behavior that is present but not used. For example, a youngster may be able to initiate a conversation with his siblings and other family members but seldom displays the same skill when encountering non-family members. A skill that has been acquired is usually displayed in only one situation. The question is, Can the child perform the task with multiple persons and across multiple settings?

Developing an Intervention Plan

In developing an intervention plan, one must decide the degree to which accommodation will be employed versus assimilation. *Accommodation* refers to modifying the physical or social environment to promote positive social interactions. Training peer mentors to interact with the child throughout the school day would be an accommodation strategy. *Assimilation* changes the child's behavior to better fit the environment. Assimilation facilitates skill development that allows the child to be more successful in social interactions. The key to a successful social skills training program is to address both accommodation and assimilation.

Peer-mediated interventions have been frequently used to promote positive social interactions among peers (Odom et al., 1985; Strain & Kohler, 1998). Peer-mediated intervention structures the physical and social environment to promote successful social interactions.

Recognizing and responding appropriately to the feelings and thoughts of others is an assimilation strategy. Several techniques have been used to promote these skills. For example, most therapy or instructional programs begin with picture cards portraying people displaying clear emotions (e.g., sadness) and then they move on to picture card illustrations of events that produce those emotions (e.g., dropping an ice cream cone on the ground). Later photographs of more ambiguous emotions—for example, annoyance and anger—are gradually introduced. After the child is responding with the name of the emotion and the thoughts of the person in the picture, video footage of similar situations is introduced.

Social stories have been used to increase the child's ability to understand sequences of social interactions. A social story portrays concepts and social rules in the form of a brief vignette. Gray (2002) provided guidelines for developing a successful social story, including:

- The story addresses the child's personal interests or needs

- The story is on a topic the child wants to read on his or her own (depending on ability level)

- The story is appropriate for the child's comprehension level

- The story uses minimally directive language to minimize oppositional reactions

Social stories can be used in conjunction with role playing. After reading a social story, the child then practices the skill introduced in the story.

Role playing consists of acting out social interactions that the child would typically encounter. For example, the child could be asked to initiate a conversation with another person while the other person is engaged in a task (e.g., writing, sorting laundry). The child would then have to ask to join in, or ask the other person to join him or her in another activity.

Video self-modeling (VSM) has proven to be one of the more effective strategies for teaching social skills. VSM in general has been more effective in teaching children with ASDs than actual live demonstrations in many instances. In VSM, children and youth learn skills by observing themselves performing the targeted skill. VSM allows the child to learn, both through observation and through personal experience. Alcantara (1994) used a video modeling technique to teach children with ASDs how to purchase items from a store, which increased the effectiveness of the children's purchasing behaviors and generalized to other stores. Charlop-Christy, Loc, & Freeman (2000) found that VSM was more effective than live modeling in teaching daily living skills to children with ASDs. In addition, the children viewing the video model demonstrated better generalization of skills across settings. Similarly, Sherer et al. (2001) demonstrated that video modeling was an effective way to teach conversation skills for some children with ASDs. LeBlanc et al. (2003) used video modeling to teach perspective taking to children with ASDs between the ages of 6 and 9.

COGNITIVE BEHAVIOR THERAPY

Cognitive behavior therapy (CBT) was developed by Aaron Beck and Albert Ellis to treat depression and other mental health problems in typical adults (Thompson & Hollon, 2006). People tend to overreact to their emotional states that they believe were caused by an external event. In CBT, the client is taught to analyze his or her implicit self-statements following external events, with the assumption that emotional reactions are triggered by our interpretation of events, not the events themselves. CBT was later transformed into various therapeutic techniques suitable for a variety of childhood emotional and behavioral disorders. CBT is the psychological treatment of choice for children with ADHD, and it is most often used in conjunction with stimulant medications (MTA Cooperative Group, 1999). When Zach, a youth with an ASD says, "Can I play with you?" to a peer and the peer replies, "In a minute," Zach is taught to analyze his interpretation of what the other child said. Perhaps Zach thinks that his friend meant, "No, I'm not going to play with you," or, "No, I don't like you." Instead, through CBT, Zach is taught to interpret his peer's comment as meaning "I'll play with you in a minute when I'm done with what I'm doing." This analysis tends to obviate the negative emotional reaction that would have occurred to the alternative interpretations.

Tony Attwood has been an active proponent of the use of CBT for treating individuals with ASDs—Asperger syndrome in particular (Attwood, 2004). There have been very few controlled trials of the use of CBT for individuals with ASDs. Sofronoff, Attwood, and Hinton (2005) evaluated the effectiveness of a brief CBT intervention for anxiety with children diagnosed with Asperger syndrome. One group received CBT for the child alone, the second group received parent training plus CBT for the child, and the third group was a waiting list control. The two intervention groups demonstrated significant decreases in parent-reported anxiety symptoms at follow-up and a significant increase in the child's ability to generate positive strategies in an anxiety-provoking situation. There was some evidence that involving parents in the CBT treatment increased efficacy. Reaven and Hepburn (2003) reported CBT of OCD in a 7-year-old girl with Asperger syndrome. Interventions were adapted in light of the child's cognitive, social, and linguistic characteristics. Obsessive-compulsive symptoms improved markedly after approximately 6 months of treatment.

In clinical practice, CBT is often combined with social skills training methods when working with higher-functioning youth with ASDs. In the example of Zach, above, the therapist might say, "Okay, what can you say to get ready to play with him?" If Zach doesn't suggest anything, the therapist can provide choices. "How about saying, 'I'll get the cards and set up the board (to play a game),' or 'I'll wait until you're through'"? After Zach decides which alternative he would choose, the therapist asks him to rehearse the entire sequence, beginning with asking his friend to play with him. By practicing multiple scenarios, Zach begins to develop a set of alternative responses to various social situations, always beginning with his interpretation of what the other person has said to him. Later, Zach reports another situation that created problems for him. "My little brother was playing with my Game Boy, so I shoved him out of the chair." "Then what happened?" the therapist asks. "My mom yelled at me and told me to stop shoving Kevin," Zach replies. "What did you think when you saw Kevin playing with your Game Boy?" the therapist asks. "He shouldn't play with my Game Boy," Zach replies. "Would it be OK if Kevin played with your Game Boy sometime?" the therapist asks. "Maybe sometime," Zach replies. "What could you say to Kevin instead of shoving him?" the therapist asks. After thinking for a minute, Zach replies, "You can play with my Game Boy after I'm through." The therapist says, "OK, that's great. Now let's practice how you can do this next time," and the therapist and Zach rehearse what he will do the next time a similar situation arises in real life. Combining CBT techniques with social skills groups—in which another child with an ASD plays the role of Zach's brother or of the child Zach approaches about playing together—can also be effective. This has the advantage of providing additional practice and increases generalizations across people Zach might encounter. Some therapists or teachers take the process one step further and accompany the target child, Zach in this case, onto the playground so that he can practice asking peers to play. These in vivo sessions are the most important because they are closest to the actual situation the youth will encounter in real life.

SUMMARY

Behavioral challenges are common among children and youth with ASDs. Parents, teachers, and therapists should try to avoid the trap of focusing exclusively on how to get rid of the problem behavior. Instead, they will find it more helpful to ask, "Why is it necessary for him to display this problem behavior?" Most behavioral challenges occur for good reasons, at least from the child's perspective. Overcoming current problems and preventing future difficulties can most effectively be accomplished by involving the key stakeholders in the child's life (e.g., parents, siblings, teachers, friends, neighbors, recreation center staff members, clergy, bus drivers). Developing an action plan requires assessing the circumstances surrounding challenging behavior (i.e., identifying setting events such as health conditions, triggers, consequences that perpetuate the problem). It also involves realistically assessing skill deficits that are preventing the child from choosing a more adaptive solution to the problem. Social skills training and cognitive behavior therapy techniques can be useful with higher-functioning and older children with ASDs. Behavioral challenges can be overcome with patience, persistence, and an ability to see the world from the child's vantage point.

8

Mental Health and Psychopharmacology in Autism Spectrum Disorders

C hildren and youth with ASDs have more mental health problems than intellectually matched and typical same-age peers (Brereton, Tonge, & Einfeld, 2006). Youth and young adults with autistic disorder appear to have greater risk of psychopathology than those with pervasive developmental disorder–not otherwise specified (PDD–NOS; Pearson et al., 2006). Among the most common mental health problems are obsessive-compulsive disorder (OCD; Kobayashi & Murata, 1998), depressive disorder (Pearson et al., 2006), and attention-deficit/hyperactivity disorder (ADHD; Lee & Ousley, 2006). Often, mental health problems are expressed differently among individuals with ASDs from those in typical individuals of the same age. Depression may be manifest primarily in irritability and social withdrawal, while anxiety may be exhibited as increased OCD systems and insomnia. Although ADHD symptoms may be similar to those in typical populations, they are less likely to involve social intrusiveness and more likely to appear as an inability to focus combined with motor restlessness.

EMOTIONAL AND BEHAVIOR PROBLEMS

When parents bring their child to a doctor for assistance with behavioral challenges, they are most often concerned about tantrums, "meltdowns," fixed compulsive routines, aggression, or self-injury. Few parents are aware of the underlying conditions causing these behavioral symptoms; they just want the behavior problems stopped. Psychotherapeutic medications are widely prescribed in an attempt to improve the behavior of people with autism spectrum disorders (ASDs) who present behavioral challenges. Some people oppose the use of psychotherapeutic medications, while those whose children have profited from medication treatment may view themselves as advocates for psychotropic drugs. That type of disagreement is similar to arguing for or against rain. When the weather has been hot and dry and the soil is becoming parched, a moderate to heavy rainfall is good fortune. But when there has already been too much rain, the soil is soaked, and there is a risk of flooding, even a modest shower can be a problem. Medications can be helpful, harmful, or inconsequential, depending on the specific circumstances.

Children and youth with ASDs can be affected by the same mental health problems other children have, but they are more prone to some than to others. Among the major health disorders are obsessive-compulsive disorder (OCD), and attention-deficit hyperactivity disorder (ADHD). Functional assessment-based behavioral intervention is always a necessary component of treating these problems; however, it is often insufficient by itself. Most of these disorders require medication as well. Deciding which medication is most appropriate requires that the child is cared for by a physician (a pediatrician, a child psychiatrist, or a pediatric neurologist) experienced with children who have ASDs. Developing a solid working relationship with a child's primary health care provider is essential. Parents are encouraged to read Luke Tsai's *Taking the Mystery out of Medications in Autism/Asperger's Syndrome,* which provides a good discussion of psychotropic medications, their mechanisms, effects, and side effects and which will help in discussing treatment options with the child's physician. Therapists and teachers will also find the book useful.

Some parents of children with ASDs seek help from doctors who prescribe psychotherapeutic drugs and others seek solutions on their own. Langworthy-Lam, Aman, and Van Bourgondien (2002) found that in North Carolina, 45.7% of individuals with ASDs were taking psychotropic drugs, 12.4% antiepileptic drugs, and 5.7% supplements for ASDs. The most commonly prescribed agents included antidepressants, which were taken by 21.7%; antipsychotics, taken by 16.8%; and stimulants, taken by 13.9%. In Ohio, 45.6% of children with ASDs were taking some form of psychotropic agent (including St. John's wort and melatonin), whereas 11.5% were taking seizure medication and 10.3% over-the-counter ASD preparations. The most common psychotropic agents included antidepressants (21.6%), antipsychotics (14.9%), antihypertensives (12.5%), and stimulants (11.3%; Aman, Lam, & Collier-Crespin [2003]).

The manner in which psychoactive drugs influence behavior can in part be understood in terms of their influence on stimulus triggers, which things are rewarding, and how often reinforcement is needed to keep the child going. A medication may make one consequence more effective in maintaining behavior than another, or it may change which of two choices is selected (e.g., doing math versus bothering a schoolmate). An antidepressant makes more serotonin available to bind to receptors. When that happens, stimuli that were previously powerfully aversive, such as teacher-task demands, may be made less aversive. Aggressive behavior that leads to avoidance of task demands is reduced. Reduced control by negative reinforcers (escape or avoidance) is the behavioral mechanism of drug action. In the following sections, some of the medications used most commonly in treating children and youth who have ASDs are discussed.

Books, chapters, and journal articles concerned with psychopharmacology and ASDs are often organized around specific symptoms. That approach understandably leads the reader to ask, "What is the best drug to treat aggression (or self-injury or tantrums)?" The answer is that there isn't any best drug for any given symptom. Any one of these symptoms can have multiple causes and contributing factors. To rationally prescribe a medicine for a child presenting disturbed behavior, one must have a reasonable idea of what is causing the problem behavior. Is the young girl having emotional outbursts because her OCD routines are being interrupted? Is the boy behaving aggressively because he has bipolar disorder? Is the child's self-injury being maintained by the release of naturally occurring opioid substances in her brain when she hurts herself? Possibly, the child's emotional lability and outbursts are an indication of a depressive disorder. As a result, this chapter is organized around underlying mental health, neurophysiological, or brain chemical conditions that are associated with emotional and behavior challenges.

Anxiety Disorders

Anxiety problems are omnipresent among children with ASDs. Evans et al. (2005) studied fears, anxiety, and phobias in children with ASDs and Down syndrome and their typical peers. They found that children with an ASD had more situational phobias and medical fears but fewer fears of harm or injury compared with the other groups. They are often afraid of unfamiliar places (e.g., doctors' offices) or mechanical devices that are disturbing to them (e.g., escalators). A 4-year-old boy with an ASD began sobbing when his family's car approached the entrance to a shopping mall. His older sister asked him what was wrong and tried to reassure him that he liked going to the mall because he could get popcorn there. As the car turned along the frontage road and drove around the opposite side of the mall he stopped crying. That was when his brother Alan figured out that Mickey was afraid of the mall entrance near the tropical rainforest restaurant that featured a life-size mechanical alligator with jaws that opened and closed. For children with ASD, fears, phobias, and anxieties are closely related to problem behaviors, whereas fears, phobias, and anxieties were less related to behavioral symptoms for other groups of children with disabilities or for typical children.

Phobias

A phobia is a persistent, irrational fear of a specific object, activity, or situation (the phobic stimulus) that results in a compelling desire to avoid it. This often leads to avoidance of the phobic stimulus or to enduring it with dread. In children, phobias may result from a single experience with a frightening stimulus (e.g., an aggressive dog). In the previous example, the boy had acquired a phobic fear of the mechanical alligator during an earlier visit to the shopping mall. He was terrified by the thought of it. Agoraphobia is one of the most common phobias associated with ASDs. The affected person experiences anxiety about being in places or situations from which escape might be difficult or in which help may not be available in the event of panic-like symptoms. Agoraphobic fears typically involve characteristic clusters of situations that include being outside the home alone; being in a crowd or standing in a line; being on a bridge; or traveling in a bus, train, or automobile. Many children and youth with ASDs attempt to avoid specific places by having behavior outbursts, because they fear they cannot leave the places if they feel a need to do so.

A *social phobia* is common among people with ASDs as well as their immediate family members. Anticipatory anxiety may begin hours or even days before an upcoming social situation (e.g., worrying every day about being thrust into a classroom full of unfamiliar children). The vicious cycle of anticipatory anxiety leads to fearful thoughts and anxiety symptoms in the feared situations, which in turn leads to less social competence in the feared social situation. People with this phobia may appear to others to be aloof or unapproachable, when in fact they are terrified, and their inept social interactions lead to further increased anticipatory anxiety about the feared situation. A teenager with Asperger syndrome might say to a peer, "I'm not good at talking to people, so I'm going to leave now." Such a remark not only labels the teenager as inept, but confuses the listener who will be unlikely to engage the teenager in conversation again. Most individuals with ASDs and social phobias avoid social or performance situations altogether, although they sometimes endure them with enormous discomfort.

Obsessive-Compulsive Disorder

Obsessive-compulsive disorder (OCD) is a mental health disorder characterized by either obsessions or compulsions or both. In obsessions,

1. Recurrent and persistent thoughts, impulses, or images are experienced at some time during the episode as intrusive and inappropriate and cause marked anxiety or distress.

2. The thoughts, impulses, or images are not simply excessive worries about real-life problems.

3. The person with the obsession attempts to ignore or suppress the thoughts, impulses, or images, or to neutralize them with other thoughts or actions.

4. Typical adults can recognize that the obsessional thoughts, impulses, or images are a product of his or her own mental processes, but children, especially those with developmental delays, usually cannot.

People with ASDs and other developmental disabilities often find it difficult to assess obsessions, and so therapists usually focus on compulsions. *Compulsions* are characterized by

1. Repetitive behaviors (e.g., ordering objects, turning light switches on and off) or mental acts (e.g., counting, repeating words silently) that the person—sometimes a higher-functioning individual—feels driven to perform, according to rules that they feel must be applied rigidly.

2. Behaviors that function to prevent or reduce distress or prevent exposure to a dreaded situation. These behaviors are not connected in a realistic way with what they are designed to prevent and are clearly excessive. Most individuals with ASDs do not realize that the repetitive behavior is excessive. Compulsive behavior is universal in ASDs.

The form compulsive behavior takes varies among individuals with ASDs, depending on intellectual level and severity of ASD symptoms. Individuals with higher IQ scores who are verbal (e.g., Asperger syndrome, PDD-NOS) often focus on specific topics (e.g., weather, dinosaurs, favorite television programs). There are individuals with high-functioning ASDs who maintain daily records of the weather conditions, including temperatures, precipitation, wind, and barometric pressure—sometimes for years—and insist on discussing meteorological phenomena with nearly everyone they encounter. People with few verbal skills are more likely to collect or fixate on specific types of objects, such as action figures, or objects that others would find a peculiar interest, such as small hardware items (e.g., coil springs, nuts, bolts, washers). Individuals with the most severe disabilities and little cognitive ability are likely to express their compulsivity through repetitive motor behavior patterns such as twirling objects or pulling loose threads from their clothing and unraveling the fabric. In the most extreme forms, these compulsive patterns include intense rocking, head weaving, and hand flapping.

Panic Attacks

Typical adults with panic attacks describe the fear as unbearable. In the midst of a panic attack, many people end up in hospital emergency rooms because they think they are dying of a heart attack or are unable to breathe. Panic attacks can be differentiated from generalized anxiety by their intermittency, and the storm-like quality with which the attack suddenly takes over the body, runs its course, diminishes, and finally stops. The discomfort is far more severe at its peak than occurs in generalized anxiety disorder. People with ASDs are more prone to situationally bound panic attacks than unprovoked panic attacks. The attack predictably occurs almost immediately following exposure to, or sometimes in anticipation of, a frightening situation (e.g., being unexpectedly called on to answer a question in the classroom). Situationally predisposed panic attacks also occur sometime *following exposure to* a situational trigger but are not as invariably associated with a particular situation. Situationally predisposed panic attacks may occur a half hour later while the child is riding home from a visit to the dentist.

Medications for Anxiety Disorders

Prescription medication treatments for different anxiety problems overlap. Choice among treatments is often based on speed of onset, side effects, and individual characteristics such as age and other health conditions.

Benzodiazepines   Among the most widely prescribed medications for managing symptoms of anxiety disorder for neurotypical people are the benzodiazepine drugs, formerly called "minor tranquilizers." They are highly effective, and there is a large difference between a dosage that relieves anxiety symptoms and a dosage that causes serious side effects. Examples are Valium (chlordiazepoxide), Librium (diazepam), and Xanax (alprazolam). These medications work by binding to the brain's gamma-aminobutyric acid (GABA) and benzodiazepine receptors. GABA is a brain chemical transmitter that puts a damper on other excitatory brain chemical systems. Overstimulation by excitatory cells in the brain can be reduced by GABA inhibiting those same brain cells. Benzodiazepine medications rapidly reduce anxiety symptoms. They have relatively few, and usually minor, side effects for most people, although in elderly people and some people with brain injuries or developmental disabilities, they may cause significant difficulties. Benzodiazepine medicines are available in generic forms, so they may cost less than some of the alternative newer antianxiety drugs. Their antianxiety and muscle relaxant effects are more apparent to the person taking a benzodiazpine drug than most of the alternative drugs used to treat anxiety. Benzodiazepines provide relatively rapid (minutes to hours) relief from anxiety while significant relief from serious anxiety symptoms may require 6–8 weeks with the Prozac (fluoxetine) family of medications and 2–4 weeks with Buspar, although in the long term, the latter may prove more effective in preventing a return of anxiety symptoms. Benzodiazepines have disadvantages. At higher daily dosages they cause drowsiness and memory problems. Also, benzodiazepine medications taken as prescribed over days and weeks lead to tolerance. The amount of relief from anxiety diminishes over time, so the dose must be increased to restore the same antianxiety effect, which can create serious problems for the person taking the medication. Tolerance may develop to the antianxiety effects, but not to some of the side effects (e.g., clumsiness, gait problems.) Benzodiazepines can aggravate self-injury by people with ASDs (cf. Barron & Sandman, 1985) and may not be a good choice to relieve anxiety before visits to the dentist or ophthalmologist because of their disinhibiting effects. Among the most common benzodiazepines are Ativan (lorazepam), Klonopin (clonazepam), Librium (chlordiazepoxide), Tranxene (chlorazepate), Valium (diazepam), and Xanax (alprazolam). They vary in speed and duration of action and clinical indications. For example, Klonopin is primarily a seizure medication and is also used in some cases to treat bipolar mania, although it has antianxiety effects as well.

Tricyclic Antidepressants with Antianxiety Effects The tricyclic antidepressants (TCAs) were the primary treatment for depression for more than 20 years until Prozac was introduced in 1988. An important side effect of TCAs discovered early on during their testing was anxiety reduction among some depressed patients. Not all TCAs have antianxiety effects—only those possessing demonstrated antianxiety effects will be discussed here. Other TCAs will be discussed when exploring treatments for depression. The antidepressant effects of TCAs may not become apparent for 2–3 weeks, although, typically, the antianxiety effects begin to occur before antidepressant effects are apparent. This can be helpful for a person suffering from both severe anxiety and major depression.

In addition to annoying side effects, some TCAs pose potentially serious dangers for some people. Most TCAs cause drowsiness, which is one of the reasons doxepin and trazadone, in particular, are often taken at bedtime. All TCAs cause dry mouth and dry eyes, and some people complain of blurred vision when receiving TCAs. Constipation is common, which is usually overcome by increased fluid intake, more exercise, and, if necessary, use of bulk laxatives. Weight gain is common with TCA treatment, sometimes as much as 15 pounds over 6 months. If TCAs are taken with other drugs that also block acetylcholine nerve fibers (e.g., antipsychotics, some antihistamines) they can cause constipation and can even precipitate a dangerous condition called *paralytic ileus*. Fortunately, this occurs only rarely.

The most potentially harmful side effect of TCAs is heart failure, although it is extremely uncommon. Patients with a history of heart arrhythmias (irregular heart beats) are poor candidates for treatment with TCAs and alternative medications for anxiety should be considered (Potter, Manjii, & Rudorfer, 1998). If there are any questions about the suitability of an individual for tricyclic treatment, a thorough heart workup including an electrocardiogram (ECG) should be conducted prior to starting medication. Because of the side effects profile of most TCAs, they are typically not used to treat children less than 12 years of age, with the exception of imipramine for bedwetting.

Specific Tricylcic Antidepressants with Antianxiety Effects   Anafranil (clomipramine) is used to treat OCD. Approximately 40% of individuals treated with clomipramine show marked improvement, and a smaller percentage experience moderate improvement. Clomipramine is also used off label for managing anxiety and panic disorder. Clomipramine is effective in reducing compulsive, repetitive activities (e.g., flapping hands, rocking, picking at string) of adults with intellectual disabilities (e.g., severe mental retardation, as well as an ASD). It is not recommended for children under 11 years of age.

Sinequan (doxepin) is FDA approved for depression and/or anxiety in neuroses and depression and/or anxiety associated with organic disease. Doxepin is widely used off label for treating people with developmental disabilities who display compulsive, repetitive behavior problems (e.g., intense rocking) and mood fluctuations. It is usually given in the evening to improve sleep and regularize daytime mood. Doxepin is not for treatment of children under 12 years of age.

Tofranil (imipramine) is indicated for treatment of depression and nighttime bedwetting; however, it is also used off label for prophylaxis of panic disorder (not FDA approved). It is not recommended for depression for children under 12 years or for enuresis only for children over 6 years. Ludiomil (maprotiline) is indicated for treatment of anxiety with depression and depression unaccompanied by anxiety.

Mark was in his early 20s when I first saw him. He had a history of very violent outbursts during which he destroyed property and struck out at anyone who was nearby. The following episode was typical:

Mark arrived home after riding in the van from work. He appeared agitated and sweaty and he was breathing heavily. The van driver said that Mark had become upset because he had to sit in the back seat of the van with two other men, when he preferred to sit in the front seat next to the driver. Once inside his group home, Mark began tearing at his shirt collar and screaming loudly. He jumped up out of his seat and began knocking over furniture, including a television resting on a nearby table. When a staff member attempted to restrain him, Mark bit the man's arm and punched him violently, causing a nosebleed. Mark's face and neck were flushed and he was perspiring heavily. Staff said that Mark's eyes looked wild and he seemed to be gasping for air. After 15 minutes or so, he began calming down and seemed completely exhausted. His shirt was drenched in sweat. He appeared to be trying to make amends by going from person to person with his head down, touching their arms or patting them on the head.

Because of previous similar episodes, Mark's psychiatrist thought that he may be schizophrenic and was hallucinating. As a result, he prescribed an anti-psychotic drug, but the medication made him drowsy and didn't stop the violent episodes. Based on Mark's history and appearance throughout the episode, I suspected that he was having panic attacks, most likely precipitated by an earlier event such as being claustrophobic on the van ride. I suggested that Mark's psychiatrist consider treating him with Tofranil, a tricyclic antidepressant widely used at that time. Mark had no further outbursts after beginning the Tofranil treatment, suggesting that the diagnosis of panic attack disorder was likely correct.

Selective Serotonin Reuptake Inhibitors with Antianxiety Effects   In 1988, Eli Lilly Company released the first in a new class of antidepressant medications designed to attack the underlying brain chemical causes of depression. The drug, Prozac (fluoxetine), took the market by storm. Prozac offered relief from depression without most of more troubling side effects of the tricyclic antidepressants such as drowsiness, dry nose and mouth, urinary retention, risk of heart problems, and low blood pressure and dizziness experienced by elderly patients.

Prozac was designed based on the assumption that depression was caused by an imbalance of the brain chemical serotonin inside and outside brain cells (in the synapses). Prozac blocks the reuptake of serotonin inside the nerve cell once it has been released, providing the free serotonin more opportunity to bind to a receptor on the adjacent cell. Because Prozac was specific to the neurotransmitter serotonin, the name *selective serotonin reuptake inhibitors (SSRIs)* was established for this new class of antidepressants.

SSRIs differ in the speed of the antidepressant and antianxiety effects and their side effects. Prozac disappears from the blood very slowly (half a dose is gone in 84 hours, compared with 21 hours for Paxil [paroxetine] and 26 hours for Zoloft [sertraline]). It is dangerous to switch from a monoamine oxidase inhibitor (MAOI) antidepressant (e.g., Parnate [tranylcypromine], Nardil [phenezine]) to an SSRI because it could precipitate a toxic reaction called *central serotonin syndrome*. SSRIs are not free of side effects, however. Nausea, common during the first week, tends to wane as the individual develops tolerance. The stomach and intestines are rich with serotonin receptors, so one way to think about the initial nausea when taking Prozac or Zoloft is that the medication is starting to work.

Because insomnia can be a problem at the beginning of SSRI treatments, the antidepressants are usually administered in the morning. Side-effect management includes waiting for tolerance to develop, reducing the dosage, or changing antidepressants. Parents should always check with their child's doctor before discontinuing SSRI medications. Among the other common SSRIs are Paxil, Zoloft, and Celexa (citalopram). Well-controlled studies have been conducted indicating that Prozac reduces symptoms of ASDs, especially perseverative behavior and intolerance for changes in routines. There is some evidence that Zoloft is effective as well.

Other antidepressant medications affect both serotonin and norepinephrine in the brain, but their effectiveness in people with ASDs has not been established. These medications include Cymbalta (duloxetine), Lexepro (escitalopram), and Effexor (venlafaxine). Blood pressure medications are used less commonly for anxiety in people with ASDs (e.g., Inderal [propranolol], Catapres, Buspar [buspirone], Atarax, Vistaril [hydroxyzine]). None of these medications is highly effective in reducing anxiety in people with ASDs, but Inderal and related antihypertensives can be useful in reducing some situational anxiety (e.g., stage fright) or difficulty falling asleep because of agitation and jitteriness.

Depression

Depression is much more common in families of individuals with ASDs, and it is presumed that it occurs more commonly in ASDs as well, although it is difficult to diagnose. When most people are anxious, they fidget, pace, appear preoccupied, and have a tense expression on their face. When people are depressed, their speech is slower, they don't seem to have interest in much of anything, they make self-deprecating remarks, they have sad facial expressions, and they express pessimism about the future. People with ASDs exhibit anxiety in ways that are similar to people without ASDs, but they lack the readily identifiable features of depression exhibited by others. They exhibit little change in their tone of voice (if they speak), they make no remarks about their feelings or the future, and they may show little change in their interests, which are already very constricted. Their facial expression changes little unless they are fearful or angry. As a result, it is difficult to accurately diagnose depression among people with ASDs.

Unipolar major depression is the most common form of depression. According to the *DSM-IV,* diagnosis depends on the presence of five or more of the following symptoms in the same 2-week period, with a definite change from usual functioning. Either depressed mood or decreased interest or pleasure must be one of the five:

1. *Mood.* For most of nearly every day, the individual appears depressed to others.

2. *Interests.* For most of nearly every day, interest or pleasure is markedly decreased in nearly all activities (noted by the individual or by others).

3. *Appetite.* There is a marked loss or gain of weight (e.g., 5 percent in one month), or appetite is markedly decreased or increased nearly every day.

4. *Sleep.* Nearly every day, the person sleeps excessively or not enough.

5. *Motor activity.* Nearly every day, others can see that the person's activity is agitated or retarded.

6. *Fatigue.* Nearly every day, the individual appears fatigued or exhibits loss of energy.

7. *Self-worth.* Nearly every day, the individual makes self-deprecating comments.

8. *Concentration.* Nearly every day, the individual appears indecisive or appears to have trouble concentrating.

9. *Death.* The person has had repeated thoughts about death or has made a suicide attempt.

Among individuals with ASDs, it is often difficult to accurately assess mood, sense of self-worth, or ability to concentrate, or whether the individual is having thoughts of death except in the highest functioning, most verbal individuals. Even then, only the most extremely depressed individuals are likely to report inner feelings or thoughts indicative of depression. The sudden emergence of frequent unprovoked crying; negative, self-deprecating comments; and/or comments about death (including recurring statements about the death of a parent, other family member, or a pet) may be a sign of potential depression in an individual with an ASD.

Among younger children with ASDs, sudden increases in aggression or self-injury, excessive crying without a provocative event, and complaints about physical symptoms (e.g., headache, stomach ache) may be signs of depression. Among adolescents and older pre-adolescent children, increased irritability, withdrawal, isolative behavior, loss of interest in previously enjoyed activities, and increased obsessionality are potential warning signs. Although it is believed that depression is common in individuals with ASDs and Asperger syndrome, there are serious diagnostic difficulties because some of the inherent characteristics of these disabilities, such as fatigue and sleep disturbance, are also core symptoms of depression (Stewart et al., 2006). In addition to these physical, behavioral, and emotional signs, a positive family history of major depressive disorder or mood disorder increases the likelihood that the signs and symptoms being witnessed may be indicative of depression in a child or adolescent with an ASD diagnosis.

Antidepressant medications can be highly effective in reducing avoidance of requests or demands by caregivers. Hellings, Kelley, Gabrielli, Kilgore, & Shah (1996) evaluated effects of the SSRI Zoloft on aggressive and self-injurious behaviors of nine adults with developmental disabilities, several of whom met diagnostic criteria for ASDs. They found that the medication reduced self-injury and aggression in eight of nine individuals. Zoloft also was found to reduce depression and anxiety problems in other psychiatric populations. McDougle et al. (1998) conducted an open trial of Zoloft and found that 57% of 42 individuals with ASDs showed significant improvement in repetitive and aggressive symptoms. Reducing anxiety increases tolerance for demands and decreases avoidance behavior (e.g., aggression, self-injury). Lewis, Bodfish, Powell, and Golden (1995) reported that the tricyclic antidepressant Anafranil (clomipramine) reduced the stereotypic and self-injurious behavior of adults with intellectual disabilities in a state residential facility, some of whom met diagnostic criteria for ASDs. Clomipramine is approved by the FDA for treatment of OCD in adult psychiatric patients. Whether the neurochemical and/or behavioral mechanisms are the same among people with ASDs and intellectual disabilities is unclear.

Medications for Depression

Individuals who suffer from depression are often less sensitive to positive reinforcers and react more strongly to negative reinforcers. Lewinsohn and colleagues postulated that depression can result from stressful events that cause the person to engage in rewarding experiences less frequently. A person who experiences few reinforcing events may suffer from the lack of availability of reinforcing events (there just isn't much in their environment that is highly satisfying) or, more often, they lack the personal skills required to effectively act on their environment. That is especially true of people with ASDs. According to this hypothesis, if an individual cannot reverse the negative balance of rewarding experiences, they are likely to withdraw even more, making matters worse (Lewinsohn, 1992). Depressed individuals have low rates of pleasant activities and obtained pleasure; their mood covaries with rates of pleasant and aversive activities. Behavioral treatments can be helpful, but sometimes they do not seem to be sufficient to relieve depression in some individuals, especially those who may be genetically prone to depression.

There is also evidence that diminished availability of serotonin in the brain is implicated in depression. Clinical studies of serotonin metabolism in major depression provide evidence for an impairment of the serotonin brain system. Deficit in L-tryptophan, a serotonin precursor, appears to be the rate-limiting step in the synthesis of serotonin and is an important factor causing depression and the response of antidepressant drugs (Maes & Meltzer, 1995).

Tricyclic Antidepressants   Tricyclic antidepressants (TCAs) were the mainstay of treatment for depression for decades. However, because of their side effects, they have been largely replaced by SSRIs and other newer antidepressants. Unpleasant side effects are most troubling with TCAs such as Elavil (amitriptyline), Anafranil (clomipramine), Sinequan (doxepin), Tofranil (imipramine), and Surmontil (trimipramine). Asendin (amoxapine), Norpramin (desipramine), Aventyl and Pamelor (nortriptyline), and Vivactil (protriptyline) cause less sedation and dry mouth and fewer visual or other side effects. TCAs must not be taken with monoamine oxidase inhibitors (MAOIs) and should be used with caution with a number of other drugs.

Selective Serotonin Reuptake Inhibitors   Since the 1990s, the drugs of choice for the treatment of major depressive disorder have been the SSRIs Prozac, Paxil, Zoloft, and Celexa because they have favorable safety profiles and lack many of the unpleasant side effects of the older tricyclic and atypical antidepressants (e.g., Desaryl [trazadone]). It is important to begin at a low-to-moderate dose and increase the daily dosage gradually as tolerance develops. Many pediatricians and child psychiatrists prescribe a much lower starting dosage for children with ASDs than for other children with anxiety or depression to avoid the agitation and insomnia that are common during the first few weeks of administration.

As with TCAs, SSRIs must not be used with MAOIs, including St. John's wort. SSRIs should not be discontinued abruptly unless an emergency or a serious side effect is present. Sudden discontinuation of SSRIs is associated with *SSRI discontinuation syndrome*, which includes dizziness, nausea, and disequilibrium. In cases where abrupt discontinuation has been necessary, administration of fresh ginger root (1,100 mg of the root) three times daily for two weeks following discontinuation has been shown to reduce gastrointestinal symptoms, but did not affect dizziness. The most important difference among the three commonly used SSRIs lies in their time course in the body. It takes 3½ days for half of the last dose of Prozac to disappear from the body, compared with less than a day for Paxil, and slightly more than a day for Zoloft.

Antidepressants Acting on Other Brain Systems

The effects of Wellbutrin (buproprion) on depression are similar to those of the SSRIs and TCAs, and its effectiveness has been shown with patients previously unresponsive to TCAs. It often begins to relieve depressive symptoms more rapidly than either SSRIs or TCAs. Wellbutrin is more activating and may cause agitation. Desaryl is an atypical antidepressant that doesn't produce its effects like any other known antidepressant. It is sedating, which can be beneficial for patients suffering from insomnia caused by their depression. Serzone (nefazodone) is chemically related to trazodone but is not approved for use in children. It has also been associated with serious liver conditions. Remero (mirtazapine) is structurally unrelated to other antidepressants available in the United States. It appears to be an effective antidepressant, although published data are inconsistent, but it has several noteworthy side effects. Little is known about its effects among individuals with ASDs. Ludiomil (maprotiline) is a cyclic antidepressant that blocks reuptake of norepinephrine at the brain-cell membrane. While it is similar to TCAs, it has a more unfavorable side effect profile, including substantial sedation, occasional blood-cell problems, increased risk of seizures, and skin reactions, making it an unattractive alternative for treating depression in most individuals.

There are very little data available regarding the effectiveness of antidepressants in treating clinical depression of people with ASDs. That is primarily because of the difficulty of diagnosing depression in this population. Among neurotypical individuals, evidence from controlled studies indicates that between 60% and 80% of people with a depressive disorder experience some degree of relief from the depressive symptoms when treated with antidepressants. Rates of improvement do not vary significantly among antidepressants (e.g., depressed mood, sleep disorder, irritability, appetite problems). Approximately one in five individuals treated with antidepressants doesn't improve or may actually feel somewhat more depressed while receiving an SSRI or a TCA. The time course of improvement depends on the specific medication, but none of the commonly prescribed medications produces a significant reduction in depression in less than 2–4 weeks, and some take as long as 6–8 weeks, depending on how the dosage is increased over that period. Results of 15 controlled clinical studies have been combined to determine the relative effectiveness of various antidepressants in reducing chronic depression. Similar results were obtained for different groups of drugs in reducing depression (e.g., TCA, SSRI, MAOI). Patients treated with TCAs were more likely to report unpleasant side effects or other complications, compared with placebos, which makes SSRIs the medication of choice in treating depression, in most instances.

Whittington et al. (2004) conducted a meta-analysis of randomized controlled trials that evaluated an SSRI versus placebo in participants aged 5–18 years. They examined remission, response to treatment, depressive symptom scores, serious adverse events, suicide-related behaviors, and discontinuation of treatment due to adverse events. They found that two studies with Prozac yielded a positive benefit-risk profile, but both Paxil and Zoloft yielded equivocal results among children with disabilities. However, subsequently, the UK Medicines and Healthcare Products Regulatory Authority banned SSRIs for children in the United Kingdom because of reports of suicidal ideation among children and adolescents, although actual suicides linked to these medications had not been reported. A recent review by Janowsky and Davis (2005) concluded that SSRIs are effective and safe in treating individuals with developmental disabilities (including ASDs) who have depression, while in another review, Wagner (2005) concluded that only Celexa, Zoloft, and Prozac were more effective than placebos in treating childhood depression. While there are differences of opinion regarding the relative efficacy of different SSRI medications in treating depression among different populations, there is general agreement that as a class they are effective in enhancing positive reinforcement and reducing avoidance.

Bipolar Disorder

Bipolar disorder is believed to be relatively uncommon in children in general, and there are no good statistics about its prevalence among children with ASDs. Classic bipolar I disorder is a major mental disorder characterized by the occurrence of one or more manic episodes and often one or more major depressive episodes. Onset is often in the teenage or young adult years. A manic episode refers to a distinct period of an abnormally and persistently elevated, expansive, or irritable mood, lasting at least 1 week. During the period of mood disturbance, three (or more) of the following manic symptoms have been present to a significant degree:

1. A feeling of inflated self-esteem or grandiosity

2. A decreased need for sleep (e.g., appear to feel rested after only 3 hours of sleep)

3. More talkative than usual or feels pressured to keep talking

4. Racing thoughts and an impatience with the pace of surrounding activities

5. Distractibility (i.e., attention too easily drawn to unimportant or irrelevant stimuli)

6. An intense increase in activities that greatly interest them combined with agitation

7. Excessive involvement in pleasurable activities that might lead to harm

Younger children and adolescents develop bipolar disorder, but usually present differently than adults. They may appear unusually happy or silly, or very irritable, angry, agitated, or aggressive. A higher-functioning teenage boy may seem to feel all-powerful and have greatly increased energy. When he talks, his speech is much too fast, he changes topics too quickly, and he cannot be interrupted. His attention moves constantly from one thing to the next.

Mental health professionals have had increased interest in *rapid cycling bipolar disorder,* defined as at least four manic episodes a year with at least one depressive interlude. Of typical adults who have bipolar disorder, 13% to 20% develop rapid cycling bipolar disorder. The average age of onset is 19 years, and it is more frequent in women than men. It is very occasionally seen in children as well. It may be precipitated by antidepressant medication or thyroid gland dysfunction. Bipolar cycles can involve mood switches occurring daily or every few days during an episode. There is very little known about rapid cycling bipolar disorder among children and adolescents with ASDs. Most of the time when a child with an ASD exhibits unpredictable episodic mood swings, on closer examination, it is due to environmental circumstances.

Mood Stabilizing Medications

Lithium (Lithobid, Eskolith) has been used to treat acute bipolar mania for nearly 60 years. When effects of lithium are compared with placebo in treating acute mania, most studies have shown that lithium is significantly superior to a sugar pill. Lithium's effects have been comparable to those of Tegretol (carbamazepine), Risperdal (risperidone), Zyprexa (alanzapine), Thorazine (chlorpromazine), and other typical antipsychotics. Open label trials as well as controlled studies indicate that lithium is effective in treating pure mania but is less often effective in treating mixed states or rapid cycling disorder. Depending on the severity of the manic symptoms, control of the manic episode is usually obtained within 4 to 10 days after the start of drug treatment. Relapse occurs within as few as 2 days if the lithium is abruptly discontinued during the manic phase. To prevent relapse of manic symptoms on an ongoing basis, a lower blood level is required.

Lithium is not recommended for young children or for nursing mothers. Nearly three quarters of people treated with lithium experience some side effects. Most are either minor or can be reduced or eliminated by lowering the lithium dose or changing the dosage schedule; however, serious side effects can occur. Lithium toxicity becomes more likely as the blood level rises. The therapeutic range of lithium in the bloodstream within which beneficial effects outweigh toxic effects is narrow, so small increases in blood level may lead to harmful effects when using lithium. Vomiting, excessive sweating, or excessive fluid intake can cause an imbalance of electrolytes in the bloodstream. Fluid loss can lead to toxicity, and excessive fluid intake can diminish the effect of lithium. Most physicians avoid using lithium for youth with ASDs because it is difficult to determine whether they are beginning to experience adverse effects.

Seizure Medications with Mood Stabilizing Effects

Tegretol is prescribed by neurologists to prevent several types of seizures. Children with mixed seizure disorders with atypical absence seizures (formally referred to as *petit mal*) or tonic-clonic seizures (formally referred to as *grand mal*) and pregnant women should not be treated with Tegretol. It was first found to have anti-manic effects in 1968 and has been widely used for that purpose since then. The American Psychiatric Association (APA) currently recommends that carbamazepine be reserved for patients unable to tolerate, or who had an inadequate therapeutic response to, lithium and Depakote. Among the more common side effects of Tegretol are blurred vision, double vision, dizziness, drowsiness, atypical muscle contractions, impaired cognition, nausea, atypical eye movements, and vomiting. Carbamazepine interacts with many other drugs, and care should be taken to check for interactions before beginning to treat patients with this medication (for up-to-date information about drug interactions see http://www.drug-interactions.com).

Depakote is primarily a seizure medication, but it is also approved for preventing migraine headaches and for treating acute bipolar mania. The APA currently recommends combined therapy with valproic acid plus an atypical antipsychotic agent or with lithium plus an antipsychotic agent as first-line drug therapy for the acute treatment of more severe manic or mixed episodes, and with one of these drugs for less severe episodes. Depakote should not be given to children under 2 years of age because of potential liver damage, to pregnant women, or to nursing mothers.

Lamictal (lamotrigine) was originally developed as a supplementary medication to reduce partial seizures when given in combination with other seizure medications. Lamotrigine is used in the maintenance therapy of bipolar I disorder. It reduces recurrences of bipolar episodes in patients who remain at risk of relapse following treatment of an acute depressive or manic episode. The APA currently recommends use of lamotrigine as an alternative to lithium, valproic acid, or divalproex. Based on current evidence, lamotrigine appears to be the treatment of choice for rapid cycling disorder. Lamotrigine should not be given to children and adolescents under 16 years of age. Fatal skin rashes have been reported in this age group.

Antipsychotics with Mood Stabilizing Effects

Clinical researchers have discovered that some of the atypical antipsychotic medications, including Clozaril (clozapine), Zyprexa (olanzapine), Risperdal (risperidone), Seroquel (quetiapine), and Geodon (ziprasidone), appear to have mood stabilizing effects. While they are generally not the first choice for treating bipolar mania, they are used increasingly when more conventional mood stabilizing medications have failed to work or in combination with lithium or other mood stabilizers.

Attention-Deficit/Hyperactivity Disorder

Nearly all children with ASDs have problems focusing their attention, and some are overly active. In most cases, these are features of an ASD and not a comorbid attention-deficit/hyperactivity disorder (ADHD) condition. However, a subset of children with ASDs also display most or all of the characteristic features of ADHD, and they usually respond favorably to the same medications as other children with ADHD. According to the *DSM-IV,*

ADHD is not supposed to be diagnosed among people who have ASDs. However, many children with ASDs who present classic signs of ADHD are treated with the same medicines used for other non-ASD patients who have ADHD.

Approximately 1 in 20 children in the general population have impairments in attention (alone), impairments in activity level (alone), or both. Chapter 2 discusses the criteria for a child diagnosed with ADHD and the three types of ADHD.

Children with ADHD of the combined type usually have the greatest difficulties. Lack of impulse control is maddening to parents and teachers of children with hyperactive ADHD. When a parent or teacher of such a child says, "Don't do that," he or she might as well be speaking to the child in a foreign language. Matters are much worse for children with ASD and ADHD-like characteristics because they do not respond well to verbal requests in the first place. Even more perplexing is the disorganization of children with inattentive ADHD. Having just told her 5-year-old daughter with Asperger syndrome and inattentive ADHD-like characteristics to put on her socks and shoes for school, the child's mother is dismayed to see her daughter's shoes and socks strewn on the floor as her daughter sits busily playing with her Dora doll. When the child's mother sternly says, "Tina, I told you to put on your socks and shoes," the child looks up with a totally confused expression on her face and says, "Oh, okay, mommy," and proceeds to put her shoes on the wrong feet.

Evidence indicates that the brains of children with ADHD interpret and react to information differently than the brains of their same-age peers, especially in situations that require sustained attention (e.g., to a teacher's spoken instruction), but they may not be distracted by other aspects of the environment (e.g., a child's voice outside the classroom). Different brain areas are responsible for selective attention and sustained attention, which do not function properly among children with ADHD. There are many causes of ADHD. Some children appear to inherit the tendency for ADHD from their parents, often their father, while others acquire ADHD because of damage to their brain during development inside the womb (e.g., from infections, exposure to alcohol or another toxin). The end result is similar: There is damage to brain structures that regulate attention, activity level, and reward mechanisms.

Stimulant Medications for Attention-Deficit/Hyperactivity Disorder

Because stimulant medications increase activity levels in most people (as well as laboratory participants), it seemed paradoxical that these medications appeared to reduce overactivity among children with ADHD. Hill (1970) first suggested that the reason stimulant medications improve the behavior of children with ADHD was that the drug enhanced the effectiveness of weak reinforcers (i.e., conditioned reinforcers) that were associated with academic tasks in school and with compliance with parental demands at home. Hill's initial laboratory study was suggestive but did not provide definitive proof of his hypothesis. Subsequently, Robbins (1975), Robbins and Sahakian (1979), and Cador, Robbins, and Everitt (1989) at Cambridge University published a series of laboratory studies demonstrating that stimulants have multiple effects, including enhancing attention mechanisms and increasing the effectiveness of weak conditioned reinforcers. These studies pointed out that the effects of stimulant medications are not really paradoxical if one understands the underlying mechanisms of the drugs' effects.

Classroom and clinical studies are rarely designed to distinguish these two effects. A student with ADHD whose school performance improves because he or she is responding more appropriately to instructional stimuli will demonstrate even greater improvement if his or her teacher increases the frequency of positive reinforcement for compliance and task completion. It is a mistake to assume that improved attention to instructional stimuli alone will sustain improved school performance. One of the reasons stimulant medications lose their effectiveness over time for some children with ADHD is that caregivers and school personnel have not provided sufficient positive reinforcement along with the improved attention the drug produces. Among many children with ADHD, a combination of stimulant medications and behavior therapy produces greater behavioral improvements than either treatment alone (MTA Cooperative Group, 1999).

There have been hundreds of clinical studies involving thousands of children with different amphetamines and methylphenidate, another stimulant for treating ADHD. Common medications used to treat ADHD include Ritalin (methylphenidate), a mixture of amphetamine products (Adderall), Dexedrine (dextroamphetamine)—including one brand with several related compounds—and Strattera (atomoxetine), which acts by a different mechanism. Methylphenidate and dextroamphetamine are short-acting medications, and dextroamphetamine spansules and methylphenidate-SR and Focalin (dexmethylphenidate) are longer-acting medications. The effects of methylphenidate, for example, usually last about 4 hours. The effects of longer-acting stimulant medications like dextroamphetamine can last up to 8 hours, although there can be wide individual variations that cannot be predicted and will only become evident once the medication is tried.

The specific dose of medication must be determined for each individual. There are recommended ranges based on body weight, but there are no consistent relations between height, age, and clinical response to a medication. A blind medication trial is often used to determine the most beneficial dosage. The child's pediatrician or child psychiatrist and pharmacist specify what dose the child is receiving, or whether it is a sugar pill (placebo) or active medication, during a particular test period. But the parents and teachers are not aware of when the medication or placebo is changed. This is done to prevent the bias of wishful thinking by parents or teachers from reporting improvements when receiving the medication, but not when receiving the placebo. The trial usually begins with a low dose that is gradually increased until clinical benefits are achieved. It is common for the dosage to be raised several times during the trial. Parents and teacher ratings are usually done using standardized scales provided by pediatricians, psychiatrists, or psychologists.

The family must weigh the pros and cons of choosing medication as part of the treatment plan for ADHD. Common immediate side effects are poor appetite and difficulty sleeping at night. Stimulant side effects are usually managed by reducing the dose and the scheduling for short-acting medications, or by changing to a prolonged-release formulation. A relatively uncommon side effect of stimulant medications may be increased eye blinking, shrugging, and a clearing of the throat. Stimulant medications can cause the emergence of a tic disorder in susceptible children. Often, but not always, the tic will disappear when the medication is stopped. For some mid-teenagers, vocal tics (e.g., throat clearing, sniffing, coughing beyond what is normal) or motor tics (e.g., blinking, facial grimacing, shrugging, head-turning) may occur as a time-limited phenomenon concurrent with ADHD. The effectiveness of stimulant medications for ADHD symptoms in ASDs has not been clearly established, although some children with ASDs and ADHD symptoms profit from stimulant drugs.

Seizure-Related Behavior Problems

The fact that there is a higher incidence of epilepsy among children and adolescents with ASDs has been recognized for many years. There also is known to be a relationship between seizure disorders and behavioral outbursts and depression. Clarke and co-workers (2005) conducted a survey of children being treated at a comprehensive epilepsy center and found that 32% had ASDs diagnoses, although that wasn't the reason for their being treated at that center. Conversely, Chez et al. (2005) found in a study of 889 people with ASD diagnoses that 60.7% had atypical EEG epileptiform activity. The most frequent sites of epileptiform impairments were localized over the right temporal region. Reinhold, Malloy, and Manning-Courtney (2005) found atypical EEG results in 85 (27%) of the 316 children evaluated for ASD at a center in Cincinnati. In a study conducted at a child development treatment center in Israel, Gabis, Pomeroy, and Andriola (2005) found that 40% of the children with ASDs seen at that center had epilepsy. McLellan and colleagues (2005) studied psychological characteristics of children from 7 months to 18 years of age who had temporal lobe epilepsy (TLE). ADHD, oppositional defiant disorder/conduct disorder, and other emotional disorders were present in about 25% of children. Thirty-eight percent were diagnosed with an ASD.

Partial epilepsy is a seizure disorder that affects only one part of the brain. Symptoms depend on which part is affected: One part of the body, or multiple body parts confined to one side of the body, may start to twitch uncontrollably. Partial seizures may involve head turning, eye movements, lip smacking, mouth movements, drooling, rhythmic muscle contractions in a part of the body, apparently purposeful movements, atypical numbness, tingling, and a crawling sensation over the skin. Partial seizures can also include sensory disturbances, such as smelling or hearing things that are not there, or having a sudden flood of emotions. Simple and complex seizures (types of partial epilepsy) are distinguished on the basis of the state of consciousness. Consciousness usually is assessed by the ability of the patient to respond to external stimuli (i.e., responsiveness). This is intact in simple partial seizures (SPS) and impaired in complex partial seizures (CPS). A third type of partial epilepsy sometimes progresses to a tonic-clonic seizure (grand mal seizure).

The most common type of partial epilepsy, called temporal lobe epilepsy (TLE), originates in the temporal lobe on either side of the brain. The seizures associated with TLE may be simple partial seizures without loss of awareness or complex partial seizures with loss of awareness. The individual loses awareness during a complex partial seizure because the seizure spreads to involve both temporal lobes, which causes impairment of memory.

A typical sequence begins with an aura. Neurotypical individuals often report feeling as though they are in a dream during the aura with an array of emotions, thoughts, and sensory experiences, some of which may be completely foreign. Some people experience hallucinations of voices, music, people, smells, or tastes. Objects may appear shrunken (micropsia) or larger (macropsia) than usual. Apparent tilting of furniture or structures has been reported. The aura may last for just a few seconds, or may continue as long as a minute or two. Lewis Carroll's description of things changing size in *Alice in Wonderland* was inspired by his experience with TLE.

Following the aura, a TLE complex partial seizure begins with a wide-eyed, motionless stare, dilated pupils, and cessation of movement. Unconscious mouth movements such as lip smacking, chewing, and swallowing may begin. Repetitive hand or leg movements, such as closing and opening one hand or extending the arm or leg repeatedly, may occur and often are accompanied by sustained head or eye turning opposite to the side of the seizure focus in the brain. Some individuals continue to react to their surroundings in what appears to be a semi-purposeful manner (these are called reactive automatisms). They also can have repetitive stereotyped manual automatisms.

A complex partial seizure may evolve to a secondarily generalized tonic-clonic seizure involving all muscles of the body. Often, when documenting a seizure, only the generalized tonic-clonic (grand mal) component of the seizure is noted. A careful history is needed to determine whether a simple seizure or a complex partial seizure occurred before the secondarily generalized seizure, which is important for prescribing the most effective treatment. Among typical individuals, usually a period of confusion follows, which distinguishes TLE from absence seizures (formally called *petit mal*), which are not associated with postseizure confusion. In addition, absence seizures are not associated with auras or with complex movements.

Numerous studies have shown that individuals with TLE are prone to depression and anxiety disorders, which are corrected for many people when treated with appropriate seizure medication. In one study, depression occurred in approximately one third of TLE patients between seizures (Devinsky, 2004). There is also a long history of reports of periodic behavioral dyscontrol episodes during which unprovoked aggression or rage outbursts occur. This is seen in individuals whose seizures involve the amygdala (on the inner surface of the temporal lobe). At times, these episodes may appear undirected and include destruction to property as well as attacks directed at people. In the past, seizures with such striking behavioral manifestations were called *psychomotor seizures.*

Because children with ASDs often have limited verbal skills and are unable to accurately report their subjective experiences, it is difficult to determine whether they are aware of what had occurred immediately before, during, and after a TLE episode. As a result, diagnosis depends on a detailed description of the sequence of events that occurs as the seizures unfold provided to a neurologist, who will most likely order an EEG to assess possible brain wave impairments consistent with a seizure disorder. It is even more helpful if parents are able to obtain a videotaped recording of an entire episode. In some instances, neurologists prefer to conduct a sleep-deprived EEG assessment that involves keeping the child awake all night and then carrying out the assessment early the next morning. This increases the likelihood of detecting EEG impairments in a child who is prone to seizures, but it may be difficult in some instances to keep a child with ASD awake all night.

Seizure Control Medications

There are more than a dozen medications used to treat different types of seizure disorders, and others are in development. This discussion will focus on drugs that have specifically been demonstrated to be effective in controlling complex partial epilepsy. The standard medications include Tegretol (carbamazepine), Depakote (valproate sodium), and Dilantin (phenytoin). Other medications that have been approved by the FDA for treating partial epilepsies are Lamictal (lamotrigine), Gabitril (tiagabine), Tranxene (clorazepate), Topamax (topirimate), and Neurontin (gabapentin). Most of these medications produce tiredness, dizziness, and fatigue, and some cause headache, double vision, coordination, and gait problems. Some seizure medications can produce serious side effects, such as blood clotting, anemia, liver damage, or serious skin rashes. Some of the newer antiepilepsy drugs have undergone little or no testing in children and thus are not yet approved for use by children. Sabril (vigabatrin), which is available in Canada but not the United States, is effective in controlling some seizures but has been reported to cause visual field constriction in some people that may not be reversible when the medication is stopped.

DOPAMINE, BRAIN OPIOIDS, AGGRESSION, AND SELF-INJURY

Aggression and self-injury are often symptoms of an underlying mental health problem or dysfunctional coping behavior. As noted previously, some aggression or self-injury is a means of escaping from unwelcome demands or situations the person finds intolerable. Other violent behavior appears to be secondary to depression or anxiety and can be treated effectively with antidepressant medications in many instances. However, some aggression and self-injury appears to have other origins. Among some individuals who engage in pervasive rocking, hand flapping, and other nonfunctional repetitive behavior, self-injury or aggression appears to be driven by other brain mechanisms. This is particularly true of those individuals with complex ASDs, that is, with dysmorphic features and global cognitive disability (Miles et al., 2005). Often, a functional assessment reveals that the behavior has no single environmental controlling variable, although aggression may at times serve as an escape function. Self-injury may occur when the individual is alone with no demands or when the person is in a noisy, busy classroom. For individuals whose aggression or self-injury does not appear to be primarily motivated by social avoidance and who exhibit few signs of anxiety or depression as previously outlined, treatment directed at possible dopamine brain impairments may be more appropriate. Brain dopamine overactivity produces irritability, hyperactivity, repetitive movements, and aggression in laboratory animals. There is limited evidence from human brain-imaging studies that supersensitivity of dopamine brain receptors contributes to their problems.

Antipsychotic Medications

The medications most often effective in treating individuals who exhibit aggressive or self-injurious behavior produce their primary effects by binding to and producing effects opposite those that typically occur at dopamine receptors in the brain, primarily D1 and D2 receptors. The older medications of these types, called *typical antipsychotics* (or neuroleptics), produced effects opposite D2 receptors with such great affinity relative to D1 receptors that they produced movement disorder problems similar to Parkinson's disease, and in some cases tardive dyskinesia, a very disfiguring movement disorder. The most commonly prescribed drugs of these types were Thorazine, Haldol, and Mellaril, although they are seldom used today.

Atypical Antispsychotic Medications

Newer atypical antipsychotic drugs have greater effects on D1 receptors than on D2 receptors and also affect the serotonin systems in the brain. Advokat, Mayville, and Matson (2000) studied side effects of older typical antipsychotic drugs and the newer atypical antipsychotics in treating individuals with developmental disabilities. They found that the side effect scores of patients receiving typical antipsychotics were 2 to 3 times higher than those for atypical antipsychotics, which were not different from scores of people receiving no medication. Numerous studies have been published revealing that Risperdal (risperidone) is effective in reducing aggression and self-injury among people with ASDs and related developmental disabilities with profiles similar to those outlined above (Zarcone et al., 2001; McDougle et al., 2005). Clozaril (clozapine) has been used successfully in several case studies and small sample reports to reduce aggression and self-injury. However, because of the risk of a serious blood disorder in a very small percentage of people receiving the drug, most doctors do not prescribe it. There is little compelling direct evidence that the other atypical antipsychotic drugs are effective, although there have been several open label trials with Geodon and Zyprexa reporting positive results. Quetiapine does not appear to be effective in reducing aggression and self-injury in ASDs (Bernard et al., 2002). Although the risks associated with atypical antipsychotics are less than the original antipsychotic drugs, there are problems nonetheless; specifically, they are capable of causing drowsiness, lethargy, and, in some cases, agitation if the dose is too high. A small percentage of treated individuals experience muscle stiffness, a mild form of Parkinson's disease that ceases when the dose is lowered or the medicine is discontinued. Geodon has been reported to produce heart rhythm problems in a few patients, which makes it unsuitable for anyone with a preexisting heart condition. Substantial weight gain, with the possibility of developing Type II diabetes, is the primary concern with atypical antipsychotics. As a result, at the present time, atypical antipsychotic medications can only be used safely for children and youth with ASDs for a confined time interval while other treatments are being put into place.

Opiate Antagonist Medication

Cataldo and Harris (1982) first suggested that a naturally occurring pain-killing substance such as beta endorphin, if it were released in the brain when an individual with an ASD or another developmental disability injures her- or himself, may serve as a reinforcer when it binds to the same opiate receptors in the brain to which addictive drugs like heroin or morphine bind. Several researchers have demonstrated that drugs that block these receptors (naloxone and naltrexone) often reduce self-injury (e.g., Thompson et al., 1994). According to this reasoning, if the person whose opiate receptors are blocked by an antagonist self injures, the reinforcing event of opiate receptor binding cannot occur.

It is likely that a child or adolescent with an ASD who injures him- or herself does so in part for social reasons, even if there is a strong brain chemical component. Symons, Fox, and Thompson (1998) evaluated the efficacy of the opiate antagonist naltrexone combined with functional communication training (FCT) for self-injury of a 12-year-old boy with an ASD, an intellectual disability, and communication impairments. Initial reductions in the overall rate of self-injurious behavior (SIB) were reported during a placebo-controlled double-blind medication trial, with further reductions noted following the addition of FCT. Similarly, Garcia and Smith (1999) evaluated the effects of naltrexone on the self-injurious behavior of two women diagnosed with profound intellectual disabilities. Both participants were exposed to pre-treatment functional analyses to determine possible social reasons for their behavior at baseline. The treatment phase consisted of continued exposure to analog assessment procedures in a multi-element format paired with daily administration of naltrexone or a placebo in a double-blind format. Naltrexone produced function-specific effects on self-injury between- and within-participants. For one participant, socially mediated head slapping (negatively reinforced) decreased with naltrexone administration, but nonsocially mediated head banging did not. For the other participant, only her nonsocially mediated self-injury was reduced with naltrexone. This study was the first to evaluate the effects of naltrexone using analog functional analysis measures.

Sandman, Touchette, Lenjavi, Marion, and Chicz-DeMet (2003) obtained a blood sample immediately after an SIB. A significant number of the participants 1) reduced their SIB at least 25% at all doses of naltrexone and 2) reduced their SIB more than 50% for at least one dose of naltrexone. There was a correlation of .67 between elevation in betaendorphin in the blood and the amount of reduction in SIB produced by naltrexone, a finding consistent with the opioid self-administration hypothesis of self-injury.

Symons, Thompson, and Rodriguez (2004) conducted a quantitative synthesis of the peer-reviewed published literature from 1983 to 2003 documenting the use of naltrexone for the treatment of SIB. Twenty-seven research articles involving 86 participants with SIB were reviewed. Eighty percent of the participants were reported to improve relative to baseline (i.e., SIB reduced) during naltrexone administration, and for 47% of participants, SIB was reduced by 50% or greater. Collectively, the foregoing data suggest that for some people with developmental disabilities, their self-injury is maintained by beta endorphin binding to opioid receptors or some similar form of opioid peptide-like activity following SIB, and that the behavioral mechanism of action of naltrexone is extinction of the self-injurious behavior.

SUMMARY

Mental health issues are common among individuals with ASDs. Much of the time, behavioral intervention strategies are capable of reducing the severity of these issues, but often, psychotropic medications have an important role to play in managing mental health issues. Anxiety and depressive disorders and ADHD are among the more common issues. Aggression and self-injury are sometimes manifestations of the foregoing conditions or they may be socially motivated. A combination of behavioral interventions, based on functional behavioral assessment methods, and psychotropic medication is often the most effective approach to overcoming these mental health issues.

9

Disabilities Associated with Autism Spectrum Disorders

L uke was born prematurely, had infantile spasms, and experienced bleeding inside his brain that produced damage to his frontal cortex. He also has a high-functioning austism spectrum disorder (ASD). Everyone likes Luke. He is exceptionally verbal, funny, and enjoyable. Luke had been told that I was coming to visit him and his parents, so he was expecting me. Luke answered the door when I rang the doorbell and greeted me with, "Hi, Travis, did you come to fix our toilet?" Apparently, the family's upstairs toilet was broken, and Luke reasoned that I must have come to repair it. I told him that I'd send one of my helpers to fix the toilet later, but that I was there to visit with him. That episode was typical of Luke. He is very socially curious and outgoing, but sometimes a bit off the mark.

Luke has very poor social judgment and limited impulse control. He occasionally blurts out profanity for no apparent reason and has periodic unprovoked behavioral outbursts. His neurologist diagnosed Luke as having frontal lobe seizures, for which he is treated with anti-epileptic medication. He is an example of a youngster with comorbid conditions: an ASD, epilepsy, and frontal lobe syndrome.

DISABILITIES COMMONLY ASSOCIATED WITH ASDs

An ASD is a concurrent condition in numerous developmental disabilities, which means that the child presents a combination of features of both disabilities. This is referred to as *syndromal autism*. Parents and teachers often wonder how that can be possible. They assume that a child either has fragile X syndrome or an ASD, not both. A variety of developmental problems can damage some of the same brain structures that are dysfunctional in autism to varying degrees. In a study of the two major types of ASDs, Miles and colleagues (2005) found that children and youth diagnosed with an ASD who also had a known genetic syndrome (e.g., de Lange syndrome) all fell within the category of complex ASD—those with dysmorphic features and/or lower intellectual functioning, who are more likely to exhibit brain differences on MRI evaluation than children with familial autism. Children with the familial form of ASDs usually have only a single disability (the ASD).

Fragile X Syndrome

Fragile X syndrome is the most common inherited cause of intellectual disability, as well as the most common known cause of ASD. Features usually include intellectual disability, ranging from learning disabilities to severe cognitive disability; an attention-deficit/hyperactivity disorder (ADHD); anxiety and unstable moods; autistic behaviors; and a long face, large ears, flat feet, and hyperextensible joints, especially fingers. Seizures (epilepsy) affect about 25% of people with fragile X. Boys are typically more severely affected than girls. Although most affected boys have intellectual disability, only one third to one half of affected girls have significant intellectual deficit; the rest have either a normal IQ or learning disabilities. Emotional and behavioral problems are common in both sexes.

About 20% of boys with fragile X meet full criteria for ASD. Most boys and some girls have some symptoms of ASD, but many tend to be very social and interested in other people. Those who also have an ASD are exceedingly shy, anxious, and exhibit repetitive behavior typical of ASDs. They often seem over-aroused and are prone to engaging in self-injury. Medications to reduce excessive arousal (e.g., Inderal, [propranolol], Tenormin [atenolol]) sometimes help manage their anxiety. Behavioral and education treatments used with other children with ASDs are also useful in children with fragile X syndrome—especially those that begin with the recognition that the child's compulsive routines are anxiety-driven and he or she is not being willfully disobedient.

In 1991, scientists discovered the gene called fragile X mental retardation–1 (FMR1) that causes fragile X syndrome. The FMR1 gene is located on the long arm of the X chromosome. Within this gene lies a region of DNA that varies in length from one person to another. Usually, the stretch of DNA falls within a range of length that would be considered "normal." In some people, however, the stretch of DNA is somewhat longer; this gene change is called a *permutation*. Although a person who carries the permutation does not usually have symptoms of fragile X, the stretch of DNA is prone to further expansion when it is passed from a mother to her children.

When the stretch of DNA expands beyond a certain length, the gene is switched off and does not produce the protein that it is normally makes. This gene change is called a *full mutation*. A boy who inherits a full mutation exhibits fragile X syndrome because his only X chromosome contains the mutated gene. A female may not be as severely affected because each cell of her body needs to use only one of its two X chromosomes and randomly inactivates the other. The Fragile X Research Foundation web site, http://www.fraxa.org, is an excellent resource for more information on this syndrome.

Dyslexia

It is becoming increasingly clear that there is a link between speech and language disabilities and ASDs. Miniscalco et al. (2006) studied a community sample of children identified with a language disorder at 6 years of age and followed them for a year. Detailed test results at age 7 years were available for 21 of the children. Thirteen of the 21 children (62%) had an ASD, atypical autism, Asperger syndrome, ADHD, or combinations of these conditions.

Dyslexia is a specific learning disability that is neurological in origin. It is characterized by difficulties with accurate and/or fluent word recognition, by poor spelling, and by decoding abilities. These difficulties typically result from an impairment in the phonological component of language. Secondary consequences may include problems in reading comprehension and reduced reading experience that can impede growth of vocabulary and background knowledge (National Reading Panel, 1998). Individuals with dyslexia process language information in an area of the brain that is different from the area of the brain individuals without dyslexia process that information. Many people who are dyslexic are of average to above average intelligence. Some people have referred to ASD as the most extreme form of dyslexia, but that is inaccurate. Although nearly all children with ASDs have language and reading problems, they also have social relationship difficulties and engage in repetitive routines that are unlike the behavior of children with dyslexia. Children with dyslexia have typical social relationships and do not engage in repetitive stereotyped routines. Some children with ASDs have reading difficulties and phonological processing problems similar to those seen in children with dyslexia and respond to the same phonetic reading strategies as children with dyslexia.

A very small percentage of children with ASDs exhibit exceptional verbal skills. Silberberg and Silberberg (1968–1969) defined the term *hyperlexia* to describe children who read at levels beyond those expected for their mental age in the face of disordered oral communication. Many parents and teachers are confused by hyperlexia, assuming it means exceptional intellectual ability. It usually does not. Most children who exhibit hyperlexia can read words and sentences early and beyond their age levels, but their comprehension is usually closer to their mental age or below. Turkeltaub et al. (2004) stated that there are three consistent features of hyperlexia:

1. The presence of a developmental disorder of communication, most often an autistic spectrum disorder

2. Acquisition of reading skills prior to age 5 without explicit instruction

3. Advanced word recognition ability relative to mental age, with reading comprehension on par with verbal ability

Prader-Willi Syndrome

Prader-Willi syndrome (PWS) is a developmental disability caused by the deletion of a section of Chromosome 15 or two copies of Chromosome 15 from their mother and none from their father. Very occasionally, other chromosomal abnormalities cause milder forms of PWS. It occurs in approximately one in 12,000 to 15,000 births. Children with PWS are distinguished by a voracious appetite, short stature, low metabolic rate, and resulting obesity. Their average IQ is 65. Approximately 15% of children with PWS also meet the diagnostic criteria for ASD. Although children with PWS are usually socially interested, they are poor at understanding others' perspectives, engage in compulsive routines similar to those seen in ASD, and are intolerant of changes in daily routines. When their expected routines are disrupted, the children exhibit tantrums. Approximately 85% of children with PWS display an unusual form of self-injury (skin picking), with onset before 5 years of age for most children (Dimitropoulos et al., 2001; Symons et al., 1999; Thompson & Butler, 2004). Educational and behavioral interventions directed at their compulsive routines are similar to those for children with ASDs (Dykens, Hodapp, & Finucane, 2000). Some parents are strongly opposed to using food reinforcement in behavioral programs for children and youth with PWS although others routinely use access to pieces of nutritious low-calorie fruit or vegetables to reinforce exercise and academic activities

To date, however, there are no truly effective treatments for the severe appetite disorder and associated obesity. Some specialists who treat children with PWS have given them a growth hormone that increases their muscle mass (thereby burning more calories) and increases their vertical growth. Psychotropic medications have generally had limited success in treating behavior problems associated with PWS, though some clinicians have used Abilify or Geodon, atypical antipsychotic medications that cause little weight gain. Two studies have suggested that Topiramate, an antiepileptic drug used as a mood stabilizer, reduced aggression and skin-picking in PWS and stopped weight gain (Shapira et al., 2004; Smathers, Wilson, & Nigro, 2003).

Angelman Syndrome

Angelman syndrome is a sister syndrome usually caused by a deletion of a section of the mother's Chromosome 15 (70%) or two copies of Chromosome 15 from the child's father (2%), with the remainder being smaller deletions or errors on other chromosomes. It has a prevalence of 1 in 25,000 births. Because the same section of Chromosome 15 is involved as in PWS and some forms of ASD, children with Angelman syndrome may also carry an ASD diagnosis. Peters, Beaudet, Madduri, and Bacino (2004) found that 42% of one sample of individuals with Angelman syndrome also met the diagnostic criteria for ASD. Unlike individuals with PWS, children with Angelman syndrome usually have severe intellectual impairments, small head size, unusual hyperkinetic limb movements, limited language, and often laugh and giggle inappropriately. Many also have seizures requiring use of antiepileptic medications. Although children with Angelman syndrome do not typically receive psychotropic medications, some doctors prescribe stimulants for hyperactivity. No specific educational or behavioral intervention strategies have been demonstrated to be uniquely effective with children with Angelman syndrome. Most programs employ a functional curriculum focusing on augmentative communication and daily living skills.

Cornelia de Lange Syndrome

The Cornelia de Lange syndrome (CdLS) is also known as the Brachman-de Lange syndrome. CdLS has an estimated birth prevalence between one in 10,000 to 30,000. There are no definitive biochemical or chromosome markers for the diagnosis. At the present time, diagnosis is made on the basis of clinical observations. The most frequently observed facial characteristics include thin, downturned lips; low-set ears; long eyelashes; and eyebrows that meet in the middle, called *synofers*. Other characteristics often associated with this syndrome include delayed growth and small stature; language delay, even in the more mildly affected; small head size; excessive body hair; and simian hand creases. Individuals may also resist being touched or show a lack of sensitivity to pain. Although significant intellectual disability is typical (average IQ is 53), some people with this disability have slightly below normal intelligence.

Malformations of the hands and feet are common and may include small hands and feet with short digits, fusing of fingers or toes, curving in of the fifth fingers, and flexion contractures at the elbows. Occasionally, fingers, hands, and forearms may be missing. Speech is often absent or minimal even in those at the higher end of the intellectual continuum. Most people with CdLS exhibit errors in articulation. Consonants are typically distorted or missing. In addition, there have been some reported observations of severe oral-motor and verbal apraxia. The majority of individuals speak very little, although they often make eye contact and appear socially interested.

Gastrointestinal problems affect a high percentage of children with CdLS. Complaints can originate from the upper GI tract, including the esophagus, stomach, and upper small intestine, although the most common is gastroesophageal reflux disease (GERD). During a home visit, the parents of an 8-year-old girl with CdLS expressed concern because their daughter was spending so much time lying on the floor masturbating. I asked them to describe her behavior to me. With some discomfort they described her lying on her back on the floor with her back arched and her arms moving repeatedly from her pubic area upward on her abdomen toward her chest. It turns out the little girl wasn't masturbating, she was experiencing extreme discomfort from GERD. In its most severe form, reflux is associated with arching of the back, eyes averted upward, and rigid flexing of the body and limbs so that if the person were laid on his or her back, only the back of the head and the heels would touch the supporting surface. Sometimes their arms flail back and forth as well. This is known as the *Sandifer Complex* and is indicative of severe pain associated with GERD. The girl's parents subsequently consulted her pediatrician about treatment for GERD.

Although some children with CdLS have few behavioral problems, many others have significant autistic behavior. Berney, Ireland, and Burn (1999) studied a sample of children with CdLS and found that the degree of intellectual disability ranged from borderline (10%) through mild (8%), moderate (18%), and severe (20%) to profound (43%). A wide variety of symptoms occurred, notably hyperactivity (40%), self-injury (44%), daily aggression (49%), and sleep disturbance (55%). These correlated closely with the presence of compulsive ASD features and with a degree of intellectual disability. Approximately three fourths of the sample displayed prominent autistic features.

Most treatments for children with CdLS emphasize physical health and well-being, which is a chronic concern. It is recommended that treatment begin early for gastrointestinal and feeding problems, hearing and visual impairment, congenital heart disease, and urinary system abnormalities. Early psychoeducational intervention programs that emphasize augmentative communication and employ visual prompting systems such as visual schedules are especially effective. Gentle guidance and redirection during instruction can be helpful because of hearing problems and lack of language. Fine motor activities, especially related to daily living skills, should take into consideration finger and hand developmental limitations. There are no generally accepted medication treatments for behavior problems in CdLS. Many physicians prescribe selective serotonin reuptake inhibitors (SSRIs) for children with CdLS who have substantial anxiety and compulsive behavior, although others rely on Abilify or Geodon for aggression and self-injury. However, there are no well-controlled studies that have evaluated the effectiveness of these medications. The Cornelia de Lange Foundation USA has a wealth of resources for parents and practitioners available on their web site (http://www.cdlsusa.org).

Tuberous Sclerosis

Tuberous sclerosis complex (TSC) is an uncommon genetic disease that causes benign tumors to grow in the brain and on other vital organs such as the kidneys, heart, eyes, lungs, and skin. Some people are so mildly affected they may find out they also have TSC only after their more severely affected child receives a diagnosis of TSC. Children have a 50% chance of inheriting TSC if one parent has the condition. Current estimates indicate that tuberous sclerosis occurs in one in 25,000–30,000 births. Some children with TSC, usually those who have an intellectual disability, are also diagnosed with an ASD. There appears to be a connection between TSC and ASD that is not understood, and active research is exploring this association. The prevalence of TSC in the ASD population is 1%–4%, whereas features of ASD are present in 25%–50% of individuals with tuberous sclerosis complex (Wiznitzer, 2004).

TSC commonly affects the central nervous system. In addition to the benign tumors that frequently occur in TSC, other common symptoms include seizures, intellectual disability, behavior problems, and skin abnormalities. TSC may be present at birth, but signs of the disorder can be subtle and full symptoms may take some time to develop. Three types of brain tumors are associated with TSC: cortical tubers, which generally form on the surface of the brain; nodules, which form in the walls of the ventricles (the fluid-filled cavities of the brain); and a type of tumor that can block the flow of fluids within the brain. The most common effect of brain manifestation is epilepsy or seizures. Seizures occur in 60%–90% of individuals diagnosed with TSC. The behavior of a child with TSC can often be difficult and trying for parents and family. Aggression, sudden rage, hyperactivity, attention deficit, acting out, obsessive-compulsive behavior, repetitive behaviors, being nonverbal when most children their age are speaking, and other autistic behaviors occur in children with TSC.

Medical management focuses on controlling seizures and psychotherapeutic drugs for hyperactivity, aggression, and sleep problems. In some cases, surgery is performed to stop otherwise uncontrollable seizures. Educational and behavioral intervention strategies for children with TSC are the same as they are for other children with *complex autism*. Depending on which brain areas are involved, children with TSC can have speech, hearing, or perceptual motor problems, which require the attention of speech therapists and/or occupational therapists. There is very little known about the effectiveness of various early intervention strategies for children with TSC, although it is prudent to intervene as one would with any other child with an ASD.

Tourette Syndrome

Gilles de la Tourette syndrome (Tourette syndrome or TS) is a neurological disorder that becomes evident in early childhood or adolescence between the ages of 2 and 15. It is estimated that 200,000 in the United States have the disorder. Tourette syndrome is characterized by multiple motor and vocal tics that have persisted more than 1 year. Tics are involuntary spasmodic muscular movements or contractions, usually of the face or extremities, but may be vocal. Many people have only motor tics or only vocal tics. The first symptoms usually are involuntary movements (tics) of the face, arms, limbs, or trunk. These tics are frequent, repetitive, and rapid. The most common first symptom is a facial tic (eye blink, nose twitch, grimace), and is replaced or added to by other tics of the neck, trunk, and limbs. Tics may also involve the entire body (e.g., kicking, stamping). Many people report what are described as premonitory urges—the urge to perform a motor activity. Other symptoms such as touching, repetitive thoughts, movements, and compulsions can occur.

Verbal tics (vocalizations) usually occur with the movements; later they may replace one or more motor tics. These vocalizations include grunting, throat clearing, shouting, and barking sounds. The verbal tics may also be expressed as coprolalia (the involuntary use of obscene words or socially inappropriate words and phrases) or copropraxia (obscene gestures). Despite widespread publicity, coprolalia/copropraxia is uncommon with tic disorders (5%–15%). Associated conditions can include attention problems (ADHD), impulsiveness, oppositional defiant disorder, obsessional-compulsive behavior, and learning disabilities. Tics run in families.

Kadesjo and Gillberg (2000) studied school-age children in the general population as well as in a countywide tic disorder clinic, screening them for tic disorder, and found that from 0.15% to 1.1% of all children had Tourette syndrome. Boys outnumbered girls by 4:1 to 6:1. Attention deficit and ASD spectrum problems (including Asperger syndrome) were common, each type of comorbidity affecting approximately two thirds of individuals with Tourette syndrome. Overall behavior problem scores were high, and affected children exhibited a marked degree of functional impairment.

Although children with TS often function intellectually like their peers, they have frequent skill deficits. Children with TS are often slow to develop printing skills and have even more difficulty with cursive writing. Children with TS often prefer to print when writing cursively, but they have difficulty forming letters and stringing them together. In addition, children with TS press so hard on the paper when handwriting that they may inadvertently break the pencil tip. During early intervention, therapy activities that help coordinate muscles in the shoulder, arm, and hand and encourage eye-hand coordination and kinesthesia later improve printing and writing. As children grow older, appropriate use of tape recorders, typewriters, or computers to assist with reading and writing can be beneficial.

Habit reversal is among the techniques that have helped reduce Tourette tics in higher-functioning verbal children. One begins by making the child aware of when he or she is exhibiting the tic. Ask the child to look into a mirror while performing the tic on purpose. Discuss with the child how his or her body moves and what muscles are being used when performing the tic. Next, ask the child to identify when a tic is starting by raising his or her hand (in school) or by saying, "That was one" (at home) when the tic occurs. If the teacher or parent sees the child engaging in the tic and the child doesn't notice, the teacher or parent should signal the child with a gesture or expression that all have agreed on.

The child is asked to record each occurrence of the tic on a 3×5 index card. Keeping track of how often it occurs makes the child more aware of engaging in the tic and provides a measure of how he or she is doing. Next, the child practices a competing response—an action replacing the tic—each time a tic is about to occur. (Ask the child to write down the competing response at the top of the 3×5 card.) The muscles used for the new action make it impossible to perform the tic. For example, instead of repeated eye blinking, the child is encouraged to very gently close his or her eyelids and hold them closed for 10 seconds. To make it more likely the child will actually engage in the competing response, ask him or her to practice the competing response while looking in the mirror. This helps the child become comfortable with the response and assures him or her that the competing response is not noticeable socially. Encourage the child to use the competing response when feeling the urge to start a tic.

Habit reversal requires persistence. Although many children will notice a decrease in their tic within a couple of days, the greatest change occurs during the second and third month. Parents and teachers need to be vigilant and should not prematurely discontinue the habit reversal procedure after only a couple of days or weeks, or it is likely that the tic will return (Christopherson, 2004; Woods, Miltenberger, & Lumley, 1996; Woods et al., 2000).

Antidopaminergic medications are the most effective drugs in treating Tourette tics. Although Haldol and Orap are the only drugs currently approved by the FDA for the treatment of Tourette syndrome, other dopamine receptor-blocking drugs and tetrabenazine, a dopamine-depleting drug, have been used to treat tics. SSRIs are recommended for the treatment of obsessive-compulsive behavior, a common comorbidity of TS, as well as ASDs (Silay & Janovic, 2005).

Attention-Deficit/Hyperactivity Disorder

Difficulties with attention are nearly universal in ASDs. As a result, the *DSM-IV* definition of attention-deficit/hyperactivity disorder (ADHD) specifies that one should not use an ADHD diagnosis if the symptoms occur exclusively during the course of a pervasive developmental disorder (PDD). However, there is growing evidence that the two conditions often overlap within the same child and may coexist as separately treatable conditions. It appears the three types of ADHD outlined in Chapter 2 may occur in a child with an ASD: inattentive, hyperactive, or a combination of inattentive and hyperactive. Although some researchers have argued that high-functioning ASD is indistinguishable from ADHD, the majority of clinical researchers disagree. Children with ADHD usually display empathy and social understanding, they enjoy interacting with others, and their language development is often similar to that of their typical peers. If they display repetitive movements, the movements are qualitatively different from the movements of children with ASDs. Repetitive routines of children with ASDs may include hand flapping, twirling, head weaving, repetitive rocking, and lining up nonfunctional objects, actions which are rarely seen among children with ADHD.

However, ADHD signs and symptoms may be seen among some children and youth with ASDs. Goldstein and Schwebach (2004) conducted a retrospective chart review of children (N = 57) diagnosed with an ASD, a PDD-NOS, or an ADHD. Questionnaire and neuropsychological test data were used to determine the severity of ADHD-like symptoms presenting among children with PDDs. Twenty-six percent of children with PDD met *DSM-IV* criteria for the combined type of ADHD. Thirty-three percent met diagnostic criteria for the Inattentive Type of ADHD and 41% did not demonstrate a number of ADHD symptoms significant enough to warrant a comorbid diagnosis of ADHD. These findings are consistent with the common clinical observation indicating that some children with PDD also experience an independent comorbid ADHD, suggesting that a comorbid diagnosis of ADHD with PDD be considered in such cases.

Within groups of children receiving structured early intervention services, it is likely that some meet the criteria of ADHD, although outcomes have not been analyzed separately for them. Clinical experience suggests that children with ASDs and more severe attention problems do best when verbal prompts are minimized and visual schedules are used combined with task completion activities (e.g., completing five problems or sorting ten red and blue socks into matching colored containers). Although some programs for children with ADHD incorporate response cost components (a mild form of punishment), this is generally not a good idea when working with children with ASDs because they tend to perseverate about losing points or tokens following an outburst. Cognitive behavior therapy (CBT) may be useful for some high-functioning children with Asperger syndrome or PDD-NOS; however, the verbal skills required may exceed the limits of many children with ASDs. Video self-rehearsal and social stories may help some children with ADHD and ASDs become more aware of their actions and their effects on others.

There is some evidence that Ritalin, the most common treatment for ADHD, is also effective in treating ADHD-like symptoms among children with ASDs. Di Martino et al. (2004) studied the effects of Ritalin on the behavior of boys with a mean age of 7.9 years with PDD and moderate-to-severe hyperactivity/impulsivity. One hour after a single Ritalin dose

(0.4 mg/kg), 40% of the children exhibited hyperactivity, stereotypes, dysphoria, or other adverse symptoms, and received no further Ritalin treatment. Those who either improved or didn't change during the 1-hour test probe were given Ritalin in an open label trial. Measures of hyperactivity and impulsivity improved significantly, although ASD core symptom measures were unaffected. No significant adverse effects were observed in children who improved while receiving Ritalin.

Down Syndrome

Down syndrome is usually caused by a child's receiving three copies of Chromosome 21 instead of two copies, although there are some cases in which DNA from two chromosomes become intermixed. Rarer are individuals who have a mixture of cells in their body that have the normal number of copies of Chromosome 21 although others have trisomy 21 (called *mosaics*). Down syndrome occurs in 1 in 650–1,000 births. Children with Down syndrome are likely to have heart and gastrointestinal problems and hearing loss. They are at greater risk for developing a rare form of leukemia.

Dykens and Hodapp (1994) studied behavioral profiles and developmental trajectories of adaptive behavior among 80 children with Down syndrome ages 1 to 11.5 years using the Vineland Adaptive Behavior Scales. Profile findings indicated a significant weakness in communication relative to daily living and socialization skills. Within communication itself, expressive language was significantly weaker than receptive skills, especially when children's overall communicative levels were above 24 months. Fidler (2005) found relative strengths in some aspects of visual processing, receptive language, and nonverbal social functioning and relative weaknesses in gross motor skills and expressive language skills.

Children with DS are often described as easygoing, cheerful, and having few behavior problems. However, as with any other developmental disability, there are exceptions, especially among individuals with more severe intellectual disability. Starr and colleagues (2005) studied 13 individuals who had DS with IQ scores between 24 and 48, using ASD diagnostic tests to determine whether they met criteria for ASDs. Five of the 13 met formal diagnostic criteria for ASD, and most of the remaining eight exhibited some ASD features. Capone and colleagues (2005) studied individuals with DS who met *DSM-IV* criteria for ASD, a comparison group of DS who displayed stereotypy movement disorder (SMD), and typical DS controls without behavior problems (N = 44). They found the lethargy and stereotypy scales of the Aberrant Behavior Checklist reliably distinguished among the groups. Kielinen and colleagues (2004) conducted a population survey of ASDs in Finland, identifying 187 children with ASDs. Of those, 12.3% also had a known genetic syndrome, among the more common being Down syndrome.

Individuals with Down syndrome who have ASDs tend to be among those with lower cognitive abilities (see Miles et al., 2005). They typically receive augmentative communication and functional adaptive skills training rather than intensive early behavior therapy (IEBT). They are also more likely to receive psychotropic medications for their behavior challenges than higher-functioning peers.

Nonverbal Learning Disorder

Myklebust (1975) coined the term *nonverbal learning disorder* (NVLD) to refer to children who have a large discrepancy between their verbal skills, which often appear normal, and their visuo-spatial skills, which are much lower than their verbal skills. Much of the subsequent work on this condition has been published by Rourke (1989), although Denckla (1983) described what appears to be the same condition using the descriptor *right hemisphere non-verbal learning and emotional disorder.* Children with NVLD may begin talking about a topic that interests them, although it is obvious that no one else is interested, and will persist in talking about that topic well beyond the time that is reasonable. The children usually have poor peer relations, engage in immature, inappropriate behavior, and have difficulty understanding social situations. They don't understand emotional signals from others. They have poor handwriting and poor overall comprehension in reading. They tend to focus on parts of objects rather than wholes. They have problems reading maps or other tasks requiring an understanding of spatial relationships such as graphs or charts. They tend to have poor perceptual motor coordination and may appear "clumsy." They are distractible and have trouble sticking to a single task. Rourke and others believe that NVLD is a right hemisphere disorder. Others in the field believe that NVLD is actually the same as Asperger syndrome. Cederlund and Gillberg (2004) studied 100 males ages 5½ to 24½ years, with an average age of 11 years 4 months, who had a clinical diagnosis of Asperger syndrome. They conducted an in-depth review of their medical records and neuropsychological test data and found a high rate (51%) of nonverbal learning disabilities (defined as Verbal IQ more than 15 points higher than Performance IQ), but otherwise there was little or no support for the notion of right-hemisphere brain dysfunction being at the core of the syndrome. They found a high incidence of ASDs among the relatives of these subjects.

The suggested strategies for working with individuals with NVLD are the same as those one would use with a child with Aspergers syndrome. Simplify the learning environment, removing extraneous materials. Structure therapy or instruction with lists and picture schedules for younger children. Have the child check off each activity as it is completed. Be concrete, avoid abstractions, and make the consequence for completing a learning task clear to the child. Caregivers are encouraged to keep verbal instructions to a minimum. The child is likely to have difficulty sorting out what is relevant from ancillary information. Social skills instruction/therapy should begin by teaching the child how to show he is listening when people speak to him. A good second step is learning to take turns, which leads to sequential reciprocal interactions. Some children have difficulty knowing how loudly to speak, depending on the listener's distance, so practicing appropriate voice volume modulation at different distances can be helpful. Social stories and VSM can be used to teach the child which situations lead to specific emotions, and how a person appears when they are experiencing a given emotion (e.g., facial expression, gestures, posture). Medications for anxiety disorder are sometimes helpful for individuals with NVLD (e.g., beta blockers, SSRI antidepressants).

SUMMARY

ASD symptoms are common in some other disabilities, and in a significant percentage of some, those symptoms lead to a co-diagnosis of an ASD. Such individuals require appropriate health care and psychoeducational services for both conditions. In some cases, it may be difficult to arrive at a definitive diagnosis because some children and youth who have very limited skills and low intellectual functioning cannot be assessed using accepted diagnostic instruments (e.g., ADOS). In those cases, the lack of appropriate social and communicative skills may reflect low cognitive functioning rather than a comorbid ASD. However, among individuals with a mild to moderate intellectual disability who are reasonably cooperative, it is usually possible to distinguish whether the child actually exhibits ASD features.

10

Caveat Emptor
Cautionary Considerations for Parents and Practitioners

A man had been having headaches and blurred vision. He had a head and neck MRI scan revealing that he had a partially blocked artery in his neck, where it enters the right side of his brain. The man asked the doctor what the likely consequences were of a partial blockage of his carotid artery, and the neurosurgeon said that it posed a substantial risk of a stroke. Although it was strongly recommended by the neurosurgeon, the man decided that he didn't want to have surgery, and so he went to an acupuncturist, who inserted needles at various points in his body. After several acupuncture treatments, the man thought his headaches didn't seem as bad and that his vision may have improved. His neighbor mentioned that she had been having severe headaches accompanied by intermittent dizzy spells and weakness in one leg. The man suggested that the neighbor try acupuncture for her headaches. Most people would think that this is a ludicrous suggestion because it is possible that the man giving the advice may have a stroke brought on by the blocked blood vessel, and he has no special expertise as a basis for making such a recommendation. It is also possible that the neighbor with the dizzy spells, weakness in one leg, and severe headaches may have a tumor or other serious neurological problem.

But this example is equivalent to what goes on every day between parents of children with autism spectrum disorders (ASDs). How often have you heard one parent tell another, or a teacher tell a colleague, "You ought to give (*fill in the intervention*) a try. It works wonders." The person making the recommendation means well, but that person's observation regarding the efficacy of the intervention may be inaccurate, and the intervention may not be appropriate for another child. It makes no more sense for parents, teachers, or therapists to select interventions for children with ASDs based on anecdotal recommendations than for a woman with serious neurological symptoms to decide to seek acupuncture treatment based on her friend's recommendation. Important treatment decisions should never be based on anecdotes, rumors, or questionable information obtained from the Internet.

Some may object to the analogy saying, "A tumor in the brain could cause paralysis or even death. What bad could happen if we tried treatment X for our child's ASD?" The most important adverse consequence is lack of commitment to an effective treatment that is truly capable of enabling a child to communicate, develop meaningful social relationships, and reduce or eliminate repetitive behavioral routines that preclude participating as a member of his or her family, with peers and teachers in school, and in activities in the community. The second detrimental repercussion is that it is a prescription for cynicism and loss of hope. Parents and practitioners who adopt ineffective strategies and techniques have their hopes dashed, often repeatedly, and eventually conclude that nothing works. Finally, it unnecessarily wastes money and time when more effective things could be done to improve the child's life. Choice of intervention matters greatly for the future of a child with an ASD.

The field of autism treatment and education has had a long history of adopting interventions based on anecdotal information. Questionable treatments have abounded, some of which continue today. Some proposed treatments have pseudoscientific credibility while others emanate from the belief that inside every child with autism is an entirely typical child attempting to escape. Since 1944, when Bruno Bettleheim opened the Orthogenic School for children with ASDs in Chicago and urged psychiatrists to treat autistic children for what he assumed was suppressed rage at what he called their "refrigerator mothers," the field has been flooded with untested and unproven remedies and teaching approaches. One after another alleged cure, treatment, or educational method has been subjected to testing only to be disproved, but many persist to this day despite contrary evidence. That raises the question why the field of autism spectrum disorders seems so prone to attracting unsound treatments and educational methods when alternative methods of proven effectiveness are available (see Chapters 5–8).

SOURCES OF PARENT VULNERABILITY

Parents of children with ASDs struggle to accept their child's disability because onset is usually gradual and they are desperately seeking to find a way to arrest the progressive changes they see occurring.

Autism Is an Invisible Disability

Autism is usually diagnosed when a child is 2–4 years old. Many children with ASDs have no distinctive physical features such as those seen in Down syndrome or Cornelia de Lange syndrome (CdLS). As a result many parents find it very difficult to accept the idea that there is not a normal child residing within the body of their son or daughter with an ASD. They face a problem similar to those faced by the wife of a man in the mid-stages of Alzheimer's dementia who looks physically the same as he has always looked, and some days does things that appear similar to those he had done in the past, but he periodically exhibits serious memory, emotional, and behavior problems. It is very difficult for the man's wife to know whether her lifetime companion is "still in there" somewhere. The same is true of parents of children with autism, especially those with the regressive form of the disorder. They want to believe the child they had hoped for is "in there somewhere" waiting to come out.

Desperately Seeking a Solution

Although parents of children with genetic syndromes seldom believe there is a treatment that will reverse their child's Down syndrome or fragile X syndrome, that belief is common among parents of children with ASDs. This presumption makes parents of children with ASDs vulnerable to those who would abuse their trust by claiming that they have the cure for autism or a treatment that will dramatically improve their child's condition. Parents feel desperate and will give nearly anything a try. Once they become emotionally invested in a proposed treatment, many parents find it difficult to abandon the idea that the treatment won't return their child to them. Parents of children with ASDs are often very tenacious, insisting that a proposed treatment will eventually prove effective even in the face of overwhelming contrary evidence. When researchers present findings revealing the treatment to which parents are committed isn't effective when thoroughly evaluated, they are often accused of dashing the parents' hopes, being viewed with suspicion or hostility. In 442 B.C., Sophocles wrote of Antigone saying, "No one likes a messenger who comes bearing unwelcome news with him." Scientists believe they have an ethical responsibility to report their findings, even though the recipients of that information find them disappointing.

WHY PARENTS USE INEFFECTIVE TREATMENTS

Parents attempt to sort out the panoply of conflicting claims regarding treatments for their children. Those offering products and services often capitalize on the fact that parents are confused and vulnerable. There are several factors that contribute to parents' willingness to try treatments that have been disproved or are of questionable effectiveness.

Opportunists Capitalize on Parents' Vulnerability

Parents seeking a panacea will find that they are a dime a dozen on the Internet. Bogus interventions fall into two broad categories: 1) pseudoscientific interventions and 2) interventions clad in the attire of spirituality, humanism, or alternative holistic medicine. Pseudoscientific interventions appeal to well-educated, independent thinkers who are willing to take the time to read and digest articles stuffed with credible sounding scientific terminology. These parents are undaunted by reference to T-Helper cells, chelation, or probiotics. Pseudoscientific offerings are replete with details about hyperpermeable intestines, gamma globulin, antifungal and enzyme therapies, all of which have a very scientific ring. But the use of scientific terms does not make the claims scientifically sound any more than the use of terms such as *self-determination* make the person who uses them ethically responsible. The proof is in the pudding, not the cook's promissory pronouncements.

The second category of proposed interventions emphasizes humanistic and spiritual concepts. They are designed to appeal to "right brain" people, those with more artistic and spontaneous emotional temperament. These approaches are often presented as philosophical positions rather than specific treatment methods, but nonetheless may be appealing to some parents seeking a solution to their child's disorder. Some incorporate concepts from Carl Rogers' theories of self-actualization. Others propose using crystals, Ayurvedic and traditional Chinese therapies as well as spiritual meditation as interventions for ASDs. These therapies are often couched in the language of mind-body wellness or holistic alternative medicine. How these theoretical notions are practically translated into concrete actions to be employed by parents, therapists, or teachers and their consequences for the development of a child with an ASD are usually left to the imagination.

Few of these interventions has objectively demonstrated efficacy and very little information is available about the safety of some biomedical remedies in children with ASDs. The Internet is awash with questionable companies selling an inconceivable array of products and services alleged to improve cognitive, emotional, and social functioning of children with ASDs. Vulnerable parents are lured into trying remedies that end up being costly over weeks, months, and sometimes much longer. Parents hope the proposed remedy will help their child, only to discover they have been duped, wasting their money and their children's precious time that could have been invested in effective interventions.

Powerful Placebo Effects

Many remedies parents have tried produced minimal changes in their children's behavior. As a result, when they embark on a newly proposed treatment, the fact that it doesn't appear to produce striking changes isn't surprising to them. They reason that if they employ the new treatment sufficiently long, perhaps it will begin to work. Parents' expectations that a new therapy will help their child are very powerful. A study using a seizure medication also used to treat some types of bipolar disorder is a case in point. Some doctors have prescribed it off-label for behavior problems in ASDs. Belsito and colleagues (2001) treated 27 boys 3–11 years old with ASD diagnoses with Lamictal for behavior problems, using a double-blind research design. They used the Autism Behavior Checklist, the Aberrant Behavior Checklist, the Vineland Adaptive Behavior Scales, the Prelinguistic-ADOS, or the Childhood Autism Rating Scale to measure possible behavioral changes caused by the medication and found no detectable effects of Lamictal on any measure. Parents were aware of when their child was receiving the drug and when he or she was receiving a placebo. Researchers independently asked parents to rate their child's behavior when receiving Lamictal, and unlike the blind evaluations by trained professionals, parents reported marked improvement during medication treatment. It is understandable that parents would want to believe they saw improvements during treatment, but desiring a positive outcome is not the same as obtaining one.

Internet Parental Grapevine

Claims about effects of potential new treatments spread like an epidemic on the parental grapevine. The common belief among parents that most children with ASDs have immune disorders is a good case in point. It appears that a subset of children with ASDs may have an immune disorder that makes them susceptible to gastrointestinal and upper respiratory infections. A pediatrician colleague describes a boy for whom he cares who periodically develops bloating and diarrhea, during which time his behavior problems worsen. Other doctors had previously treated the boy with psychotherapeutic medications that had little effect on his behavior problems. After conducting laboratory tests of gastrointestinal bacteria and fungal growth, my pediatrician colleague treated the youngster with antibiotics to reduce the overgrowth of intestinal bacteria and the gastrointestinal problems and behavior problems disappeared.

When parents of similarly afflicted children hear about the successful treatment of the boy discussed above, they begin pressuring their children's doctors to treat their children's behavior problems with antibiotics. Most don't have an immune problem or overgrowth of intestinal bacteria. In most cases, the behavior problems of children with ASDs are socially based. Within days, transmission of rumors about an alleged link between immune disorders and ASDs spreads like wildfire on the Internet. Parental testimonials are reproduced on electronic mailing lists, passed on to others, and pasted on web sites throughout the world. A claim by one parent becomes a fact within hours and is a worldwide phenomenon within days, often on the basis of very little information and no evidence from a controlled study.

Skepticism About Pharmaceuticals

The general public has become increasingly skeptical about pharmaceutical treatments because they occasionally hear of prescription drugs being withdrawn due to potentially dangerous side effects. News reports of cozy relationships between pharmaceutical companies and some doctors have made matters much worse. The public isn't generally aware that all prescription drugs go through an elaborate testing process in order to come to the market, and drugs with significant problems never make it to the pharmacy. Although prescription medications must have demonstrated efficacy, their ability to reduce problem behavior in any given case is unpredictable, and they rarely solve the problem alone.

By contrast, over-the-counter herbal medications and dietary supplements are not considered drugs and therefore aren't required to undergo the same type of demanding FDA-supervised testing. As a result, there is no way of knowing whether they are effective or whether they would possess similar risks as prescription drugs if they had undergone the same type of scrutiny. Because parents haven't heard about these substances being withdrawn from the market by the FDA, they are left with the misimpression that over-the-counter supplements must be safer. What many parents often don't realize is that the FDA doesn't have information about the safety of herbal or other over-the-counter remedies, so unless there is a sudden well-publicized series of serious illnesses or deaths associated with a dietary supplement, there is no way to know if they are safe.

Delayed Onset

Some medications prescribed by doctors have side effects, and onset of positive treatment effects may be delayed. Some antidepressant medications used to treat anxiety and obsessive-compulsive disorder (OCD) in people with ASDs take as long as 4–6 weeks to produce optimal effects, but for the first 2 weeks may cause agitation, insomnia, and irritability in some individuals. Parents are understandably intolerant of treatments with such delayed onsets, especially if the treatment makes their child's behavior worse in the short term. Parents want prompt results and are often disappointed when those results are not forthcoming. That leads parents to search for a more immediate solution, even if that solution is a placebo.

Effort and Cost

Most effective interventions for children with autism are labor intensive, time consuming, and costly. Treatments appealing to parents or teachers are often presented by their proponents as quick fixes requiring little effort. At least initially, they appear to be less costly than many traditional pharmaceuticals or intensive psychological or educational therapies. The child is given pills several times daily. No other changes in the parents' lives are necessary. Some unorthodox biomedical treatments are administered months apart. Treatment in a hyperbaric oxygen chamber, although expensive, may seem less onerous for parents than having to carry out intensive behavior therapy activities daily.

PROBLEMS WITH INAPPROPRIATE AND INEFFECTIVE TREATMENTS

Several treatments have emerged over the past 15 years that grew out of preliminary studies that looked promising but could not be replicated. In other cases, treatments developed for other populations have been inappropriately implemented for children with ASDs. Focusing on ineffective treatments reduces the commitment to evidence-based practices.

Treatments Based on Preliminary Clinical Findings

Some treatments have been proposed by clinicians, who believed their remedy was scientifically sound, but it wasn't. Typically, those proposing the new treatment have a theoretical basis for their beliefs and, after limited testing in a few individuals, concluded that the treatment was safe and effective. Regrettably, their preliminary findings are often reported before the treatment has been subjected to more rigorous testing with properly diagnosed individuals, appropriate control conditions, and unbiased raters who are unaware of the treatment conditions. That is what happened with the use of Secretin to treat ASD symptoms. Karoly Horvath, a gastroenterologist, and his colleagues (1998) gave intravenous Secretin, a pancreatic hormone, to three children who, according to their parents, had an ASD. Dr. Horvath had not confirmed the diagnosis using standardized methods. The parents were aware of the treatment conditions, as were Dr. Horvath and his colleagues, none of whom were ASD specialists. The parents reported remarkable recovery from autism symptoms, which Horvath and his co-workers accepted at face value. A firestorm of demands by parents for Secretin treatment for children with ASDs ensued. After the initial report, 16 well-controlled, double-blind studies with carefully characterized groups of children with ASDs were conducted to evaluate Secretin's effectiveness. None of them found any signs of reversal of ASD symptoms as a result of Secretin treatment.

Treatments Developed for Other Populations

Several treatments have been effective for other populations or conditions and also have been claimed to be effective for people with ASDs without any corroborating evidence.

Facilitated Communication

Some interventions have proven helpful with other populations, and by extrapolation were inappropriately extended to children with autism. That was the case with facilitated communication, a communication intervention developed in Australia making it possible for individuals with severe speech apraxia and dystonia to communicate by selecting letters or words printed on a board with a pointer. People with severe speech and oral-motor apraxia are unable to coordinate mouth, tongue, and lip movements with exhaling air across their vocal cords to produce reliable word sounds. Individuals in Australia with apraxia who used facilitated communication had receptive language, responding appropriately to speech from others but were unable to produce speech. Most young children with ASDs have little receptive language and few have severe apraxia, and therefore the technique was not an appropriate alternative communication intervention for them.

After seeing facilitated communication at work with individuals with severe apraxia on a visit to Australia, an American educator returned to the United States and began using facilitated communication with individuals with ASDs. In this process, a "facilitator" supported the hand or arm of a person with autism, who is told to spell out a message using a list of letters, numbers, or words and a pointing device held in his or her hand. It is claimed that the facilitator helps individuals move their hands to the letter or word they wish to select but does not influence their choice. Proponents claimed that it enabled such individuals to communicate. Soon after the technique was introduced in the United States, claims arose that individuals with ASDs and severe intellectual disabilities used facilitated communication to produce complete sentences, including statements such as "I am not retarded," or sophisticated assertions about the legal rights of individuals with developmental disabilities. Parents of a 7-year-old girl with an ASD, who also had significant intellectual disability, told me that when their daughter started communicating via facilitated communication, she began creating poetry. They showed me some of her poetry, which they said had been transcribed by her teacher. Later in the conversation, they discussed their plans for where she might attend college. My heart was heavy when I realized the depth of their belief that their daughter, who had a severe intellectual disability, was actually very bright, creative, and destined for a professional future, all based on what her teacher alleged was the little girl's communication via facilitated communication.

A case in New York involved a 16-year-old girl with an ASD and no speech who had allegedly accused her father and both grandfathers of sexual molestation, using facilitated communication. The facilitator was apparently not aware that both grandfathers had been dead for many years. There was no evidence of any kind to corroborate the allegations. Both parents faced criminal charges—the father for the alleged molestation, and the mother for not reporting the father. The case was before the court for more than 10 months. A state judge's verdict was that the allegations made by facilitated communication lacked credibility and the charges were dismissed. Similar cases before the courts were dismissed as well. Subsequently, a series of controlled scientific studies demonstrated that facilitated communication is invalid because the outcome is actually determined by the facilitator. Although it appears that most facilitators were not aware of it, the teachers or speech therapists serving as facilitators were apparently responsible for selecting the letters or words, not the person with the ADS.

Hyperbaric Oxygen Chamber

Although *hyperbaric oxygen chamber* treatment can be useful for promoting healing of certain types of injuries, it has no established efficacy in treating ASDs. Hyperbaric oxygen treatment is approved by the FDA to facilitate healing of certain wounds and to treat carbon monoxide poisoning, thermal burn healing, and other physiological applications. Numerous clinics and treatment programs in the United States and Canada advertise hyperbaric oxygenation for treating autism, usually based on the claim that it increases blood flow to specific brain areas. Several manufacturers and distributors of hyperbaric chambers have been issued warning letters by the FDA for advertising the use of hyperbaric oxygen treatment for unapproved conditions, including autism, for which there is no evidence of treatment success. Hyperbaric oxygen treatment has known side effects including middle-ear damage, lowering of seizure threshold, pulmonary edema, and possible heart failure (Wang, Calhoun, & Mader, 2002).

Lack of Commitment to Evidence-Based Practices

The field of education has had a limited history of employing evidence-based practices. A dramatic case in point was the adoption of whole-language reading instruction by the California State Board of Public Instruction in 1987. It had previously been demonstrated in well-controlled studies that direct instruction focusing on basic reading skills (i.e., phonics and phonetics) was among the most effective methods for teaching reading, including to disadvantaged children. Optimal results are often obtained using a combination of direct instruction and whole language once students begin to read. In the mid-1980s, the whole-language theory of reading instruction swept through California. Over the next 8 years, following adoption of an exclusively whole-language approach to reading instruction, California's fourth-grade reading scores plummeted to near the bottom (Azimov, 1998). Most children must be taught to read through a structured and protracted process in which they are made aware of sounds and the symbols that represent those sounds, and then they learn to apply these skills automatically and attend to meaning (National Reading Panel, 2000). Lack of commitment to making intervention decisions based on solid empirical evidence was a costly mistake by California's educational policy makers.

ASD instruction has encountered some of the same problems in public schools experienced in teaching reading. Decisions regarding instructional strategies are largely left up to individual teachers and their special education supervisors within school districts, many of whom received their training prior to the 2001 publication by the National Research Council *Educating Young Children With Autism* (Lord & McGee, 2001). Some colleges of education continue to approach the selection of instructional strategies as a philosophical choice rather than one based on empirical evidence. At times, individual schools and entire districts adopt ASD educational strategies based on theories of typical child development and philosophies of education rather than on evidence of the strategies' effectiveness. Often school personnel select practices based on the personal preferences developed during their teacher training many years earlier, rather than on evidence of the effectiveness of the practices.

WHO IS RESPONSIBLE FOR MY CHILD'S CONDITION?

The mother of a child with fetal alcohol syndrome is aware that drinking during her pregnancy caused her child's disability, and she suffers the guilt that comes with that knowledge. Parents of children with Down syndrome know that failure of Chromsome 21 to separate properly during early cell division caused their child's condition.

Making Sense of the Unexplainable

We all try to make sense of important events that seem inexplicable. Tragic incidents that appear capricious are particularly troubling. Various cultures have different ways of arriving at an understanding of unexpected events that befall them. In the remarkable story, *The Spirit Catches You and You Fall Down* (Fadiman, 1997), a clash between Western medical understanding of the causes of a child's epilepsy and those of the Hmong culture in which epileptic seizures are interpreted as a sacred gift, are powerfully portrayed. The American doctors sought to find the physiological cause of the child's seizures, while the child's parents were grateful for the child's gift. When an automobile spins out of control on wet pavement and ends up in the ditch where it collides with a tree, the highway patrol may blame the driver for driving too fast, the driver may blame the automobile manufacturer, and the automobile manufacturer may blame the engineers who designed the highway. Someone must be responsible. It is possible, however, that they all are responsible in varying ways. We live in a world in which we believe each adverse event must be linked to a specific cause and to a person responsible for that cause. When a cause is not known, there is a tendency to assign a cause based on presuppositions, biases, and preferences. That has been especially true over the past decade in the field of autism spectrum disorders.

Searching for the Culprit

Parents of children with an ASD understandably do not want to believe that there was something they did that caused their child's condition. It is preferable to assume that perhaps some medicine the mother received during pregnancy, toxin exposure, an immunization containing a destructive virus or mercury caused their child's autism. Parents reason that the company that made the vaccine or the doctor who administered it must be held accountable for their child's condition. Perhaps, they think, some heavy metal or infectious agent remains in their child's body, and with appropriate treatment, the ASD will disappear. Chelation is among the most popular treatments to remove hypothesized residual mercury or other heavy metal that might be in the child's body, although there is usually no evidence that a toxin is present. As discussed in Chapter 2, controlled studies conducted to date indicate that this does not appear to be a viable explanation. But, as with other proposed treatments, antipodal information from controlled studies often angers parents of children with an ASD because it raises doubts about their belief concerning who and what is responsible for their child's condition.

WHEN IS A TREATMENT REALLY A TREATMENT?

The public is bombarded by stories about new treatments or educational methods for children with ASDs in the mass media and have no way of knowing whether they are really as effective as they claim to be.

The Mass Media Thrives on Man-Bites-Dog Stories

Reporters often produce television, radio, and newspaper stories in which a previously untested treatment being used in a local clinic or by a practitioner who is reported to have made remarkable changes for a child with an ASD. The story's lead often presents the local clinician as the little guy tilting the windmill of the scientific establishment. It often doesn't matter whether there is any convincing evidence that the treatment actually had anything to do with claims of improvement or recovery; what matters is how sensational the report can be made (Riggott, 2005).

Regrettably, reporters at times make no distinction between treatments of proven effectiveness and disproved methods. Two treatment methods are presented to the reader or viewer as though they are comparably effective alternative treatments, each represented during interviews with professionals from competing camps. The phenomenon is similar to news reports about global warming in which the impression has often been created that there are significant differences of opinion in the scientific community about the phenomenon, when the only dissenting opinions are those of a small number of scientists who are paid employees of large energy companies. In the case of treatments for children with ASDs, there is broad agreement among autism experts about the effectiveness of intensive early behavior therapies, selective serotonin reuptake inhibitor (SSRI), and atypical antipsychotic medications, although these facts are seldom included in news reports.

Evidence of Treatment Effectiveness

Parents, teachers, and other practitioners are faced with the difficult task of deciding when a treatment or educational method is really a treatment and when is it wishful thinking. Any intervention for which reimbursement is sought from federal or state agencies, or private insurance companies, should be expected to meet minimum standards of evidence of efficacy and safety. Parents who wish to spend their own money on novel treatments may find it useful to consider adopting similar guidelines. What can parents and practitioners look for in deciding whether claims that a new treatment is effective are sound? To determine whether a treatment is effective, it must be subjected to objective testing employing guidelines similar to the following:

1. *Diagnosis:* All the people receiving a test treatment that is being evaluated must have the same condition or disability. If three people are coughing, one wouldn't expect the antibiotic erythromycin to reduce the cough regardless of the cause of the cough. A person who has asthma or another who has an allergy would be unlikely to profit from an antibiotic. Only the person who has a bacterial infection in their lungs and bronchioles is likely to show improvement when treated with erythromycin. An herbal remedy is unlikely to consistently improve reading performance by three elementary school children if one has autism and is non-verbal, a second has poor vision and needs glasses, and a third has attention deficit hyperactivity disorder (ADHD). In testimonials or reports from poorly controlled studies, the people being treated are often not properly diagnosed. As a result, the people receiving the test treatment include an assortment of different conditions, some of which may be appropriate for the test treatment and others inappropriate. At the end of the day, there will be no way to know whether the failure to observe a consistent treatment effect is because the treatment truly wasn't effective or because some of the people receiving the medication had conditions that were not appropriate for the treatment being tested. ASD study samples are often mixed

by age, sex, degree of disability, and co-morbid conditions. It would be surprising if some of these factors did not influence the effectiveness of a given intervention.

At times, an intervention may be effective for a subgroup of people with an ASD diagnosis (e.g., those with Asperger syndrome or high-functioning autism who are verbally competent), but relatively ineffective for others. Proponents of treatments occasionally imply that a treatment that is effective with only a fraction of people is effective with all the people who have a similar diagnosis. When comparing outcomes across studies in which groups receiving treatments were not comparable, one must take care in concluding that one treatment is superior to another.

2. *Proper Controls:* One group of people is given the test treatment or intervention and a second group is given an identical appearing version of pill or similar appearing psychological or educational intervention that does not include the critical component thought to be responsible for the treatment effect. Alternatively, during one period, a person receives an intervention, although during a second they receive an identical appearing placebo, or a standard intervention that has limited effectiveness. By comparing the outcome under the two conditions, it is possible to determine whether the intervention had a real effect.

3. *Unbiased Evaluators:* Someone other than the person administering the intervention must judge whether there is any difference in the person's condition after the treatment, or if the two groups of people (i.e., one receiving the medicine, the other taking a placebo) really differ in outcome. If the administrator of the treatment is aware of when the person is receiving the active intervention and when that person is receiving a placebo or a control treatment, the administrator cannot evaluate the intervention's effects without bias. The administrator's hopes and beliefs about the intervention's effects may prejudice his or her rating, which means that an independent person with no stake in the outcome must evaluate any changes.

4. *Consistent and Valid Intervention:* The intervention must be dependable in quality, must be administered consistently according to established guidelines, and must be administered for long enough periods of time to have an opportunity to be effective. With educational or psychological interventions, the validity with which the intervention was administered has to be evaluated through independent observation (i.e., was the intervention reliably implemented as specified?). In medication studies, the correct dose must be taken regularly for a long enough period to have an opportunity to produce the necessary neurochemical changes to produce an effect. A preadolescent girl with an ASD and significant behavioral

challenges was prescribed an SSRI antidepressant. Her mother complained that the medication wasn't helping. When I inquired about the dose her daughter was receiving, the woman indicated that she adjusted the dose from day to day depending on how her daughter was behaving. In addition, she said that if her daughter had few problems for several days, she stopped giving her the medication. There would be no way of knowing whether the SSRI might have helped her daughter's problem behavior because the mother didn't administer it reliably in the prescribed daily dosage, which is necessary to produce a measurable clinical effect.

5. *One Treatment at a Time:* When testing effects of an intervention, usually only one treatment at a time is given. If two or more interventions occur concurrently, it is impossible to know which is responsible for the outcome. In medication treatment trials for participants for whom another medication has been given for an extended period for another reason (e.g., to control blood pressure), at times the second medication may be continued while testing a new medicine, but that has to be determined on a case-by-case basis depending on the medication being tested. Some medication combinations can be dangerous or even fatal.

6. *Starting or Stopping Other Interventions:* Other interventions may not be started or stopped during the period the test treatment is being evaluated. Diet, herbal medications, or speech therapy may also change the person's behavior and should be held constant through the period the test intervention is being evaluated. Some people adopt the "everything but the kitchen sink" approach, trying various combinations of treatment at the same time, or, worse yet, starting some and stopping others during the period they are trying to test the new intervention. With so many variables, there will be no way of knowing whether the new treatment is effective.

7. *Valid Quantitative Outcome Assessments:* Standardized ways of evaluating a person's behavioral and/or psychological condition must be used before, during, and after treatment, usually validated rating scales, checklists, or other proven paper and pencil scales for measuring medication effects. Impressions such as "He is doing much better" need to be supplemented by use of quantitative measures that have been shown in other studies to be sensitive to similar treatments. Usually, scales or tests broken down into specific areas of interest (e.g., irritability, agitation, anxiety) are rated or scored before, during, and after treatment. Sometimes improvement may occur in one symptom (e.g., anxiety) but show little or no improvement in others. At times, changes occur slowly, and general ratings such as "much better" or "worse" usually fail to detect smaller changes, which can be important. One of the most common problems in informal treat-

ment evaluations is the use of a single measure on one day before treatment and another single measure at the end of treatment. Either day may happen to be an especially good or bad day, which would constitute an inaccurate overall picture of change.

8. *Adequate Sample Size:* Finally, enough people have to be tested with the new treatment to be confident that the results weren't a spurious finding. Most parents who try a new proposed treatment for their child believe that they see a positive outcome and are often convinced that the treatment will work for their friends' children, who seem to have the same problem. The parents of a child given dietary supplements who appears to improve during intervention are likely to recommend that their friends who have a child with an ASD give the same supplements a try. Before concluding that a treatment is effective for most people with a given condition, it is important to try the treatment on a larger group of people who really have the same condition.

Failure to observe similar outcomes for most of the people tested does not deny the possibility of the positive outcome for those who saw improvement—their impressions may be valid. But it does alert us to the possibility that not everyone whose parents believe have the same condition will profit equally. Parents who are considering giving their child a new proposed treatment should know whether a promising new intervention is effective for those same problems among children with roughly the same characteristics in 20%, 50%, or 80% of those tested, and this can't be known until a large group of people is tested. If 80% of people tested show improvement, one has more reason to be optimistic about outcome. However, if only 20% of people tested show improvement, the treatment probably has a limited likelihood of working in a given case.

SUMMARY

The belief that a treatment will result in recovery or dramatic improvement of a child with autism despite all the contradictory evidence appears to be related to the phenomenon of cognitive dissonance first studied by the social psychologist Leon Festinger and his colleagues (Festinger, Reiken, & Schachter, 1956). Festinger and colleagues read a newspaper report about a group of people in Lake City, Minnesota, and the nearby town of Collegeville who seemed to believe the genuineness of extraterrestrial messages allegedly received by their leader, Mrs. Marian Keech (a fictitious name used in Festinger's report). Mrs. Keech was alleged to have received messages from spiritual beings on other planets called the Guardians. She said that the Guardians made messages flow through her hand by "automatic writing," and eventually a small but devoted group of followers gathered around her. One day, the Guardians were said to have sent a message foretelling a great flood that would encompass the Earth. Although the group members were upset at first, additional messages indicated that those who believed in the Guardians' lessons sent via Mrs. Keech's automatic writing would survive. Spacemen would arrive just before the hour of the calamity on December 21st and save them by evacuating them to another planet. Festinger and his colleagues traveled to Lake City, infiltrated the group, and waited to observe what would happen on December 22, when the world would remain unchanged. Their question was, What happens to those who believe intensely in an anticipated outcome when confronted with the dissonance of the prophecy failing? The psychologists hypothesized that group members in Lake City, who formed a tightly knit group around Mrs. Keech, would not be deterred by the prophecy failing. As a way of reducing their dissonance, they would actually strengthen their implicit belief in her genuineness, whereas the members in the neighboring Collegeville, waiting alone in their homes without a support group, would weaken their belief, possibly even rejecting the prophecy as being a hoax. When the predicted flood did not occur, Festinger's expectations based on dissonance theory were confirmed: The Collegeville members denounced Mrs. Keech as a fraud, although the Lake City members called a press conference to reaffirm their belief in Mrs. Keech's prophecy and continued in subsequent weeks to proselytize their beliefs to outsiders saying that God had spared the world this time, but that the people had better mend their ways. According to the Lake City group's reasoning, if their persuasion led more people to adopt their belief, that would validate their position.

Festinger argued that for such a process to occur, there must be firm conviction (e.g., immunization causes autism); there must be public commitment to this conviction (e.g., letters to the editor, presentations at conferences, testimony before committees); the conviction must be amenable to unequivocal disconfirmation (e.g., through empirical research by many investigators in different countries); such unequivocal disconfirmation must occur (e.g., numerous studies have failed to find such a relationship); and, lastly, social support must be available to the believer subsequent to the disconfirmation (e.g., a flurry of letters, electronic mailing list commentaries, articles, proclamations by parents continuing to contend that immunization causes ASDs). Their connectedness via the Internet for many in the ASD community creates a virtual support group similar to that surrounding Mrs. Keech in Lake City. There are scores of electronic mailing lists accessed by parents and practitioners on which one can nearly always find someone who reports that a remedy or method improved their child's or student's functioning. Mutual affirmation of the validity of their beliefs reduces cognitive dissonance arising from evidence that the treatment is ineffective or the alleged cause isn't really a cause of ASDs. They reason that if so many others agree that a treatment is effective, or that immunization causes ASDs, it must be true.

Insisting that a treatment for a child with an ASD will cure him or her or dramatically improve his or her condition in the face of overwhelming contradictory evidence may limit a child's access to a more effective intervention. It can also be a disservice to other parents who are misled into committing to an ineffective remedy. There is no dearth of cure-alls and nostrums from which to choose. It is truly a matter of let the buyer beware, caveat emptor. Parents are highly vulnerable to exploitation by unscrupulous purveyors of all manner of alleged remedies and interventions with promises of dramatically improved lives for children with ASDs. Some imply that cures are possible, and parents, feeling desperate, may resort to desperate measures. Some treatments have pseudoscientific roots, while others emanate from the belief that a typical child resides, waiting to be unshackled, within every child with an ASD. Various holistic and spiritual treatments promise improvements in a child's humanity, without providing a practical road map to guide parents or practitioners. Very few of these treatments do much to improve the children's functioning or the quality of their lives. Therapists and educators are often attracted to interventions that promise to be less time consuming, labor intensive, and costly. Quick fixes are nearly always illusory. The lack of tradition of employing evidence-based practices in some fields of allied health sciences and education continue to present challenges to the field. But parents and practitioners have an alternative. They can insist that purveyors of treatments provide reasonable objective evidence, following established clinical or educational research guidelines, when they attempt to convince others of the value of a proposed treatment. In the absence of such information, parents and practitioners are wise to be wary.

Appendix A

RESOURCES

Note: The Internet Uniform Resource Locators (URLs) listed for each resource were correct and active at the time this book was published. URLs change frequently and therefore readers may later find it necessary to use a search engine to locate some sites using the organizational name.

Organizations

American Academy of Child and Adolescent Psychiatry;
    http://www.aacap.org/index.ww
American Academy of Pediatrics; http://www.aap.org/
American Psychological Association; http://www.apa.org/
Association for Behavior Analysis; http://www.abainternational.org/
Autism Society of America; http://www.autism-society.org/
Autistic Society of Canada; http://www.autismsocietycanada.ca/
Autism Speaks; http://www.autismspeaks.org/
Center for Disease Control; http://www.cdc.gov/
Council for Exceptional Children; http://www.cec.sped.org/
Cure Autism Now; http://www.cureautismnow.org/site/
First Signs; http://www.firstsigns.org/
U.S. Food and Drug Administration Consumer Magazine; http://www.fda.
    gov/fdac/306_toc.html
Families of More Advanced Individuals with Autism, Asperger Syndrome,
    and Pervasive Developmental Disorder/Not Otherwise Specified;
    http://www.asperger.org/index.html
National Alliance for Autism Research; http://www.naar.org/naar.asp
National Autistic Society (UK); http://www.nas.org.uk/
National Institute of Child Health & Human Development;
    http://www.nichd.nih.gov/
National Institute on Deafness and Other Communication Disorders;
    http://www.nidcd.nih.gov/
National Institute of Mental Health; http://www.nimh.nih.gov/
Organization for Autism Research; http://www.researchautism.org/
United States Office of Special Education Programs http://www.ed.gov/
    about/offices/list/osers/osep/index.html?src=mr

PUBLICATIONS

Professional References: Books and Policy Statements

American Academy of Child and Adolescent Psychiatry Working Group on Quality Issues. (1999). Practice parameters for the assessment and treatment of children, adolescents, and adults with autism and other pervasive developmental disorders. *Journal of the American Academy of Child and Adolescent Psychiatry, 38*(12 Suppl), 55S–76S.

American Academy of Pediatrics Committee on Children with Disabilities. (2001). The pediatrician's role in the diagnosis and management of autistic spectrum disorder in children. *Pediatrics, 107,* 1221–1226.

Association for Behavior Analysis Autism Special Interest Group (SIG) Guidelines for Consumers of Applied Behavior Analysis Services to Individuals with Autism and Related Disorders Revision. Adopted September 15, 2004, from Cambridge Center for Behavioral Studies; http://www.behavior.org/autism/

Bauman, M.L., & Kemper, T.L., (2006). *The neurobiology of autism* (2nd ed.). Baltimore: Johns Hopkins University Press.

Filipek, P.A., Accardo, P.J., Aswal, S., Baranek, G.T., Cook, E.H. Jr., Dawson, G., et al. (2000). Practice parameter: Screening and diagnosis of autism: Report of the Quality Standards Subcommittee of the American Academy of Neurology and the Child Neurology Society. *Neurology, 55,* 468–479.

Institute of Medicine. (2004). *Immunization safety review: Vaccines and autism.* Washington, DC: National Academies Press.

Lord, C.E., & McGee, J. (2001). Educating children with autism. Committee on Educational Interventions for Children with Autism, Division of Behavioral and Social Sciences and Education. Washington, DC: National Academy Press.

McConnell, S.R. (2002). Interventions to facilitate social interaction for young children with autism: Review of available research and recommendations for educational intervention and future research. *Journal of Autism and Developmental Disorders, 32*(5), 351–372.

Simpson, R., deBoer-Ott, S., Griswold, D., Myles, B., Byrd, S., Ganz, J., et al. (2005). *Autism spectrum disorders: Interventions and treatments for children and youth.* Thousand Oaks, CA: Corwin Press.

Volkmar, F.R., Rhea, P., Klin, A., & Cohen, D.J. (2005). *Handbook of autism and pervsive developmental disorders, assessment, interventions, and policy* (3rd ed.). New York: Wiley.

Journals

Note: Journals with asterisks are autism-specific; the remainder include articles on autism as well as other disabilities and applied problems.

* Autism; http://www.sagepub.co.uk/journal.aspx?pid=105478&sc=1
Focus on Autism and Other Development Disabilities; http://www. proedinc.com/ Scripts/default.asp
Journal of Applied Behavior Analysis; seab.envmed.rochester.edu/jaba/
Journal of Applied Research in Intellectual Disabilities; www.blackwell publishing.com/journal.asp?ref=1360-2322&site=1
*Journal of Autism and Developmental Disorders; http://www.ovid.com/site/ catalog/journal/270.jsp?top=2&mid=3&bottom=7&subsection=12
Journal of Intellectual Disability Research; www.blackwellpublishing.com/ journal.asp?ref=0964-2633
Journal of Special Education; www.ingentaconnect.com/content/proedcw/jse
Research in Developmental Disabilities; http://www.elsevier.com/wps/find/ journaldescriptoin.cws_home/826/description#description

Books for Practitioners: Evidence-Based References

Bondy A., & Frost, L. (2001). *A picture's worth: PECS and other visual communication strategies in autism.* Bethesda, MD: Woodbine House.

Carr, E.G., Levin, L., McConnachie, G., Carlson, J.I., Kemp, D.C., & Smith, C.E. (1994). *Communication-based intervention for problem behavior: A user's guide for producing positive change.* Baltimore: Paul H. Brookes Publishing Co.

Handleman, J.S., & Harris, S.L. (2006). *School-age education programs for children with autism.* Austin, TX: Pro-Ed.

Harris, S.L., & Handleman, J.S. (Eds.). (2000). *Preschool education programs for children with autism* (2nd ed.). Austin, TX: Pro-Ed.

Koegel, R.L., & Koegel, L.K. (2005). *Pivotal response treatments for autism: Communication, social and academic development.* Baltimore: Paul H. Brookes Publishing Co.

Maurice, C., Green, G., & Luce, S.C. (1996). *Behavioral intervention for young children with autism: A manual for parents and professionals.* Austin, TX: Pro-Ed Publishers.

McClannahan, L.E., & Krantz, P.J. (1999). *Activity schedules for children with autism: Teaching independent behavior.* Bethesda, MD: Woodbine House.

Mesibov, G., & Howley, M. (2003). *Accessing the curriculum for pupils with autistic spectrum disorders: Using the TEACCH programme to help inclusion.* Oxford, UK: David Fulton.

Mesibov, G.B., Shea, V., & Schopler, E. (2004). *The TEACCH approach to autism spectrum disorders.* New York: Springer.

O'Neill, R.E., Horner, R.H., Albin, R.W., Sprague, J.R., Storey, K., & Newton, J.S. (1997). *Functional assessment of problem behavior: A practical assessment guide* (2nd ed.). Pacific Grove, CA: Brooks/Cole Thomson Learning.

Prizant, B.M., Wetherby, A.W., Rubin, E., Laurent, A.C., & Rydell, P.J. (2005). *The SCERTS model program planning and intervention: A comprehensive educational approach for young children with autism spectrum disorders.* Baltimore: Paul H. Brookes Publishing Co. *{Note: Though components of the SCERTS model have been studied empirically, there are currently no controlled pre-post evaluations of the efficacy of the entire SCERTS approach.}*

Quill, K.A. (2000). *Do-watch-listen-say: Social and communication intervention for children with autism.* Baltimore: Paul H. Brookes Publishing Co.

Siegel, B. (2003). *Helping children with autism learn: A guide to treatment approaches for parents and professionals.* Oxford, UK: Oxford University Press.

Comprehensive Treatment Programs and Individuals Providing Training

Vincent Carbone (Verbal Behavior); http://www.drcarbone.net/

Emory University Autism Center (Walden Model); http://www.psychiatry.emory.edu/programs/autism/

Institute for Child Development (NYSU Binghamton); http://icd.binghamton.edu/icdext/teach/561RS02.html

Lovaas Institute (UCLA); http://www.lovaas.com/

New England Center for Children; http://www.necc.org/

Princeton Child Development Institute; http://www.pcdi.org/

Relationship Development Intervention: RDI (Steven Gutstein); http://www.rdiconnect.com/RDI/AboutSG.asp

STARS School (James Partington; Verbal Behavior); http://www.behavioranalysts.com/

TEACCH (University of North Carolina); http://www.teacch.com/

UCSB Koegel Autism Research Center (Pivotal Response Training) http://kady.education.ucsb.edu/autism/

Major Autism Research Centers and Contact Information

Boston University, Boston, MA; Helen Tager-Flusberg, Ph.D; Susan Folstein, MD; E-mail: htagerf@bu.edu

Institute of Psychiatry, Kings College, London, UK; Michael Rutter; http://internal.iop.kcl.ac.uk/ipublic/staff/profile/external.aspx?go=10273

Kennedy Krieger Institute, Baltimore, MD; Rebecca Landa, Ph.D.; Mark Batshaw, M.D.; e-mail: owenska@kennedykrieger.org

Mt. Sinai School of Medicine, New York, NY; Eric Hollander, M.D.; Joseph Buxbaum, M.D.; e-mail: eric.hollander@mssm.edu

University of California, Davis, Sacramento, CA; Sally Rogers, Ph.D.;
e-mail: sjrogers@ucdavis.edu

University of California, Los Angeles, Los Angeles, CA; Marian Sigman,
Ph.D.; Daniel Geschwind, M.D.; http://www.autism.ucla.edu

University of Cambridge, Cambridge, UK; Simon Baron-Cohen;
http://www.autismresearchcentre.com/arc/

University of Goteborg, Annedals Clinics, Department of Child and
Adolescent Psychiatry, Goteborg, Sweden; Christopher Gillberg

University of North Carolina, Chapel Hill, NC; Joseph Piven, M.D.; James
Bodfish, Ph.D.; http://www.fpg.unc.edu/~NDRC/

University of Pittsburgh, Pittsburgh, PA; Nancy Minshew, Ph.D.; http://
www.pitt.edu/~nminshew

University of Rochester Medical Center, Rochester, NY; Patricia
Rodier, Ph.D.; Susan Hyman, M.D.; e-mail: Patricia_Rodier@mrmc.
rochester.edu

University of Texas Health Science Center at Houston (Affiliated Program)
Houston, TX; Katherine Loveland, Ph.D.; http://www.uth.tmc.edu/
schools/med/psychiatry/msi/chdr2/autism.htm

University of Utah, Salt Lake City, UT; William McMahon, M.D.;
http://utahautismresearchprogram.genetics.utah.edu/

University of Washington, Seattle, WA; Geraldine Dawson, Ph.D.;
Elizabeth Aylward, Ph.D.; http://depts.washington.edu/uwautism/
research/participation.html

Yale University, New Haven, CT; Fred Volkmar, M.D.; Ami Klin, Ph.D.;
http://info.med.yale.edu/chldstdy/

The Internet

Internet sites listed below provide useful, generally valid and trustworthy
information about autism spectrum disorders. There are also currently
more than 1,800 Yahoo groups devoted to autism and countless message
boards and forums. MSN includes a smaller number of autism groups.
These groups are not included in this list because of the great variability
in the information posted on these sites. Sites that are operated by major
organizations such as the Autism Society of America or federal agencies
are listed above by organization.

ASPEN; http://www.aspennj.org/index.html

Asperger's Disorder Home Page; http://www.aspergers.com/

Association for Science in Autism Treatment; http://www.asatonline.org/

Autism and PDD Support Network; http://www.autism-pdd.net/

Autism Resources (links); http://www.autism-resources.com {*Note: A relatively unselective list of several hundred autism links of varying trustworthiness.*}

Family Village; http://www.familyvillage.wisc.edu/index.htmlx *{Note: This highly reliable site, hosted by the Waisman Center at the University of Wisconsin, includes a wealth of information about a large number of disabilities, including autism.}*

Geneva Centre for Autism (Toronto, Canada); http://www.autism.net/index.php

Signs of Autism.com; http://www.signsofautism.com/

Appendix B

GLOSSARY

This glossary includes three categories of terms: technical, health, and education. Technical terms refer to behavioral or psychological assessment and intervention concepts and methods. Health terms refer to concepts and procedures used by state or federal health agencies (e.g., Medicaid) as requirements for reimbursement of services. Education terms apply to state and federal concepts and methods applied by the U.S. Office of Education and state departments of education. Health terms are indicated by the letter *H*, education terms are followed by the letter *E*, and technical terms are without a letter designation.

ABC Analysis: A record of events 1) occurring before a target response has occurred, 2) the behavior of concern, and 3) what happens after that target response has occurred. An ABC analysis is often useful in identifying situations giving rise to challenging behavior and what happens afterward that maintains recurrence of that response.

Activity Reinforcer: An activity made available to a child on completion of an educationally or therapeutically desired response that increases the recurrence of the desired behavior; for example, for many children with an autism spectrum disorder, swinging on a swing is an effective activity reinforcer following seatwork.

Antecedent Stimulus: Some aspect of the situation that sets the occasion for a specific response (e.g., Stimulus: "What is your name?"; Response: "Tom"). Sometimes antecedent stimuli set the occasion for problem behavior (e.g., Stimulus: "Put on your shoes"; Response: Puts fingers in her ears).

Antihypertensive Medications: Several medications originally developed to treat high blood pressure are also prescribed because of their mildly calming effects in autism spectrum disorders. Children who are "wired" and have great difficulty calming down before bedtime are sometimes given one of these medications, which are generally safe with few side effects. Among the more common are Tenormin, Inderal, and Catapres, all having mild antianxiety effects and reducing excessive arousal in some people.

Aphasia: Impairment in the understanding or transmission of ideas by language—reading, writing, or speaking—that is due to injury or disease of the brain centers involved in language.

Applied Behavior Analysis (ABA): The application of the scientific principles of behavior analysis to improving the behavior and functioning of people in a variety of applied settings. There is a common belief that ABA refers specifically to a type of therapy for children with autism developed by Ivar Lovaas. This is incorrect. Autism ABA therapies vary considerably and include verbal behavior, pivotal response training, incidental teaching, as well as Lovaas's discrete trial method. All employ the same common principles outlined in "Some Current Dimensions of Applied Behavior Analysis (Baer, Wolf, & Risley [1968]) but differ widely in details about how those principles are applied.

Asperger Syndrome: An autism spectrum disorder first identified by Hans Asperger in Austria in 1944. According to *DSM-IV* (299.80) children with Asperger syndrome have qualitative impairment in social interactions; restricted and stereotyped interests, which cause clinically significant impairment in social and other important areas of functioning; no significant delay in language development; and no significant delay in cognitive development or age-appropriate self-help skills. *H*

Assessment of Basic Language and Learning Scales (ABLLS-R): An assessment instrument developed by James Partington for determining baseline skill levels, for setting goals, and for monitoring progress.

Attention–Deficit/Hyperactivity Disorder (ADHD): Six or more of the symptoms of *inattention* or six or more symptoms of *hyperactivity/impulsivity* have persisted for at least six months to a degree that is maladaptive and inconsistent with developmental level. ADHD may be inattentive, hyperactive-impulsive, or both. According to *DSM-IV* criteria, a child with an autism spectrum disorder cannot also have ADHD, which many experts believe makes no sense because many kids with autism spectrum disorders appear to have ADHD as well. *H*

Atypical Antipsychotics: Newer antipsychotic medication with a lower risk of causing involuntary movements or muscle stiffness. Some atypical antipsychotics are effective in relieving the symptoms of schizophrenia, such as anhedonia and social withdrawal. Atypical antipsychotics are widely used to treat violent and self-injurious behavior in autism spectrum disorders. Examples include clozapine, olanzapine, risperidone, and quetiapine. Most but not all atypical antispychotics cause weight gain. *H*

Autism Diagnostic Observation Schedule (ADOS): A complex diagnostic procedure for differentially diagnosing autism spectrum disorders that was developed by Lord, Rutter, DiLavore, and Risi in 1999. The ADOS is intended to be used by experienced clinicians; training in their use is necessary. For these reasons, and because of its length, it is most appropriate as part of a comprehensive evaluation within specialty clinics. The ADOS assesses the diagnostic criteria of the current *DSM-IV* and *ICD-10* criteria and quantifies separately the three domains that define autism spectrum disorders: social reciprocity, communication, and restricted, repetitive behaviors and interests. It takes about 45 minutes to administer. Most experts consider it the "gold standard" in autism diagnosis.

Autistic Disorder: An autism spectrum disorder characterized by a combination of qualitative impairment in social interaction and communication and restricted repetitive and stereotyped patterns of behavior, interests, and activities, with an onset prior to 36 months of age. See DSM-IV-TR 299.80 for details. Autistic disorder differs from PDD-NOS (see below) in that the latter category is used when there is a severe and pervasive impairment in the development of reciprocal social interaction associated with impairment in either verbal or nonverbal communication skills, or with the presence of stereotyped behavior, interests, and activities. In other words, communication dysfunction and repetitive stereotyped behavior are not both necessary for a PDD-NOS diagnosis, but they are necessary for an autistic disorder diagnosis. *H, E*

Autism Spectrum Disorders (ASDs): A group of neurodevelopmental disabilities characterized by impairments in social relationships and communication, with excessively narrow interests and/or repetitive routines. ASDs include autistic disorder, pervasive developmental disorder-not otherwise specified, and Asperger syndrome. *H, E*

Avoidance: Behavior that leads to removal of a situation or stimulus that is unpleasant or disliked by the person doing the avoiding, prior to a major aversive event. Avoidance is negatively reinforced behavior. A child with an autism spectrum disorder who has had great difficulty in school may scream and tantrum when his mother tells him to put on his coat in the morning prior to leaving for school.

Back-Up Reinforcer: In a behavior therapy plan, a child's behavior may be immediately rewarded with check marks, stars, or points, which are then exchanged at a later time for a preferred activity or material reward. The back-up reinforcer is the consequence received at a later time when enough points, check marks, or stars have been earned.

Backward Chaining: Teaching a complex sequence of skills (e.g., in handwashing) beginning near the end of the sequence (e.g., drying hands on a towel), and then adding additional links to the sequence one at a time (e.g., turning off the faucet, rinsing hands, and so forth) until the child is able to perform the entire sequence from the beginning (e.g., turning on the faucet and then wetting hands) to the end (e.g., hanging up the towel).

Baseline: The performance level before any treatment has begun. Baseline may be a measure of how often a problem behavior occurs, or the percent of occasions on which a child responds correctly before therapy begins.

Behavior Therapist (BT): A therapist who has a minimum of a bachelor's degree or equivalent experience working with children with autism and/or related disabilities. They must also have a minimum of 2,000 hours of experience to be mental health professionals. BTs typically have had coursework in applied behavior analysis or related programming and supervised experience working with children using applied behavior analysis principles or techniques. *H*

Behavioral Contingency: The specific conditions that must be met for a reinforcer to be delivered; for example, every other correct response to a specified cue is rewarded with praise.

Checklist for Autism in Toddlers (CHAT): The Checklist for Autism in Toddlers (CHAT) is a screening checklist developed in the United Kingdom that consists of 23 yes or no items. Items pertain to social relatedness and have the best discriminability between children diagnosed with and without autism or pervasive developmental disorder. The M-CHAT, a revised version created for use in the United States, is a potentially useful instrument for the early detection of autism, but it is not a diagnostic test.

Childhood Autism Rating: A 15-item rating scale developed by Schopler, Reichler, and Renner for screening for possible autism. The Childhood Autism Rating is intended for children over 2 years of age. Physicians, special educators, school psychologists, speech pathologists, and audiologists who have experience with children with autism can be trained to use the rating scale. It is not intended to be a definitive diagnostic tool by itself.

Childhood Disintegrative Disorder (Heller's Syndrome): A form of autism spectrum disorder described by Dr. Theodor Heller in 1908 (hence it is sometimes called Heller's syndrome). The child develops apparently typically until 2–3 years, and then loses language, social, fine, and gross motor skills. Once the regression has begun, the child's behavioral characteristics are indistinguishable from severe autism. Some researchers believe it is a specialized form of regressive autism, although others contend that it is qualitatively different and more severe. *H*

Clinical Evaluation of Language Fundamentals (CELF-4): A language assessment test for 5–8-year-olds. Four subtests provide a Total Language Score to determine if a problem exists and whether a child qualifies for services. CELF-4 also determines the nature of the language disorder: the student's language strengths and weaknesses; receptive language and expressive language scores; and language structure, language content, language content and memory, and working memory scores. The person administering the test should be a licensed speech pathologist or psychologist trained in administering and interpreting the CELF-4.

Complementary and Alternative Medicine: Complementary and alternative medicine is a group of medical, health care, and healing systems other than those included in mainstream health care in the United States. Complementary and alternative medicine includes the worldviews, theories, modalities, products, and practices associated with these systems and their use to treat illness and promote health and well-being. Examples of complementary medicine are ayurvedic medicine, chiropractic, homeopathic medicine, naturopathic medicine, meditation, hypnosis, herbal therapies, special diets, orthomolecular medicine, massage, reikei, and therapeutic touch. *H*

Complex Autism: One of two major subtypes of autism associated with more severe disability, lower IQ score, more language and social impairment, more EEG and MRI abnormalities, subtle physical features that appear different from their family's (e.g., ears, teeth, spacing of eyes). Complex autism does not run in families. The male-to-female sex ratio is 3:1, although in essential autism the sex ratio is 6:1. Response to treatment is usually less favorable than essential autism (Miles et al., 2005).

Compulsion: An intense tendency to engage in repetitive ritualistic behavior such as hand washing, ordering items, or repeating words silently that aims to prevent or reduce distress or prevent some dreaded event or situation. The person feels driven to perform such actions in response to an obsession or according to rules that must be applied rigidly, even though the behaviors are recognized to be excessive or unreasonable. Compulsions in people with developmental disabilities may be less clearly related to reducing anxiety. Individuals with autism spectrum disorders seldom view them as unreasonable or excessive. *H*

Conditioned Reinforcer: A conditioned reinforcer is a reinforcer that gains its rewarding properties through repeated pairing with another reinforcer. For example, during initial familiarization with a child, therapists repeatedly pair themselves with other rewarding events and activities (e.g., tickling, hugging, sips of beverage, preferred food items). Hence, the staff takes on conditioned reinforcing properties.

Contingencies, Reinforcement: The conditions that must be satisfied for a reinforcer to be presented. Contingencies include stimulus events prior to a response, the number of occurrences and the timing of a specific response, and the consequence following occurrence of the specified response. Contingencies may be simple (e.g., when asked to say the name of a printed word the child does so, thereby earning a treat). Contingencies may also be complex, specifying how often a reinforcer is delivered over a period of time (e.g., a child is given praise following a desired response an average of once every 2 minutes, but the interval between successive praising may be as short as 30 seconds and as long as 5 minutes).

Contrived Reinforcer: A reinforcer that is not natural to a situation or the response being made. If a child requests "Milk" and is given a drink of milk, that is a natural reinforcing consequence that is logically tied to the response. If a child points to a picture of a glass of milk and says "Milk" and is given a penny as a reward, that is a contrived reinforcer that is not natural to the situation or the response that was made. It is usually less effective.

Developmental Delay: A chronological delay in the appearance of typical developmental milestones achieved during infancy and early childhood, caused by organic, psychological, or environmental factors. The term *significant developmental delay* refers to a delay in a child's development, in adaptive behavior, cognition, communication, motor development, or social development to the extent that, if not provided with special intervention, it may adversely affect his or her educational performance in age-appropriate activities. The term does not apply to children who are experiencing a slight or temporary lag in one or more areas of development, or a delay that is primarily due to environmental, cultural, economic disadvantage, or lack of experience in age-appropriate activities. A developmental delay need not lead to a lifelong developmental disability, although that may occur in some instances. *H, E*

Developmental Disability: A disability that is present at birth, or emerges early in life, which affects cognitive, social, language, psychomotor, and/or other functioning necessary to get along in life. Developmental disabilities are considered lifetime disabilities that require specialized support services. *H, E*

Diagnostic and Statistical Manual of Mental Disorders (DSM-IV-TR, 4th ed.). (2000). American Psychiatric Association. The DSM-IV includes the diagnostic criteria for the most common mental disorders including: description, diagnosis, treatment, and research findings. It is the main diagnostic reference of mental health professionals in the United States. A *DSM* diagnosis is required in order to be reimbursed for mental health services. *H*

Differential Reinforcement: Reinforcement of specific responses, but not other similar appearing responses, occurring after presentation of an antecedent stimulus. Differential reinforcement may apply to some aspect of a response, such as how forcefully it occurs (e.g., speaking more loudly) or how rapidly it occurs (e.g., within a certain amount of time following a request).

Differential Reinforcement of Incompatible Behavior: Reinforcement of a response or an aspect of a response that cannot be made while also engaging in a problem behavior. For example, reinforcing use of hands to button an item of clothing to reduce hand flapping; the child cannot button and hand flap at the same time.

Discrete Trial Therapy: Behavior therapy in which isolated opportunities for learning a skill are presented one trial at a time by presenting a stimulus (or cue) and reinforcing correct responding (e.g., pointing, naming) to that stimulus. Successive trials are separated by intertrial intervals during which no discriminative stimuli are presented and responses are either precluded or are not reinforced. Discrete trial therapy is useful when first beginning therapy with a child with poor attention and very limited skills, and when introducing a new, very difficult discrimination. As a practical matter, very few intensive early behavior therapy programs use discrete trial therapy methods exclusively throughout all therapy.

Discrimination: Responding specifically and selectively to one stimulus (or aspect of a stimulus) after a history of having been reinforced for doing so.

For example, a child's pointing to the red square and not a green square when a therapist says, "Point to red."

Drug: A drug is defined (by the FDA) as a substance recognized by an official pharmacopoeia or formulary that is intended for use in the diagnosis, cure, mitigation, treatment, or prevention of disease, and that (other than food) is intended to affect the structure or function of the body. *H*

Dyslexia: A specific reading disability due to a defect in the higher cortical processing of graphic symbols and their sounds. Dyslexia is different from reading retardation which may, for example, reflect intellectual disability or cultural deprivation. *H, E*

Early Childhood Special Education (ECSE): Early childhood special education must be available to pupils from birth to 7 years of age who have a substantial delay or disorder in development or have an identifiable sensory, physical, mental, social/emotional condition or impairment known to hinder typical development and who need special education. There are specific rules and criteria regarding 0–3-year-old and 3–6-year-old children. *E*

Echolalia: A form of speech common in very young typical children and older children with autism, in which the child repeats back to a speaker exactly what they have said verbatim. In many cases, echolalic verbalizations are repeated over and over, rather than just once. Echolalia may be immediate in response to a spoken utterance by another person or delayed (e.g., repeating a TV ad hours later). Echolalia is a form of speech but usually does not communicate information. *H, E*

Educational Activity: An educational activity is an activity that is typically part of a school's curriculum, such as reading, spelling, or math. Under federal Medicaid regulations of intensive early behavior therapy services, activities that are primarily educational in nature cannot be reimbursed. Intensive early behavior therapy is for the purpose of treating the core symptoms of autism, communication, and socialization and reducing repetitive focused interests and behavior. Whether an educational activity is taking place in a school setting or at home, it may not be part of an intensive early behavior therapy program plan. Intensive early behavior therapy can take place in school if the primary purpose is to improve and a child with an autism spectrum disorder's social skills and communication with peers, or to reduce repetitive fixed routines that interfere with the child's social functioning in school. *H, E*

Effective (Medical Treatment): Under the Kefauver-Harris Drug Amendments of 1962 (amending the Food, Drug, and Cosmetic Act of 1938), a drug is considered to be effective that has been designated as such by the Food and Drug Administration on the basis of "substantial evidence." Such evidence was defined by Congress as "… adequate and well-controlled investigations, including clinical investigations, by experts qualified by scientific training and experience to evaluate the effectiveness of the drug involved." Similar criteria are applied to other medical treatments. *H*

Electroencephalography (EEG): A method for measuring the electrical activity on the surface of the brain usually used to detect impairments such as epilepsy. Most clinical EEG machines have 16 or 32 very small circular electrodes that are taped to the surface of the scalp. The small electrodes detect minute changes in brain electrical activity that are amplified by the EEG device and translated into tracings on paper or a computer screen. The person feels nothing during the EEG test other than the electrodes stuck to his or her scalp. *H*

Errorless Discrimination Learning: Learning to respond differentially to two or more stimuli without making incorrect responses in the course of skill acquisition. Errorless discrimination learning typically involves beginning with an extremely simple discrimination that is well within a child's ability to perform, and then as skills improve, very gradually making the discrimination increasingly difficult—at each step making certain the child can perform the task with few if any errors.

Essential Autism: One of two major autism subtypes (cf. Miles et al., 2005) characterized by somewhat higher IQ score, better social and language skills, fewer neurological impairments, and generally better response to treatments. Children with essential autism usually exhibit no physical dysmorphic features. Essential autism runs in families and is much more common in boys than girls (6:1).

Evidence-Based Medicine: The conscientious, explicit, and judicious use of current best evidence in making decisions about the care of individuals. The practice of evidence-based medicine means integrating individual clinical expertise with the best available external clinical evidence from systematic research. *Individual clinical expertise* means proficiency and judgment clinicians acquire through experience and clinical practice. *Best available external clinical evidence* means clinically relevant research from basic or from individual-centered clinical research. External clinical evidence can invalidate previously accepted diagnostic tests and treatments and replace them with new ones that are more powerful, more accurate, more efficacious, and safer (Sackett, Rosenberg, Gray, Haynes, & Richardson [1996]). *H*

Extinction: Weakening a learned behavior by making certain no reinforcing event occurs following occurrences of that response. For example, a child has learned that if she cries at mealtime, her babysitter will give her ice cream. No longer giving her ice cream when she cries will be followed by an initial increase in crying (called an extinction burst) and then reduced crying; that is, it will extinguish.

Family Skills Training: A major purpose of intensive early behavior therapy is to enable parents to acquire the skills to promote the development of their children with autism spectrum disorders on their own. In family skills training a psychologist or behavior therapist works with the parents, teaching them techniques and procedures to continue their child's skill development in the absence of intensive early behavior therapy staff. *H*

Functional Behavior Class: A group of different appearing responses that serve the same function or purpose. A child may scream, throw food, and hit a sibling, all in order to gain the parents' attention. They all belong to a single functional class of "attention-getting behavior."

Functional (Behavioral) Assessment: A process that seeks to identify the problem behavior a child may exhibit, to determine the function or purpose of the behavior, and to develop interventions to teach acceptable alternatives to the behavior. The process is as follows: 1) identify the behavior that needs to change, 2) collect direct observational data on the behavior, 3) develop a hypothesis about the reason for the behavior based on the behavior's typical antecedents and consequences, 4) evaluate possible health or other social conditions that may be contributing to the behavior problem, and 5) implement a behavior intervention based on the foregoing analysis.

Functional Magnetic Resonance Imaging (fMRI): An image of living tissue at work; in autism spectrum disorders it is usually of the brain. fMRI is not usually done as a clinical diagnostic procedure, only for research and very specialized clinical purposes. A standard MRI device is used (see MRI below). An image of the brain at work is obtained while resting; then, following presentation of a stimulus (e.g., pictures of faces, spoken words), brain activity is measured again. The difference in level of brain activity when resting as compared with when being stimulated by a specific task, creates a functional image; that is, which brain structures are at work when processing the specific information in question. Several brain structures have been repeatedly found to be functioning minimally or not at all among individuals with autism spectrum disorder using fRMI scanning methods. **H**

Generalization: Responding to stimuli and situations that resemble those used during teaching or therapy, but that differ from them. Learning to respond to different therapists involves generalization across people. Learning to display the same response at home and school is generalization across situations.

Gilliam Autism Rating Scale: A 42-item rating scale describing the characteristic behaviors of persons with autism in the categories of stereotyped behaviors, communication, and social interaction. A structured interview form is used to gather diagnostically important information from the child's parents.

Imitation: Refers to reproducing the same response as that produced by a model. Imitation can be gross motor (placing hand on your head), fine motor (wiggling your fingers), or verbal (saying a word).

Incidental Teaching: Teaching a skill within the context of typical daily activities rather than at a table or in a more isolated situation designated for therapy. For example, teaching a child to appropriately greet the mail delivery person when he or she delivers mail, rather than practicing greetings in a separate room in a simulation of a mail delivery situation.

Individual Skills Training: Behavior therapists or instructional staff work with each child on goals mutually agreed on by parents and intensive early behavior therapy staff. The specific procedures employed are called individual skills training and are targeted at the core autism symptoms. Progress in individual skills training is monitored regularly by onsite staff. At least once monthly, progress is reviewed, and an in-depth review is conducted every 6 months.

Individual Treatment Program (ITP): An ITP is a detailed plan that addresses a child's individual needs based on measures of baseline skills (both strengths and weaknesses) that are designed to improve the child's functioning. ITP goals are stated in quantitative measurable terms. Parents and team members work together to develop the ITP. Parents are able to revisit the ITP for a given 6-month period, modify plans, and if progress is faster than expected, help set new goals. *H*

The International Statistical Classification of Diseases and Related Health Problems (10th ed., ICD-10): The 10th edition of a classification system of diseases, health conditions, and procedures developed by the World Health Organization, which represents the international standard for the labeling and numeric coding of diseases and health-related problems. Within this system, all diseases and conditions are assigned numbers in hierarchical order. There are small differences in the terms and criteria in *DSM-IV* and *ICD-10,* but in most instances they are of no practical significance. Services to children with autism spectrum disorders must be assigned *ICD-10* codes for medical reimbursement. *H*

Inter-Observer Agreement: Sometimes two people looking at the same situation may see different events occurring. When this happens there is little inter-observer agreement. All measures should be periodically checked by instructional or therapy staff who independently observe the child's behavior to determine whether they are seeing the same things occurring. Parents are welcome to participate as observers to obtain another independent measure of how a child's behavior is changing over time.

Interval Time Sampling: A method of estimating how often a problem behavior occurs by dividing the day into blocks of time (e.g., 15-minute intervals) and recording whether the behavior of concern (e.g., aggression) did or did not occur during a given block of time. This is called a partial interval time sample, which provides two kinds of information: 1) the number of blocks of time over the day that the problem occurred and 2) the time periods during which there were more or fewer problems (e.g., fewer between 8:30 A.M. and noon). That makes it easier to identify what seems to aggravate or reduce the problem (see Touchette scatter plot).

Kanner's Syndrome: The name for autism prior to the redefinition under the *DSM-IV* classification system. It was sometimes called *classic autism.* Leo Kanner was the first clinical scientist to describe autism among 12 children seen at his clinic at Johns Hopkins University in 1943. Kanner identified the three core symptoms of autism. *H*

Licensed Clinical Social Worker: A licensed clinical social worker has received a master's degree in social work from a program accredited by the Council on Social Work Education or a doctoral degree in social work and, either as part of the master's or doctorate degree program or in postgraduate studies, had a clinical social work concentration and completed supervised clinical field training. These social workers have competed 3,000 hours of supervised practice, including at least 1,000 hours of face-to-face client contact and *DSM-IV* diagnosis and treatment of individuals in not less than 2 years, approved by the social worker section. In addition, they must pass a state social work exam and the national American Board of Examiners in Clinical Social Work exam. Clinical social workers specialize in assisting clients with mental health concerns connected with necessary services as well as providing direct mental health services themselves.

Licensed Psychological Practitioner: Some states also license individuals who have earned a master's or doctoral degree or the equivalent of a master's degree in a doctoral program with a major in psychology from a regionally accredited educational institution meeting the standards the State Board of Psychology has established by rule, including successful completion of the required predegree supervised professional experience. They must pass the national and state board examinations. Licensed psychological practitioners must be supervised by a licensed psychologist (1 hour per every 20 hours of client contact).

Licensed Psychologist: A licensed psychologist has completed a Ph.D. or PsyD from an accredited doctoral program in psychology. He or she must have completed an approved internship and postdoctoral practicum (a minimum of one year) and must pass state and national examinations of the Association of State and Provincial Boards of Psychology and the State Board of Psychology.

Magnetic Resonance Imaging (MRI): A method used to visualize the structure of living tissue. In children with an autism spectrum disorder, an MRI is usually taken of the brain. The device uses a large magnet surrounding the person to detect changes in the orientation of water molecules in tissue, which is what creates the image. MRI is effective in imaging soft tissue, but X-rays or CT scans are usually better for bone. MRI may not always distinguish between tumor tissue and edema fluid. A structural MRI will not indicate how well brain tissue is functioning—only the location of specific structures and whether there appears to be any impairments (see fMRI). *H*

Maintenance: Intermittent practice and reinforcement of a learned skill to assure that it will continue to be exhibited in daily life at home, school, and in the community.

Modeling: A therapy method in which another person demonstrates the form of response that is defined as correct (e.g., eating with a spoon). This serves as the cue for the child's response, which is to reproduce the same response form as closely as possible. Modeling is a good method for refining the skill level of a response that the child already is attempting.

Mood Stabilizer: A medication given to prevent excessive mood swings, either mania or depression, in individuals with bipolar disorder. Examples include lithium, Tegretol, and Depakote. *H*

Multiple Disabilities (Dual Diagnosis): The diagnosis of more than one disorder or disability within a single individual. There is typically one disability defined as the primary disability (e.g., autism) and secondary disabilities that affect the expression of the primary disability (e.g., specific language disorder, obsessive-compulsive disorder). *H*

Natural (Intrinsic) Consequences: Consequences of a child's behavior that are logically related to their actions. When a child puts on her clothing in the morning, she can go outdoors and play. Playing outdoors is a natural consequence. Contrived consequences have no logical relation to the behavior displayed. When a child puts on her clothes in the morning, her mom gives her a candy, which has no logical relation to dressing. Natural consequences usually are more effective in maintaining a child's behavior.

Negative Reinforcer: An aversive event whose removal following a child's response increases the likelihood of that behavior occurring again under the same circumstances. If a child dislikes speech therapy and slaps her face on entering the therapist's room, the therapist is unlikely to force her into participating in speech therapy. The child leaves and has avoided speech therapy. *{Note:* Negative reinforcement is NOT the same as punishment.}

Observational Learning: Observational learning is similar to modeling in that the child learns components of skills and consequences that will be forthcoming by observing another person. It differs in that the child is not necessarily imitating a specific response pattern (e.g., how to hold a pencil, button a blouse). Instead, the child is learning a general method for overcoming an obstacle or obtaining a desired consequence. A child with autism spectrum disorders may learn from watching another child at school how to request assistance in the classroom.

Obsessions: Obsessions 1) are recurrent and persistent thoughts, impulses, or images that are inappropriate and that cause marked anxiety or distress; 2) the thoughts, impulses, or images are not simply excessive worries about real-life problems; 3) the person attempts to ignore or suppress such thoughts, impulses, or images, or to neutralize them with some other thought or action; 4) in typical populations the person recognizes that the obsessional thoughts, impulses, or images are a product of his or her own mind (not imposed from without), but people with autism spectrum disorders generally do not recognize that the recurring thoughts or fears arise from within. *H*

Occupational Therapy: The evaluation, planning, and implementation of a program of purposeful activities to develop or maintain adaptive skills necessary to achieve the maximal physical and mental functioning of the individual in his or her daily pursuits. Occupational therapy includes evaluation and treatment of developmental impairments, play, and leisure performance; the use of manual and creative activities; guidance in the selection and use of adaptive equipment; and specific exercises to enhance functional performance. Occupational therapy is conducted by licensed occupational therapists and occupational therapy assistants. Occupational therapists must have attained a bachelor's degree from an accredited American Occupational Therapy Association program or have completed educational preparation deemed equivalent and not less than 24 weeks of supervised field work.

Overcorrection: Following a child's response that has disruptive effects on the environment—for example, intentionally throwing a cup of juice—a child may be required to not only clean up the juice from the floor, but to also wipe the kitchen table and the kitchen countertops. Cleaning up the juice from the floor would be "correction," the other cleaning tasks would be "overcorrection." This aversive method is often counterproductive, not very effective, and not recommended.

Panic Attacks: Discrete periods of sudden onset of intense apprehension, fearfulness, or terror. During these attacks there are symptoms such as shortness of breath or smothering sensations, palpitations, pounding heart, or accelerated heart rate, chest pain or discomfort, choking, and fear of losing control. Panic attacks may be unexpected (uncued), in which the onset of the attack is not associated with a situational trigger and instead occurs "out of the blue"; situationally bound, in which the panic attack almost invariably occurs immediately on exposure to, or in anticipation of, a situational trigger ("cue"); or situationally predisposed, in which the panic attack is more likely to occur on exposure to a situational trigger but is not invariably associated with it. Some children with autism spectrum disorders are prone to panic attacks, but they are difficult to diagnose due to the child's lack of ability to report how he or she feels. *H*

Pediatrician, Developmental Behavioral: Developmental pediatricians have completed requirements for an M.D., a general pediatrics residency, and then a 2-year fellowship (advanced training) in children's developmental problems, especially developmental disabilities. Some developmental behavioral pediatricians emphasize developmental problems similar to mental health disorders, such as ADHD, dyslexia, autism spectrum disorders, tantrums, and so forth, although others focus on neurological aspects of developmental disorders (e.g., epilepsy, cerebral palsy, hearing, visual problems). In identifying the most appropriate doctor for their child, parents should seek information about the primary scope of the practice of the pediatrician they are considering. *H*

Pediatrician, General: An M.D. with additional training in the primary care for children between the ages of newborn and 17 years. Many general pediatricians have had very little training or experience with autism. Their primary practice will be general medical problems such as ear infections, gastrointestinal problems, sleep difficulties, and other general health problems. *H*

Phobia: A persistent, irrational fear of a specific object, activity, or situation (the phobic stimulus) that results in a compelling desire to avoid it. This often leads either to avoidance of the phobic stimulus or to enduring it with dread. In children with autism spectrum disorders, phobias may result from a single experience with a frightening stimulus, such as an aggressive dog. *H*

Positive Behavior Support: The application of a behaviorally based systems approach to enhancing the capacity of families, schools, and communities to design effective environments that improve the link between evidence-based practices and the environments in which an individual is educated, works, or lives. Attention is focused on creating and sustaining primary (schoolwide or company wide), secondary (classroom, residence), and tertiary (individual) supports that improve personal, health, social relationships, family life, and recreational activities for all individuals with behavioral challenges by making problem behavior less effective, efficient, and relevant and desired behavior more functional. *E*

Positive Reinforcer: A commodity or an event presented following a child's response that increases the likelihood of that behavior occurring again under the same circumstances.

Premack Principle: Access to a higher likelihood activity will serve as a reinforcer for performing a less likely activity. Sometimes called "Grandma's Rule"; that is, "You can go out to play as soon as you clean up your room." The principle was introduced by psychologist David Premack.

Preschool Language Scale: The preschool language scale provides measures of developmental milestones, primarily measures of young children's receptive and expressive language. For younger children it focuses on interaction, attention, and vocal/gestural behaviors, although for 5- and 6-year-olds, there are more items targeting early literacy and phonological awareness skills that tap school readiness. The preschool language scale includes a caregiver questionnaire in which parents or caregivers share their knowledge of the child's typical communication at home. It requires 20–45 minutes and graduate training in testing and interpretation of assessments.

Primary Reinforcer: Something (usually a commodity) that is reinforcing without any prior experience and which tends to be universal across people. When a child has gone without the primary reinforcer in question for some time (e.g., hasn't eaten since breakfast) the value of the reward increases (e.g., a snack at 10:30 A.M.). The most common examples are foods or beverages. In practice, nearly all reinforcers used in behavior therapy are "learned" in the sense that children have had experience with them and they are often associated with pleasurable activities, such as having dessert at mealtime, treats at a restaurant, cake at a birthday party, and so forth.

Prior Authorization: Legal authorization that is requested by a service provider of a state funding agency or insurance company to begin services to a child. If services begin without a prior authorization, it is possible that the funding agency may not agree to pay for the provided services. Prior authorization requests must be accompanied by an individual treatment plan that justifies the number of hours of specific types of services. *H*

Probe: Presentation of a few trials with a new stimulus or task, embedded within a block of familiar trials, to determine whether the child has the ability to display the skill in question. Alternatively, after a skill has been trained and is in a maintenance phase, periodically a test trial is conducted to determine whether the skill is maintained. In both cases, the single or small number of test trials are called probes.

Professional Boundaries: Professional boundaries refer to the appropriate relationships between therapy and instructional staff and the child, parents, and other family members. Professional boundaries are spelled out in the code of ethics of the licensed psychologist supervising services, and by the agencies that fund services. While staff working in a family's home, or working closely with the family through a school program, usually develop close, warm relationships with the family, it is important to maintain a professional rather than a personal relationship between family and staff.

Risks to professional boundaries include: 1) contacts between staff and the family outside of the therapy situation (e.g., going out to dinner together, attending family events); 2) accepting or exchanging gifts other than very small items on the child's birthday; 3) discussion and disclosure of personal information by the therapist to the family (e.g., about relationship with boyfriend or parents) or by the family to the therapy staff (e.g., intimate marital matters); 4) therapy staff performing non-therapy tasks for the family, either as a favor or for pay (e.g., babysitting, household chores, transporting the child).

Staff members who violate professional boundaries are usually reprimanded or dismissed, depending on the seriousness of the infraction. In home-based services, parent behavior that is interpreted by staff members as inappropriate, such as sexual remarks, suggestive comments about appearance, or attempts to impose personal religious or other beliefs on staff members, will lead to a warning and if continued may lead to discontinuation of services. *H, E*

Progress Notes: At the conclusion of each shift, one staff member who has been the lead person on that shift is required to record in writing the beginning time, end time, the nature of activities undertaken during that shift, an indication of the child's progress, and suggestions for changes or things to which staff in the next shift should be alerted. At each six-month submission of an individual treatment plan prior authorization request to the Department of Human Services, samples of progress notes must be included for review. *H*

Prompt: A stimulus (verbal, gestural, or manual) presented to a child designed to assist in initiating a desired response. During initial therapy, prompts often involve manual guidance and/or gestures such as pointing. As therapy progresses, prompts become largely verbal. As skill levels increase, verbal prompts are gradually faded both in time (e.g., the therapist waits longer to give the child an opportunity to respond) and intensity (e.g., therapist may say the prompt more quietly).

Punishment, Negative: Removal of a desired positive reinforcer immediately following a challenging behavior in an effort to reduce the recurrence of the undesired response—for example, turning off a video game.

Punishment, Positive: Presenting an unpleasant stimulus immediately following an undesirable behavior—for example, spanking. Positive punishment procedures are prohibited in most programs.

Receptors, Neurochemical: Chemically defined areas of a cell (specialized protein) that initiate a biological response on uniting with chemically complementary areas of natural neurochemicals or drugs.

Regressive Autism: Approximately 30% of children with autism appear to have been developing relatively typically until 18 months to 2 years of age; then over a period of weeks or months, their skills decline and they develop progressively increasing symptoms of autism. The cause(s) of such regressive autism are unknown. Children with regressive autism appear to respond similarly to therapy and have prognoses similar to other children who had symptoms of autism within the first year of life. Regressive autism is more common in essential autism. *H*

Reinforcement, Negative: Removal of a stimulus following a response making it likely that the child will repeat that response in the future under the same circumstances. For example, a child learns that if he screams and covers his ears when he is asked to respond to his parents' requests, they stop making demands. Screaming and covering his ears is negatively reinforced.

Reinforcement, Positive: Consequences of a child's behavior that increase the likelihood that it will occur again in the future under similar circumstances. For example, parents' praise and hugs may increase the recurrence of helping set the table.

Reinforcer Menu: A printed, handwritten, or visual list of images of possible reinforcing commodities or activities that is made available to a child following completion of a desired response.

Reinforcer Sampling: During initial development of a child's therapy program, behavior therapists and senior behavior therapists expose the child to a variety of commodities and activities that have the potential for serving as reinforcers. Those that are effective in strengthening the child's behavior in learning specific skills are retained as part of the child's reinforcement menu.

Reinforcer Survey: (see Reinforcer Sampling)

Relationship Development Intervention (RDI): A therapy developed by Steven Gutstein, Ph.D., a clinical psychologist based in Houston, TX. It emphasizes the importance of the relationship between parents and child (see http://www.rdiconnect.com/RDI/).

Response Cost: A procedure intended to reduce challenging behavior by attaching a cost to making the undesired response—that is, removal of a reinforcer. It is similar to time out, except that instead of entirely eliminating access to positive reinforcement for a period of time, points or tokens are taken away contingent on the problem behavior. Frequently, a power struggle emerges between the child and adult as each attempt to remove a token occurs, which may lead to further problem behavior.

Response Topography: The form and appearance of a response. Usually the form of a response, such as fussing, hitting a sibling, and making repeated noises, is less important than the function it serves, such as avoiding a task. Several response topographies may be very different but serve the same purpose, and may all serve the same purpose of demanding adult attention. They have different topographies but serve the same function and belong to the same response class.

Selective Serotonin Reuptake Inhibitor (SSRI): A medication used to treat anxiety and depression that produces its effects in part by increasing the amount of serotonin that is available in the brain. It does so by preventing the recycling of serotonin molecules (called re-uptake) into brain cells. SSRI's have numerous other effects as well. They are widely used to reduce anxiety and compulsive behavior in children and adults with autism spectrum disorders. Their main side effects are insomnia, nausea, agitation, and increased irritability during the first week or two of treatment. There is usually a 2–4 week delay between the beginning of treatment with an SSRI and visible therapeutic effects. SSRIs generally have fewer side effects than the older tricyclic antidepressants. Common SSRIs are Prozac, Paxil, and Celexa. *H*

Self-Injury (Self-Injurious Behavior): Repetitive behavior similar to stereotypies often occurring many times per day that causes (or may cause) damage to the body of the person engaging in the behavior. Self-injury is most common among people with autism spectrum disorders, fragile X syndrome, Cornelia de Lange syndrome, and individuals with severe intellectual disabilities. Common examples are head hitting and hand-biting. Self-injury is not the same as occasional self-harm by people with schizophrenia, borderline personality disorder, or other psychotic conditions.

Sensory Integration Therapy: The term "sensory integration" was coined by Jean Ayres, who assumed that each sense works with the others to form a composite picture of who we are physically, where we are, and what is going on around us. She proposed that sensory integration is the brain function responsible for producing this composite picture. It is the organization of sensory information for on-going use (see Ayres, 1979). None of the interventions based on this theory has produced lasting changes in the functions among children with autism spectrum disorders that they are alleged to correct according to the National Academy of Sciences report *Educating Young Children with Autism*. *E*

Serotonin: A brain chemical transmitter or messenger that carries information from one nerve cell to another. Serotonin is elevated in brain tissue from some people with autism spectrum disorders due to reduced number of receptors to which serotonin can bind; that is, the brain attempts to compensate for fewer receptors by making more serotonin. Serotonin abnormalities are associated with depression, anxiety, and sleep difficulties. A chemical precursor to serotonin, tryptophan, is found in chicken, turkey, most meats, milk, tuna fish, soybeans, cabbage, kidney beans, lima beans, oats, pistachios, poppy seed, pumpkin seed, spinach, wheat, and evening primrose seed. Foods high in tryptophan promote sleep by increasing brain serotonin.

Shaping: Reinforcing approximations to the correct topography of response in a series of successive approximations. Shaping is a useful way of refining the form and accuracy of a response.

Speech-Language Pathologist (SLP): A specialist who evaluates and treats communication disorders. An SLP is sometimes called a speech therapist or speech pathologist. SLPs usually have an M.A. in their specialty, as well as a Certificate of Clinical Competence (CCC) earned by working under supervision. Some states also require a state license and examination. *H, E*

Stereotyped Movements: Repetitive, seemingly driven, and nonfunctional motor behavior (e.g., hand shaking or waving, body rocking, head banging, mouthing of objects, self-biting, picking at skin or body orifices, hitting one's own body). Sometimes people in the autism spectrum disorders field have called them "self-stims" or "stims," which has the unfortunate effect of seeing them as independent behavior rather than as part of the overall adaptive and maladaptive coping behavior of the individual. Stereotypies are most common during prolonged periods of boredom and intense excitement or anxiety. At times self-stimulation is an avoidance response as well. *H*

Supervising Psychologist: Under most state guidelines, home or private center-based intensive early behavior therapy must be supervised by a qualified licensed psychologist or licensed psychological practitioner who is credentialed by the relevant state agency and the other insurance companies reimbursing such services. Supervising psychologists must have specific training in, and knowledge of, autism spectrum disorders and must have clinical experience designing, implementing, and supervising psychological services to children with autism spectrum disorders. *H*

Task Analysis: A complex task is broken down into a series of sub-components, each of which can be taught individually and then combined.

Theory of Mind (Mind Blind): A complex discrimination based on verbal and visual information obtained from speech and facial expressions of others. The ability to ascribe thoughts, desires, knowledge, and intentions to other people based on a history of having correctly drawn inferences about those private events in the past. The term "mind blindness" was coined by Simon Baron-Cohen to refer to this impairment in autism spectrum disorders (see Baron-Cohen, Cosmides, & Tooby [1997]).

Time Out: Withdrawal of the opportunity to earn positive reinforcement for some period of time following a problem response. Time out is only meaningful if the situation from which the child is being "timed out" is rich with positive reinforcement. If the situation is one the child dislikes and in which he or she earns few reinforcers, removing the child to a separate area (e.g., behind a screen) isn't time out.

Time Sampling: Recording how often a specific behavior occurs over a period of time, usually broken down into short observation periods (e.g., 5 minutes per hour).

Token Reinforcement: Any tangible immediate reinforcer provided following a desired response that is accumulated and then exchanged for a back-up reinforcer at a later time. Tokens may be check marks, stars, beans in a jar, or actual physical tokens. Token reinforcement is used when providing a tangible reinforcer (e.g., food in the midst of a therapy activity such as talking) or providing access to a preferred play activity would disrupt the ongoing therapy.

Touchette Scatter Plot: A given observation period (e.g., the school day) is broken down into 15- or 60-minute blocks, and anytime a specific target behavior occurs, a mark is made in the appropriate time block. At the end of the day, the result is a record of the pattern of instances of problem behavior by time of day. It is an inexpensive way of identifying high probability problem periods.

Tricyclic Antidepressants (TCAs): An older group of antidepressants that are effective in treating depression and anxiety disorders such as obsessive-compulsive disorder. TCAs have unpleasant side effects and are seldom used with very young children, although some doctors prescribe them in very low dosages to help with sleep. Among the more common TCAs are Elavil, Sinequan, and Desaryl. Desaryl is often given to older children and adolescents with autism spectrum disorders as a sleep aid. Anafranil is specifically prescribed for obsessive-compulsive disorder. Side effects include dry mouth, drowsiness, blurred vision, and constipation. *H*

Verbal Behavior: Refers to B.F. Skinner's book by that title, *Verbal Behavior* (1957). It was an analysis of speech and writing in terms of the speaker's current motivational state, current stimulus circumstances, past history, and genetic constitution.

Vincent Carbone (see http://www.drcarbone.net/) has developed an incidental teaching approach to behavior therapy with children with autism that he calls "Verbal Behavior," which is based on behavior analytic principles and addresses some concepts in Skinner's book. Some practitioners and parents are understandably confused by the fact that similar behavior analytic techniques have adopted the same term but insist that they are very different from one another.

Vineland Adaptive Behavior Scale: Two hundred ninety-seven items that provide a general assessment of adaptive behavior. It is administered to a parent or caregiver in a semi-structured interview format. It covers communication, daily living skills, and socialization and motor skills for children age birth to 18 years. An optional maladaptive behavior domain is included in interview editions to measure undesirable behaviors. Examiner must have completed a doctoral (or in some cases master's) degree program that included training (through coursework and supervised practical experience) in the administration and interpretation of clinical instruments. Requires 40–60 minutes.

Wechsler Intelligence Scale for Children: A test of general intelligence in children age 6 through 16 years. Test must be administered and interpreted by a doctoral psychologist or trained psychometrist. The test includes numerous subtests that measure individual cognitive abilities. The result is a verbal scale, a performance scale, and a full-scale score. Experienced examiners place more emphasis on individual scale and subscale scores than total scores, especially for special needs children.

White Matter (Overgrowth in Autism): Several studies have shown that between 2–8 years of age, some children experience an overgrowth of white matter beneath the brain's cerebral cortex. White matter is the fatty white insulation that surrounds nerve fibers and is essential for preventing signals from one nerve fiber from jumping over to another. In those individuals beyond 8 or 9 years of age the amount of white matter declines to a much lower level. There is some evidence suggesting that overgrowth of white matter may be related to an inflammatory or immune response of some kind, but this is not known for certain.

REFERENCES

Ayres, A.J. (1979). *Sensory integration and the child.* Los Angeles: Western Psychological Services.

Baron-Cohen, S., Cosmides, L., & Tooby, J. (1997). *Mindblindness.* Cambridge, MA: MIT Press.

Lord, C.E., Rutter, M., DiLavore, P.C., & Risi, S. (1999). Autism Diagnostic Observation Schedule-WPS (WPS Edition). Los Angeles: Western Psychological Services.

Miles, J.H., Takahashi, T.N., Bagby, S., Sahota, P.K., Vaslow, D.F., Wang, C.H., et al. (2005). Essential versus complex autism: Definition of fundamental prognostic subtypes. *American Journal of Medical Genetics A., 135* (2), 171–180.

Sackett, D., Rosenberg, W.M., Gray, J.A., Haynes, R.B., & Richardson, W.S. (1996). Evidence-based medicine: What it is and what it isn't. *British Medical Journal, 312,* 71–72.

Schopler, E., Reichler, R.J., DeVellis, R.F., & Daly, K. (1980). Toward objective classification of childhood autism: Childhood Autism Rating Scale (CARS). *Journal of Autism and Developmental Disorders, 10,* 91–103.

Skinner, B.F. (1957). *Verbal behavior.* New York: Appleton Century Crofts.

Kefauver-Harris Drug Amendments Act of 1962, PL 87–781.

References

Advokat, C.D., Mayville, E.A., & Matson, J.L. (2000). Side effect profiles of atypical antipsychotics, typical antipsychotics, or no psychotropic medications in persons with mental retardation. *Research in Developmental Disabilities, 21,* 75–84.

Afzal, M.A., Ozoemena, L.C., O'Hare, A., Kidger, K.A., Bentley, M.L., & Minor, P.D. (2006). Absence of detectable measles virus genome sequence in blood of autistic children who have had their MMR vaccination during the routine childhood immunization schedule of the UK. *Journal of Medical Virology, 78,* 623–630.

Albin, R.W., Lucyshyn, J.M., Horner, R.H., & Flannery, K.B. (1996). Contextual fit for behavioral support plans: A model for "goodness of fit." In L.K. Koegel, R.L. Koegel, & G. Dunlap (Eds.), *Positive behavior support: Including people with difficult behavior in the community.* Baltimore: Paul H. Brookes Publishing Co.

Alcantara, P.R. (1994). Effects of videotape instructional package on purchasing skills of children with autism. *Exceptional Children,* 40–55.

Altman, R., & Kanagawa, L. (1994). Academic and social engagement of young children with developmental disabilities in integrated and nonintegrated settings. *Education and Training in Mental Retardation and Developmental Disabilities, 29,*184–193.

Aman, M., Aman, M.G., Arnold, L.E., McDougle, C.J., Vitiello, B., Scahill, L., Davies, M., et al. (2005). Acute and long-term safety and tolerability of risperidone in children with autism. *Journal of Child and Adolescent Psychopharmacology, 15*(6), 869–884.

Aman, M.G., Lam, K.S., & Collier-Crespin, A. (2003) Prevalence and patterns of use of psychoactive medicines among individuals with autism in the Autism Society of Ohio. *Journal of Autism & Developmental Disorders, 33,* 527–534.

American Academy of Pediatrics. Committee on Children with Disabilities. (2001). The pediatrician's role in the diagnosis and management of autistic spectrum disorder in children. *Pediatrics, 107,* 1221–1226.

American Psychiatric Association. (2000). *Diagnostic and statistical manual of mental disorders* (4th ed.). Washington, DC: Author.

Anderson, S.R., Avery, D.L., DiPietro, E.K., Edwards, G.L., & Christian, W.P. (1987). Intensive home-based early intervention with autistic children. *Education and Treatment of Children, 10,* 352–366.

Ashwin, C., Baron-Cohen, S., Wheelwright, S., O'riordan, M., & Mullmore, E.T. (2006). Differential activation of the amygdala and the "social brain" during fearful face-processing in Asperger Syndrome. *Neuropsychologia.* (E-pub ahead of print)

Asperger, H. (1944). Die 'autistischen psychopathen' im kindesalter, *Archiv fur Psychiatrie und Nervenkrankheiten, 117,* 76–136. Translated by Uta Frith (Ed.). (1991). *Autism and Asperger Syndrome.* Cambridge UK: Cambridge University Press.

Attwood, T. (2004). *Exploring feelings: Cognitive behavior therapy to manage anxiety.* Arlington, TX: Future Horizons.

Austin, J.K., Harezlak J., Dunn, D.W., Huster, G.A., Rose, D.F., & Ambrosius, W.T. (2001). Behavior problems in children before first recognized seizures. *Pediatrics, 107,* 115–122.

Ayres, A.J. (1972). Improving academic scores through sensory integration. *Journal of Learning Disabilities, 5,* 338–343.

Ayres, A.J. (1979). *Sensory integration and the child.* Los Angeles: Western Psychological Services.

Ayres, A.J., & Tickle, L.S. (1980). Hyper-responsivity to touch and vestibular stimuli as predictor of positive response to sensory integration procedures by autistic children. *American Journal of Occupational Therapy, 34,* 375–381.

Azimov, A. (1998, December 11). Schools given new direction on 3 R's: More math earlier, switch to phonics. *San Francisco Chronicle,* p. A–29.

Baer, D.M., Wolf, M.M., & Risley, T.R. (1968). Some current dimensions of applied behavior analysis. *Journal of Applied Behavior Analysis, 1,* 91–97.

Bambara, L.M., & Kern L. (2005). *Individualized supports for students with problem behaviors: Designing positive behavior plans.* New York: Guilford Press.

Bambara, L.M., Koger, F., Katzer, T., & Davenport, T.A. (1995). Embedding choice in the context of daily routines: An experimental case study. *Journal of the Association for Persons with Severe Handicaps, 20*(3), 185–195.

Baron-Cohen, S. (1997) *Mindblindness: An essay on autism and theory of mind.* Cambridge, MA: MIT Press.

Baron-Cohen, S., Ring, H.A., Wheelwright, S., Bullmore, E.T., Brammer, M., Simmons, A., & Williams, S.C. (1999). Social intelligence in the normal and autistic brain: An MRI study. *European Journal of Neuroscience, 11,* 1891–1898.

Barrett, S. (2004). *Consumer health: A guide to intelligent decisions* (8th ed.). New York: McGraw-Hill.

Barrett, S. *QuackWatch* http://www.quackwatch.org/

Barron, J., & Sandman, C.A. (1985). Paradoxical excitement to sedative-hypnotics in mentally retarded clients. *American Journal of Mental Deficiency, 90*(2), 124–129.

Bates, E., & Dick, F. (2002). Language, gesture, and the developing brain. *Developmental Psychobiology, 40,* 293–310.

Bauman, M.L., & Kemper, T.L. (1985). Histoanatomic observations of the brain in early infantile autism. *Neurology, 35,* 866–874.

Bauman, M.L., & Kemper, T.L. (1994). Neuroanatomic observations of the brain in autism. In M.L. Bauman & T.L. Kemper (Eds.), *The neurobiology of autism* (pp. 119–145). Baltimore: Johns Hopkins University Press.

Bauman, M.L., & Kemper, T.L. (2005). Neuroanatomic observations of the brain in autism: a review and future directions. *International Journal of Developmental Neuroscience, 23,* 183–187.

Belsito, K.M., Law, P.A., Kirk, K.S., Landa, R.J., & Zimmerman, A.W. (2001) Lamotrigine therapy for autistic disorder: A randomized, double-blind, placebo-controlled trial. *Journal of Autism Developmental Disorders, 31,* 175–181.

Benaisch, A.A., & Tallal, P. (2002). Infant discrimination of rapid auditory cures predicts later language impairment. *Behavioral and Brain Research, 136,* 31–49.

Bernard, L., Enayati, A., Roger, H., Binstock, T., & Redwood, L. (2002). A systematic review of the use of atypical antipsychotics in autism. *Journal of the Psychopharmacology Bulletin, 1,* 93–101.

Berney, T.P., Ireland, M., & Burn, J. (1999). Behavioural phenotype of Cornelia de Lange syndrome. *Archives of Disease in Childhood, 81,* 333–336.

Besag, F.M. (2004). Behavioral aspects of pediatric epilepsy. *Epilepsy and Behavior, 5,* (Suppl. 1), S3–13.

Bettelheim, B. (1950). *Love is not enough: The treatment of emotionally disturbed children.* New York: Free Press.

Bettelheim, B. (1967). *The empty fortress: Infantile autism and the birth of the self.* New York: Free Press.

Biklen, D. (1993). *Communication unbound: How facilitated communication is challenging traditional views of autism and ability/disability.* New York: Teachers College Press.

Bishop, D.V., Maybery, M., Maley, A., Wong, D., Hill, W., & Hallmayer, J. (2004). Using self-report to identify the broad phenotype in parents of children with autism spectrum disorders: A study using the Autism-Spectrum Quotient. *Journal of Child Psychology and Psychiatry and Applied Disciplines, 45,* 1431–1436.

Boddaert, N., Chabane, N., Belin, P., Bourgeois, M., Royer, V., Barthelemy, C., et al. (2004). Perceptions of complex sounds in autism: Abnormal auditory cortical processing in children. *American Journal of Psychiatry, 161,* 2117–2120.

Brereton, A.V., Tonge, B.J., & Einfeld, S.L. (2006). Psychopathology in children and adolescents with autism compared to young people with intellectual disability. *Journal of Autism and Developmental Disorders, 36,* 863–870.

Bricker, D., Squires, J., & Mounts, L. (1999). *Ages & Stages Questionnaires (ASQ): A parent-completed, child-monitoring system.* Baltimore: Paul H. Brookes Publishing Co.

Brill, M.T. (2001). *Keys to parenting the child with autism* (2nd ed.). Hauppauge NY: Barron's Educational Series.

Bromley, J., Hare, D.J., Davison, K., & Emerson, E. (2004). Mothers supporting children with autistic spectrum disorders: Social support, mental health status and satisfaction with services. *Autism, 8,* 409–423.

Brooks, P.H., & Haywood, H.C. (2003). A preschool mediational context: The Bright Start curriculum. In A.S.-H. Seng, L.K.-H. Pou, & O.-S. Tan (Eds.), *Mediated learning experience with children: Applications across contexts* (pp. 98–132). Singapore: McGraw-Hill Education (Asia).

Butter, E.M., Wynn, J., & Mulick, J.A. (2003). Early intervention critical to autism treatment. *Pediatric Annals, 32,* 677–684.

Cador, M., Robbins, T.W., & Everitt, B.J. (1989). Involvement of the amygdala in stimulus-reward associations: Interaction with the ventral striatum. *Neuroscience, 30,* 77–86.

Capone, G.T., Grados, M.A., Kaufmann, W.E., Bernard-Ripoll, S., & Jewell, A. (2005). Down syndrome and comorbid autism-spectrum disorder: Characterization using the aberrant behavior checklist. *American Journal of Medical Genetics A, 134,* 373–380.

Carbone, V.J., Lewis, L., Sweeney-Kerwin, E.J., Dixon, J., Louden, R., & Quinn, S. (2006). A comparison of the approaches for teaching VB functions: Total communication vs. vocal-alone. *Journal of Speech Language Pathology and Applied Behavior Analysis, 1,* 181–182.

Carbone, V.J., Morgenstern, B., & Zecchin-Tirri, G. (2006). *An analysis of instructional methods as motivational variables.* Manuscript submitted for publication.

Carr, E.G., Dunlap, G., Horner, R.H., Koegel, R.L., Turnbull, A.P., Sailor, W., et al. (2002). Positive behavior support: Evolution of an applied science. *Journal of Positive Behavior Interventions, 4,* 4–16, 20.

Carr, E.G., & Durand, V.M. (1985). Reducing behavior problems through functional communication training. *Journal of Applied Behavior Analysis, 18,* 111–126.

Carr, E.G., Reeve, C.E., & Magito-McLaughlin, D. (1995). Contextual influences on problem behavior in people with developmental disabilities. In L.K. Koegel, R.L. Koegel, & G. Dunlap (Eds.), *Positive behavioral support: Including people with difficult behavior in the community* (pp. 403–423). Baltimore: Paul H. Brookes Publishing Co.

Carr, J.E., & Chong, I.M. (2005). Habit reversal treatment of tic disorders: A methodological critique of the literature. *Behavior Modification, 29,* 858–875.

Carta, J., Simmons Estes, J.S., Schiefelbusch, J., & Terry, B.J. (2000). *Project Slide.* Sopris West Educational Services; http://www.sopriswest.com/

Cataldo, M.F., & Harris, J. (1982). The biological basis of self-injury in the mentally retarded. *Analysis and Intervention in Developmental Disabilities, 7,* 21–39.

Cederlund, M., & Gillberg, C. (2004). One hundred males with Asperger syndrome: A clinical study of background and associate factors. *Developmental Medicine and Child Neurology, 46,* 652–660.

Centers for Disease Control and Prevention (2006). *How common are autism spectrum disorders (ASDs)?* Retrieved April 2006 from http://www.ced.gov/ncbddd/autism/asd_common.htm

Charlop-Christy, M.H., Loc, L., & Freeman, K.A. (2000). A comparison of video modeling with in vivo modeling for teaching children with autism. *Journal of Autism and Developmental Disorders, 30,* 537–552.

Chez, M.G., Chang, M., Krasne, V., Coughlan, C., Kominsky, M., & Schwartz, A. (2005). Frequency of epileptiform EEG abnormalities in a sequential screening of autistic patients with no known clinical epilepsy from 1996–2005. *Epilepsy and Behavior, 8,* 267–271.

Christenson, S.L., & Conoley, J.C. (1992). *Home-school collaboration: Enhancing children's academic and social competence.* Silver Spring, MD: NASP.

Christenson, S.L., & Sheridan, S.M. (2001). *Schools and families: Creating essential connections for learning.* New York: Guilford Press.

Christopherson, E. (2004, August). *How to eliminate habits like thumbsucking with simple behavior modification*; retrieved January 20, 2007 from http://www.dbpeds.org/articles/detail.cfm?id=112

Clarke, D.F., Roberts, W., Daraksan, M., Dupuis, A., McCabe, J., Wood, H., et al. (2005). The prevalence of autistic spectrum disorder in children surveyed in a tertiary care epilepsy clinic. *Epilepsia, 46,* 1970–1977.

Cohen, W., Hodson, A., O'Hare, A., Boyle, J., Durranit, T., McCartney, E., et al. (2005). Effects of computer-based intervention through acoustically modified speech (FastForWord) in severe mixed receptive-expressive language impairment: Outcomes from a randomized controlled trial. *Journal of Speech, Language and Hearing Research, 48,* 715–729.

Cooperman, T., Obermeyer, W., & Webb, D. (2003). *Consumerlab.Com's guide to buying vitamins & supplements: What's really in the bottle*; Consumerlab.com LLC

Couper, J.J., & Sampson A.J. (2003). Children with autism deserve evidence-based intervention. *Medical Journal of Australia, 178,* 424–425.

Crosland, K.A., Zarcone, J,R., Lindauer, S.E., Valdovinos, M.G., Zarcone, T.J., Hellings, J.A., & Schroeder, S.R. (2003). Use of functional analysis methodology in the evaluation of medication effects. *Journal of Autism and Developmental Disorders, 33*(3), 271–279.

Cullen, C., & Mappin, R. (1998). An examination of the effects of gentle teaching on people with complex learning disabilities and challenging behaviour. *British Journal of Clinical Psychology, 37*(Pt 2), 199–211.

Dadson, S., & Horner, R.H. (1993). Manipulating setting events to decrease problem behaviors: A case study. *Teaching Exceptional Children, 25,* 53–55.

Dawson, G., & Watling, R. (2000). Interventions to facilitate auditory, visual, and motor integration in autism: A review of the evidence. *Journal of Autism and Developmental Disorders, 30*(5), 415–421.

DeFosse, L., Hodge, S.M., Makris, N., Kennedy, D.N., Caviness, V.S. Jr., McGrath, L., et al. (2004). Language-association cortex asymmetry in autism and specific language impairment. *Annals of Neurology, 56*(6), 755–756.

Demichelli, V., Jefferson, T., Rivetti, A., & Price, D. (2005). Vaccines for measles, mumps and rubella in children (review): The Cochrane Collaboration (classification C115). London: Wiley.

Denckla, M.B. (1983). The neuropsychology of social-emotional learning disabilities. *Archives of Neurology, 40,* 461–462.

Devinsky, O. (2004). Diagnosis and treatment of temporal lobe epilepsy. *Reviews in Neruological Diseases, 1,* 2–9.

Di Martino, A., Melis, G., Cianchetti, C., & Zuddas, A. (2004). Methylphenidate for pervasive developmental disorders: Safety and efficacy of acute single dose test and ongoing therapy: An open-pilot study. *Journal of Child and Adolescent Psychopharmacology, 14,* 297–298.

Dimitropoulos, A., Feurer, I., Butler, M., & Thompson, T. (2001). Emergence of compulsive behavior and tantrums in children with Prader-Willi syndrome. *American Journal on Mental Retardation, 106*(1), 39–51.

Duarte, C.S., Bordin, I.A., Yazigi, L., & Mooney, J (2005) Factors associated with stress in mothers of children with autism. *Autism, 4,* 416–427.

Dunlap, G., & Fox, L. (1999). A demonstration of behavioral support for young children with autism. *Journal of Positive Behavior Interventions, 1,* 77–87.

Dunn, D.W., Austin, J.W., Caffrey, H.M., & Perkins, S.M. (2003). A prospective study of teachers' ratings of behavior problems in children with new-onset seizures. *Epilepsy and Behavior, 4,* 26–35.

Dunn, W. (1997). The sensory profile: A discriminating measure of sensory processing in daily life. *Sensory Integration Special Interest Section Quarterly, 20.* Bethesda, MD: American Occupational Therapy Association.

Durand, V.M. (2002). *Severe behavior problems: A functional communication training approach.* New York: Guilford Press.

Durand, V.M., & Crimmins, D.B. (1992). *The Motivation Assessment Scale administration guide.* Topeka, KS: Monaco & Associates.

Dyer, K., Dunlap, G., & Winterling, V. (1990). Effects of choice making on the serious problem behaviors of students with severe handicaps. *Journal of Applied Behavior Analysis, 23,* 515–524.

Dyer, K., & Larson, E.V. (1997). Developing functional communication skills: Alternatives to aberrant behavior. In E. Cipani & N.N. Singh (Eds.), *Practical approaches to the treatment of severe behavior problems.* Sycamore, IL: Sycamore Publishing.

Dykens, E.M., Hodapp, R.M., & Evans, D.W. (1994). Profiles and development of adaptive behavior in children with Down syndrome. *American Journal on Mental Retardation, 98,* 580–587.

Dykens, E.M., Hodapp, R.M., & Finucane, B. M. (2000). *Genetics and mental retardation syndromes: A new look at behavior and interventions.* Baltimore: Paul H. Brookes Publishing Co.

Eisenhower, A.S., Baker, B.L., & Blacher J. (2005). Preschool children with intellectual disability: Syndrome specificity, behaviour problems, and maternal well-being. *Journal Intellectual Disability Research, 49,* 657–671.

Ermer, J., & Dunn, W. (1998). The sensory profile: A discriminant analysis of children with and without disabilities. *American Journal of Occupational Therapy, 52,* 283–290.

Emory University Autism Center; retrieved January 29, 2007, from http://www.psychiatry.emory.edu/PROGRAMS/autism/overview.html

Ernst, E. (Ed.). (2006). Focus on alternative and complementary therapies (FACT). *Pharmaceutical Press* (ISSN:1 465–3753).

Esler, A.N., Godber, Y., & Christenson, S.L. (2002). Best practices in supporting home school collaboration. In A. Thomas & J. Grimes (Eds.), *Best practices in school psychology IV* (pp. 389–411). Bethesda, MD: The National Association of School Psychologists.

Evans, D.W., Canavera, K., Kleinpeter, F.L., Maccubbin, E., & Taga, K. (2005). The fears, phobias and anxieties of children with autism spectrum disorders and Down syndrome: Comparisons with developmentally and chronologically age matched children. *Child Psychiatry and Human Development, 36,* 3–26.

Farroni, T., Csibra, G., Simion, F., & Johnson, M.H. (2002). Eye contact detection in humans from birth. *Proceedings of the National Academy of Sciences USA, 99,* 9602–9605.

Fecteau, S., Lepage, J.F., & Theoret, H. (2006). Autism spectrum disorder: Seeing is not understanding. *Current Biology, 16,* R131–133.

Festinger, L., Riecken, H., & Schachter, S. (1956). *When prophecy fails.* Minneapolis: University of Minnesota Press.

Fidler, D.J. (2005). The emerging Down syndrome behavioral phenotype in early child-hood: Implications for practice. *Infants and Young Children, 18,* 86–103.

Fishman, S.N., Wolf, L.C., & Noh, S. (1989). Marital intimacy in parents of exceptional children. *Canadian Journal of Psychiatry, 34,* 519–525.

Food and Drug Administration, *FDA Consumer Magazine*; retrieved January 20, 2007, from http://www.fda.gov/fdac/default.htm

Food and Drug Administration, *Warning letters to hyperbaric oxygen device manufacturers*; retrieved January 17, 2007, from http://www.fda.gov/foi/warning_letters/m3449n.pdf; http://www.fda.gov/foi/warning_letters/m5272n.pdf

Forest, M., & Lusthaus, E. (1989). Promoting educational equality for all students: Circles and maps. In S. Stainback, W. Stainback, & M. Forest (Eds.), *Educating all students in the mainstream of regular education.* Baltimore: Paul H. Brookes Publishing Co.

Frankel, M.G., Happ, F.W., & Smith, M.P. (1975). The relation of historical and contem-porary theories to functional teaching. In Franke, M.G., Happ, F.W., & Smith M.P. (Eds.), *Functional teaching of the mentally retarded.* Springfield, Ill: Charles C. Thomas.

Freeman, N.L., Perry, A., & Factor, D.C. (1991). Child behaviours as stressors: Replicating and extending the use of the CARS as a measure of stress: A research note. *Journal of Child Psychology and Psychiatry and Applied Disciplines, 32,*1025–1030.

French, J.E. (2000). Itard, Jean-Marie-Gaspard. In A.E. Kazdin (Ed.). *Encyclopedia of psy-chology.* New York: Oxford University Press.

Fuchs, D., Fuchs, L.S., Al Otaiba, S., Thompson, A., Yen, L., McMaster, K.N., et al. (2001). K-PALS: Helping kindergartners with reading readiness: Teachers and researchers in partnership. *Teaching Exceptional Children, 33*(4), 76–80.

Fuchs, D., Fuchs, L.S., & Burish, P. (2000). Peer-assisted learning strategies: An evidence-based practice to promote reading achievement. *Learning Disabilities Research and Practice, 15*(2), 85–91.

Fuchs, L.S., Fuchs, D., Kazdan, S., & Allen, S. (1999). Effects of peer-assisted learning strategies in reading with and without elaborated help giving. *Elementary School Journal, 99,* 201–220.

Gabis, L., Pomeroy, J., & Andriola, M.R. (2005). Autism and epilepsy: Cause, consequence, comorbidity or coincidence. *Epilepsy and Behavior, 7,* 652–656.

Garcia, D., & Smith, R.G. (1999). Using analog baselines to assess the effects of naltrex-one on self-injurious behavior. *Research in Developmental Disabilities, 20,* 1–21.

Gaynor, J.F. (1973). The "failure" of J.M.G. Itard. *Journal of Special Education, 7*(4), 439–445.

Ghaziuddin, M., Butler, E., Tsai, L., & Ghaziuddin, N. (1994). Is clumsiness a marker for Asperger syndrome? *Journal of Intellectual Disability Research, 38,* 519–527.

Gizzolati, G., & Craighero, L. (2004). The mirror-neuron system. *Annual Review of Neuroscience 27,* 169–192.

Glasco, F.P. (2000). Detecting and addressing developmental and behavioral problems in primary care. *Pediatric Nursing, 26,* 251–257.

Golan, O., & Baron-Cohen, S. (2006). Systematizing empathy: Teaching adults with Asperger syndrome or high-functioning autism emotions using interactive media. *Development and Psychopathology, 18,* 591–617.

Gold, N. (1993). Depression and social adjustment in siblings of boys with autism. *Journal of Autism and Developmental Disorders, 23,*147–163.

Goldstein, H. (1999, December 13–14). Communication intervention for children with autism: A review of treatment efficacy. Paper presented at the First Workshop of the Committee on Educational Interventions for Children with Autism, National Research Council. Florida State University, Gainesville, Florida.

Goldstein, S., & Schwebach, A.J. (2004). The comorbidity of pervasive developmental dis-order and attention deficit hyperactivity disorder: Results of a retrospective chart review. *Journal of Autism and Developmental Disorders, 34,* 329–339.

Gordon, C.T., State, R.C., Nelson, J.E., Hamburger, S.D., & Rapoport, J.L. (1993). A double-blind comparison of clomipramine, desipramine, and placebo in the treatment of autistic disorder. *Archives of General Psychiatry, 50,* 441–447.

Gray, C. (2002). *The new social story book: Illustrated edition.* Arlington, TX: Future Horizons.

Gray, S.W., & Klaus, R.A. (1965). An experimental preschool program for culturally deprived children. *Child Development, 36,* 887–898.

Greenough, W.T., & Black, J.E. (1992). Induction of brain structure by experience: Substrates for cognitive development. In M.R. Gunnar & C.A. Nelson (Eds.), *Developmental Behavior Neuroscience, 24,* 155–200. Hillsdale, NJ: Lawrence Erlbaum Associates.

Greenspan, S.J., & Wieder, S. (2006). *Engaging autism: Helping children relate, communicate and think with the DIR Floortime approach.* Cambridge, MA: Da Capo Press.

Greenspan, S.J., Wieder, S., & Simons, R. (1998). *The child with special needs: Encouraging intellectual and emotional growth.* New York: Perseus Books.

Greenwood, C.R., Hou, L.S., Delquadri, J., Terry, B.J., & Arreaga-Mayer, C. (2001). Classwide peer tutoring program: A learning management system. In J. Woodward & L. Cuban (Eds.), *Technology, curriculum, and professional development: Adapting schools to meet the needs of students with disabilities* (pp. 61–86). Thousand Oaks, CA: Corwin.

Greier, D.A., & Greier, M.R. (2003a). An assessment of thimerosal on childhood neurodevelopmental disorders. *Pediatric Rehabilitation, 6,* 97–100.

Greier, D.A., & Greier, M.R. (2004). A comparative evaluation of the effects of MMR immunization and mercury doses from thimerisol-containing childhood vaccines on the population prevalence of autism. *Medical Science Monitor, 11,* LE13–14.

Greier, M.R., & Greier, D.A. (2003b). Neurodevelopmental disorders after thimersol-containing vaccines: A brief communication. *Experimental Biology and Medicine, 228,* 660–664.

Grigg-Damberger, M. (2004). Neurologic disorders masquerading as pediatric sleep problems. *Pediatric Clinics of North America, 51,* 89–115.

Gutstein, S.E. (2004). The effectiveness of relationship development intervention in remediating core deficits of autism-spectrum children. *Journal of Developmental and Behavioral Pediatrics, 25,* 375.

Gutstein, S.E., & Sheely, R.K. (2002). *Relationship development intervention with children, adolescents, and adults.* London: Jessica Kingsley.

Harris, S., Handleman, J., Gordon, R., Kristoff, B., & Fuentes, F. (1991). Changes in cognitive and language functioning of preschool children with autism. *Journal of Autism and Developmental Disorders, 21,* 281–290.

Harris, S.L. (1986). Parents as teachers: A four- to seven-year follow-up of parents of children with autism. *Child & Family Behavior Therapy, 8,* 39–47.

Harris, S.L., & Glasberg, B.A. (2003). *Siblings of children with autism: A guide for families* (2nd ed.). Bethesda, MD: Woodbine House.

Harris, S.L., & Handleman, J.S. (2000). Age and IQ at intake as predictors of placement for young children with autism: A four- to six-year follow-up. *Journal of Autism and Developmental Disorders, 30,* 137–142.

Hart, B.M., & Risley, T.R. (1982). *How to use incidental teaching for elaborating language.* Lawrence, KS: H & H Enterprises.

Hastings, R.P. (2003). Child behaviour problems and partner mental health as correlates of stress in mothers and fathers of children with autism. *Journal of Intellectual Disability Research, 47,* 231–237.

Hastings, R.P., & Johnson, E. (2001). Stress in UK families conducting intensive home-based behavioral intervention for their young child with autism. *Journal of Autism and Developmental Disorders, 31,* 327–336.

Hastings, R.P., Kovshoff, H., Ward, N.J., degli Espinosa, F., Brown, T., & Remington, B. (2005). Systems analysis of stress and positive perceptions in mothers and fathers of preschool children with autism *Journal of Autism Developmental Disorders, 35,* 635–644.

Hattori, J., Ogino, T., Abiru, K, Nakano, K., Oka, M., & Ohtsuka, Y. (2006) Are pervasive developmental disorders and attention-deficit/hyperactivity disorders distinct disorders? *Brain and Development, 28,* 371–374.

Hellings, J.A., Kelley, L.A., Gabrielli, W.F., Kilgore, E., & Shah, P. (1996). Sertraline response in adults with mental retardation and autistic disorder. *Journal of Clinical Psychiatry, 57,*(8), 333–336.

Hellings, J.A., Zarcone, J.R., Crandall, K., Reese, R.M., Marquis, J., Fleming, K., et al. (2001). Weight gain in a controlled study of risperidone in children, adolescents, and adults with mental retardation and autism. *Journal of Child and Adolescent Psychopharmacology, 11*(3), 229–238.

Herbert, J.D., Sharp, I.R., & Gaudiano, B.A. (2002). Separating fact from fiction in the etiology and treatment of autism: A scientific review of the evidence. *The Scientific Review of Mental Health Practice, 1*(1), 23–43.

Hesse, S., Muller, U., Lincke, T., Barthel, H., Villmann, T., Angermeyer, M.C., et al. (2005). Serotonin and dopamine transporter imaging in patients with obsessive-compulsive disorder. *Psychiatry Research, 140,* 63–72.

Hill, R.T. (1970). Facilitation of conditioned reinforcement as a mechanism of psychomotor stimulation. In E. Costa & S. Garattini (Eds.), *Amphetamines and related compounds.* New York: Raven Press.

Hollander, E., Anagnostou, E., Chaplin, W., Esposito, K., Haznedar, M.M., Licalzi, E., et al. (2005). Striatal volume on magnetic resonance imaging and repetitive behaviors in autism. *Biological Psychiatry, 58,* 226–232.

Honda, H., Shimizu, Y., & Rutter, M. (2005). No effect of MMR withdrawal on the incidence of autism: A total population study. *Journal of Child Psychology and Psychiatry and Applied Disciplines, 46,* 572–579.

Horner, R.H. (1999). Positive behavior supports. *Focus on Autism and Other Developmental Disabilities, 15*(2), 97–105.

Horner, R.H., Day, H., & Day, J.R. (1997). Using neutralizing routines to reduce problem behavior. *Journal of Applied Behavior Analalysis, 30,* 601–613.

Horner, R.H., Dunlap, G., Koegel, R.L., Carr, E.G., Sailor, W., Anderson, J., et al. (1990). Toward a technology of "nonaversive" behavioral support. *Journal of the Association for Persons with Severe Handicaps, 15,* 125–132.

Horner, R.H., Sugai, G., Todd, A.W., & Lewis-Palmer, T. (1990). Elements of behavior support plans: A technical brief. *Exceptionality, 8*(3), 205–215.

Horton, R. (2004). The lessons of MMR. *Lancet, 363,* 747–749.

Horvath, K., Stefanatos, G., Sokolski, K.N., Wachtel, R., Nabors, L., & Tildon, J.T. (1998). Improved social and language skills after secretin administration in patients with autism spectrum disorders. *Journal of the Association of Academic Minority Physicians, 9,* 9–15.

Howlin, P., Baron-Cohen, S., & Hadwin, J. (1998). *Teaching children with autism to mindread: A practical guide for teachers and parents.* New York: John Wiley & Sons.

Huebner, R.A., & Emery, L.J. (1998). Social psychological analysis of facilitated communication: Implications for education. *Mental Retardation, 36,* 259–268.

Humphrey, G. (1962). Introduction. In J.M.G. Itard, *The wild boy of Aveyron.* New York: Appleton-Century-Crofts.

Huttenlocher, P.R., & de Courten C. (1987). The development of synapses in striate cortex of man. *Human Neurobiology, 6,* 1–9.

Immunization Safety Review Committee. (2004). *Immunization safety review: Vaccines and autism institute of medicine.* Washington, DC: National Academies Press.

Individuals with Disabilities Education Act (IDEA) of 1990, PL 101-476, 20 U.S.C. §§ 1400 *et seq.*

Individuals with Disabilities Education Improvement Act of 2004, PL 108-446, 20 U.S.C. §§ 1400 *et seq.*

Ingersoll, B., & Schreibman, L. (2006). Teaching reciprocal imitation skills to young children with autism using a naturalistic behavioral approach: Effects on language, pretend play and joint attention. *Journal of Autism and Developmental Disorders, 36,* 487–505.

Itard, J.M.G. (1962). *The wild boy of Aveyron.* (G. Humphrey & M. Humphrey, Trans.). New York: Appleton-Century-Crofts. (Original works published 1801 and 1806).

Iwata, B.A., Dorsey, M.F., Slifer, K.J., Bauman, K.E., & Richman, G.S. (1982). Toward a functional analysis of self-injury. *Analysis and Intervention in Developmental Disabilities, 2,* 3–20.

Jahr, E., Eldevik, S., & Eikeseth, S. (2000). Teaching children with autism to initiate and sustain cooperative play. *Research in Developmental Disabilities, 21,* 151–169.

Janowsky, D.S., & Davis, J.M. (2005). Diagnosis and treatment of depression in patients with mental retardation. *Current Psychiatry Reports, 7,* 421–428.

Jones, V., & Prior, M. (1985). Motor imitation abilities and neurological signs in autistic children. *Journal of Autism and Developmental Disorders, 15,* 37–46.

Just, M., Cherkassky, V.L., Keller, T.A., & Minshew, N.J. (2004). Cortical activation and synchronization during sentence comprehension in high-functioning autism: Evidence of underconnectivity. *Brain, 127* (Pt 8), 1811–1821.

Kadesjo, B., & Gillberg, C. (2000). Tourette's disorder: Epidemiology and comorbidity in primary school children *Journal of American Academy of Child and Adolescent Psychiatry, 39,* 548–555.

Kaminen, N., Hannula-Jouppi, K., Kestila, M., Lahermo, P., Muller, K., Kaaranen, M., et al. (2003). A genome scan for developmental dyslexia confirms linkage to chromosome 2p11 and suggests a new locus on 7q32. *Journal of Medical Genetics, 40,* 340–345.

Kamps, D.M., Leonard, B.R., Vernon, S., Dugan, E.P., Delquadri, J.C., Gershon, B., et al. (1992). Teaching social skills to students with autism to increase peer interactions in an integrated first-grade classroom. *Journal of Applied Behavior Analysis, 25,* 281–288.

Kane, J., Luiselli, J.K., Dearborn, S., & Young, N. (2004–2005, Fall–Winter). Wearing a weighted vest as a intervention for children with autism/pervasive developmental disorder. *The Scientific Review of Mental Health Practice, 3*(2), 19–24.

Kanner, L. (1943). Autistic disturbances of affective contact. *Nervous Child, 2,* 217–250.

Kanner, L. (1967). Medicine in the history of mental retardation. *American Journal of Mental Deficiency, 72*(2), 65–170.

Kaye, J.A., del Mar Melero-Montes, M., & Jick, H. (2001). Mumps, measles, and rubella vaccine and the incidence of autism recorded by general practitioners: A time trend analysis. *British Medical Journal, 322,* 460–463.

Kellerman, G.R., Fan, J., & Gorman, J.M. (2005). Auditory abnormalities in autism: Toward functional distinctions among findings. *CNS Spectrums, 10,* 748–756.

Kennedy, C.H., & Itonken, T. (1993). Effects of setting events on the problem behavior of students with severe disabilities. *Journal of Applied Behavior Analysis, 26,* 321–327.

Kennedy, C.H., & Thompson, T. (2000). Health conditions contributing to problem behavior among people with mental retardation and developmental disabilities. In M.L. Wehmeyer & J.R. Patton (Eds.), *Mental retardation in the 21st century* (pp. 211–231). Austin, TX: PRO-ED.

Kielinen, M., Rantala, H., Timonen, E., Linna, S.L., & Moilanen, I. (2004). Associated medical disorders and disabilities in children with autistic disorder: A population-based study. *Autism, 8,* 49–60.

Klein, K.D., & Diehl, E.B. (2004). Relationship between MMR vaccine and autism. *Annals of Pharmacotherapy, 38,* 1297–1300.

Klin, A., Jones, W., Schultz, R., Volkmar, F., & Cohen, D. (2002). Visual fixation patterns during viewing of naturalistic social situations as predictors of social competence in individuals with autism. *Archives of General Psychiatry, 59,* 809–881.

Ko, D.Y., & Sahai-Srivastava, S. (1996–2006). Temporal Lobe Epilepsy. *E-Medicine (from WebMD)* Retrieved January 18, 2007, from http://www.emedicine.com/NEURO/ topic365.htm

Kobayashi, R., & Murata, T. (1998). Behavioral characteristics of 187 young adults with autism. *Psychiatry and Clinical Neuroscience, 52,* 383–390.

Koegel, R.L., Carter, C.M., & Kern Koegel, L. (1999). Setting events to improve parent–teacher coordination and motivation for children with autism. In J.K. Luiselli & M.J. Cameron (Eds.), *Antecedent control: Innovative approaches to behavioral support* (pp. 167–186). Baltimore: Paul H. Brookes Publishing Co.

Koegel, R.L., & Koegel, L.K. (Eds.). (1995). *Teaching children with autism: Strategies for initiating positive interactions and improving learning opportunities.* Baltimore: Paul H. Brookes Publishing Co.

Koegel, L.K., Koegel, R.L., & Carter, L.M. (1998). Pivotal responses and the natural language teaching paradigm. *Seminars in Speech and Language, 9,* 355–371.

Koegel, R.L., Schreibman, L., Good, A., Cerniglia, L., Murphy, C., & Koegel, L. (1989). *How to teach pivotal behaviors to children with autism: A training manual.* Santa Barbara: University of California.

Koegel, R.L., Schreibman, L., Loos, L.M., Dirlich-Wilhelm, H., Dunlap, G., Robbins, F.R., & Plienis, A.J. (1992). Consistent stress profiles in mothers of children with autism. *Journal of Autism and Developmental Disorders, 22,* 205–216.

Landau, W.M., & Kleffner, F.R. (1957). Syndrome of acquired aphasia with convulsive disorder in children. *Neurology, 7,* 523–530.

Langworthy-Lam, K.S., Aman, M.G., & Van Bourgondien, M.E. (2002). Prevalence and patterns of use of psychoactive medicines in individuals with autism in the Autism Society of North Carolina. *Journal of Child and Adolescent Psychopharmacology, 12,* 311–321.

Larsson, E.V. (2002). Involving parents in therapy. In O.I. Lovaas (Ed.), *Teaching children with developmental disabilities.* Austin, TX: PRO-ED.

Lawry, J., Danko, C., & Strain, P. (1999). Examining the role of the classroom environment in the prevention of problem behaviors. In S. Sandall & M. Ostrosky (Eds.), *Young exceptional children: Practical ideas for addressing challenging behaviors* (pp. 49–62). Longmont, CO: Sopris West and Denver, CO: DEC.

LeBlanc, L.A., Coates, A.M., Daneshvar, S., Charlop-Christy, M.H., Morris, C., & Lancaster, B.M. (2003). Using video modeling and reinforcement to teach perspective taking skills to children with autism. *Journal of Applied Behavior Analysis, 36,* 253–257.

Lee, D.O., & Ousley, O.Y. (2006). Attention-deficit/hyperactivity disorder symptoms in a clinic sample of children and adolescents with pervasive developmental disorders. *Journal of Child and Adolescent Psychopharmacology, 6,* 737–746.

Leonard, L.B. (1998). *Children with specific language impairment.* Cambridge, MA: MIT Press.

Levy, S.E., & Hyman, S.L. (2005). Novel treatments for autistic spectrum disorders *Mental Retardation and Developmental Disabilities Research Reviews, 11,* 131–142.

Lewinsohn, P. (1992). Control your depression (Rev. Ed.). New York: Fireside.

Lewis, M.H., Bodfish, J.W., Powell, S.B., & Golden, R.N. (1995) Clomipramine treatment for stereotype and related repetitive movement disorders associated with mental retardation. *American Journal on Mental Retardation, 100,* 299–312.

Lewis, M.H., Bodfish, J.W., Powell, S.B., Parker, D.E., & Golden, R.N. (1996) Clomipramine treatment for self-injurious behavior of individuals with mental retardation: A double-blind comparison with placebo. *American Journal on Mental Retardation,100,* 654–665.

Lord, C.E., & McGee, J.G. (2001). *Educating children with autism* (pp. 98–100). Committee on Educational Interventions for Children with Autism, Division of Behavioral and Social Sciences and Education, National Research Council. Washington, DC: National Academies Press.

Lord, C.E., McGee, J.G., Lovaas, O.I., Berberich, J.P., Perloff, B.F., & Schaffer, B. (1966). Acquisition of imitative speech by schizophrenic children. *Science, 151,* 705–707.

Lord, C.E., Pickles, A., McLennan, J., Rutter, M., Bregman, J., Folstein, S., et al. (1997). Diagnosing autism: Analyses of data from the autism diagnostic interview. *Journal of Autism and Developmental Disorders, 27*(5), 501–517.

Lord, C.E., Risi, S., Lambrecht, L., Cook, E., Leventhal, B., DiLavore, P., et al. (2000). The ADOS-G (Autism Diagnostic Observation Schedule-Generic): A standard measure of social and communication deficits associated with autism spectrum disorder. *Journal of Autism and Developmental Disorders, 30,* 205–223.

Lord, C.E., Rutter, M., DiLavore, P.C., & Risi, S. (1999). *Autism Diagnostic Observation Schedule-WPS (WPS Edition).* Los Angeles: Western Psychological Services.

Lovaas, O.I. (1980). Behavioral teaching with young autistic children. In B. Wilcox & A. Thompson (Eds.), *Critical issues in educating autistic children and youth* (pp. 220–233). Washington DC: U.S. Department of Education, Office of Special Education.

Lovaas, O.I. (1987). Behavioral treatment and normal educational and intellectual functioning in young autistic children. *Journal of Consulting and Clinical Psychology, 55,* 3–9.

Lundberg, I., Frost, J., & Peterson, O. (1988). Effectiveness of an extensive program for stimulating phonological awareness in preschool children. *Reading Research Quarterly, 23*(3), 263–268.

Maag, J. (2001). *Power struggles: Managing resistance and building rapport.* Longmont, CO: Sopris West.

Mace, F.C., Hock, M.L., Lalli, J.S., West, B.J., Belfiore, P., Pinter, E., & Brown, D.T. (1988). Behavioral momentum in the treatment of noncompliance. *Journal of Applied Behavior Analysis, 21,*123–141.

Maes, M., & Meltzer, H.Y. (1995) The serotonin hypothesis of major depression. In F. Bloom & D. Kupher (Eds.), *Psychopharmacology: The fourth generation of progress* (pp. 933–944). New York: Raven Press.

Malone, R.P., Maislin, G., Choudhury, M.S., Gifford, C., & Delaney, M.A. (2002). Risperidone treatment in children and adolescents with autism: short- and long-term safety and effectiveness. *Journal American Academy of Child Adolescent Psychiatry, 41,* 140–147.

Mandell, D.S., Walrath, C.M., Manteuffel, B., Sgro, G., & Pinto-Martin, J.A. (2005). The prevalence and correlates of abuse among children with autism served in comprehensive community-based mental health settings. *Child Abuse and Neglect, 129,* 1359–1372.

Massey, G.N., & Wheeler, J.J. (2000). Acquisition and generalization of activity schedules and their effects on task engagement in a young child with autism in an inclusive preschool classroom. *Education and Training in Mental Retardation and Developmental Disabilities, 35,* 326–335.

Matson, J.L. (2006). Determining treatment outcome in early intervention programs for autism spectrum disorders: A critical analysis of measurement issues in learning based interventions. *Research in Developmental Disabilities.* (May 5 E-pub ahead of print)

McClannahan, L.E., & Krantz, P.J. (1993). On systems analysis in autism intervention programs. *Journal of Applied Behavior Analysis, 26,* 589–596.

McClannahan, L.E., & Krantz, P.J. (1994). The Princeton Child Development Institute. In S.L. Harris & J.S. Handleman (Eds.), *Preschool education programs for children with autism* (pp. 107–126). Austin, TX: PRO-ED.

McClannahan, L.E., & Krantz, P.J. (2005). *Teaching conversation to children with autism: Scripts and script fading.* Bethesda. MD: Woodbine House.

McCracken, J.T., McGough, J., Shah, B., Cronin, P., Hong, D., Aman, M.G., et al. (2002). Risperidone in children with autism and serious behavioral problems. *New England Journal of Medicine, 347,* 314–321.

McDougle, C.J., Holmes, J.P., Carlson, D.C., Pelton, G.H, Cohen, D.J., & Price, L.H. (1998). A double-blind placebo-controlled study of risperidone in adults with autistic disorder and other pervasive developmental disorders. *Archives of General Psychiatry, 55,* 633–641.

McDougle, C.J., Kresch, L.E., & Posey, D.J. (2000). Repetitive thoughts and behavior in pervasive developmental disorders: Treatment with serotonin reuptake inhibitors. *Journal of Autism and Developmental Disorders, 30,* 427–435.

McDougle, C.J., Naylor, S.T., Cohen, D.J., Volkmar, F.R., Heninger, G.R., & Price, L.H. (1996). A double-blind, placebo-controlled study of fluvoxamine in adults with autistic disorder. *Archives of General Psychiatry, 53,* 1001–1008.

McDougle, C.J., Scahill, L., Aman, M.G., McCracken, J.T., Tierney, E., Davies, M., et al. (2005). Risperidone for the core symptom domains of autism: Results from the study by the autism network of the research nits on pediatric psychopharmacology. *American Journal on Mental Retardation, 106,* 525–538; retrieved January 31, 2007, from http://ici2.umn.edu/preschoolbehavior/strategy/htm

McEachin, J.J., Smith, T., & Lovaas, O.I. (1993). Long-term outcome for children with autism who received early intensive behavioral treatment. *American Journal on Mental Retardation, 97,* 359–372.

McEvoy, M., Reichle, J., & Davis, C. (1995). *A replication and dissemination of model of inservice training and technical assistance to prevent challenging behavior in young children with disabilities.* Minneapolis: Center for Early Education and Development, University of Minnesota.

McGee, G.G., Almeida, M.C., Sulzer-Azaroff, B., & Feldman, R.S. (1992). Promoting reciprocal interactions via peer incidental teaching. *Journal of Applied Behavior Analysis, 25,* 117–126.

McGee, J.G., Krantz, P.J., & McClannahan, L.E. (1986). An extension of incidental teaching procedures to reading instruction for autistic children. *Journal of Applied Behavior Analysis, 19,* 147–157.

McLellan, A., Davies, S., Heyman, I., Harding, B., Harkness, W., Taylor, D., et al. (2005). Psychopathology in children with epilepsy before and after temporal lobe resection. *Developmental Medicine and Child Neurology, 47,* 666–672.

McWilliam, R.A. (1996). *Rethinking pull-out services in early intervention: A professional resource.* Baltimore: Paul H. Brookes Publishing Co.

McWilliam, R.A. (2000). Recommended practices in interdisciplinary models. In S. Sandall, M. E. McLean, & B.J. Smith (Eds.), *DEC recommended practices in early intervention/early childhood special education* (pp. 47–52). Denver, CO: DEC.

McWilliam, R.A., & Bailey, D.B. (1992). Promoting engagement and mastery. In D.B. Bailey & M. Wolery (Eds.), *Teaching infants and preschoolers with disabilities* (2nd ed., pp. 229–256). Columbus, OH: Merrill.

McWilliam, R.A., & Bailey, D.B. (1995). Effects of classroom social structure and disability on engagement. *Topics in Early Childhood Special Education, 15,* 123–147.

Micali, N., Chakrabarti, S., & Fombonne, E. (2004). The broad autism phenotype: Findings from an epidemiological survey. *Autism, 8,* 21–37.

Miles, J.H., Takahashi, T.N., Bagby, S., Sahota, P.K., Vaslow, D.F., Wang, C.H., et al. (2005). Essential versus complex autism: Definition of fundamental prognostic subtypes. *American Journal of Medical Genetics A., 135*(2), 171–180.

Miniscalco, C., Nygren, G., Hagberg, B., Kadesjö, B., & Gillberg C. (2006). Neuropsychiatric and neurodevelopmental outcome of children at age 6 and 7 years who screened positive for language problems at 30 months. *Developmental Medicine and Child Neurolology, 48,* 361–366.

Minshew, N.J, Goldstein, G., & Siegel, D. (1997). Neuropsychologic functioning in autism: Profile of a complex informational processing disorder. *Journal of the International Neuropsychological Society, 3,* 303–316.

Mitchell, S., Brian, J., Zwaigenbaum, L., Roberts, W., Szatmari, P., Smith, I., et al. (2006). Early language and communication development of infants later diagnosed with autism spectrum disorder *Journal of Developmental and Behavioral Pediatrics, 27*(2), S69–78.

Moes, D.R., & Frea, W.D. (2002). Contextualized behavioral support in early intervention for children with autism and their families. *Journal of Autism and Developmental Disorders, 32*(6), 519–533.

Moes, D., Koegel, R.L., Schreibman, L., & Loos, L.M. (1992). Stress profiles for mothers and fathers of children with autism. *Psychological Reports, 71,*1272–1274.

Molloy, C.A., Morrow, A.L., Meinzen-Derr, J., Dawson, G., Bernier, R., Dunn, M., et al. (2006). Familial autoimmune thyroid disease as a risk factor for regression in children with autism spectrum disorder: A CPEA study. *Journal of Autism and Developmental Disorders,* 317–324.

Montessori, M. (1988). *The Montessori method* (Reissue Edition). New York: Schocken Books.

MTA Cooperative Group. (1999). A 14-month randomized clinical trial of treatment strategies for attention-deficit/hyperactivity disorder. *Archives of General Psychiatry, 56,* 1073–1086.

Myklebust, H.R. (1975). Non-verbal learning disabilities: Assessment and intervention. In H.R. Myklebust (Ed.), *Progress in learning disabilities: Vol. 3* (pp. 85–121). New York: Grune & Stratton.

National Council Against Health Fraud. (2002). *NCAHF Policy Statement on Chelation Therapy,* 8–10; retrieved January 18, 2007, from www.ncahf.org

National Educational Goals Panel, Goal 8. (1990). U.S. Department of Education. *What is the National Education Goals Panel?* Retrieved January 18, 2007, from http://govinfo. library.unt.edu/negp/page3–17.htm

National Institutes of Health, National Center for Complementary and Alternative Medicine; http://nccam.nih.gov/

National Institutes of Health, Office of Dietary Supplements. International Bibliographic Information on Dietary Supplements (IBIDS) Database; http://dietary supplements. info.nih.gov/health_information/ibids.aspx

National Reading Panel. (1998). *Teaching children to read: An evidence-based assessment of the scientific research literature on reading and its implications for reading instruction.* Washington, DC: National Institute of Child Health and Human Development, the National Institute for Literacy, and the U.S. Department of Education.

National Reading Panel. (2000). *Teaching children to read.* Washington, DC: National Institute of Child Health and Human Development, NIH, DHHS. (Report of the National Reading Panel: Teaching Children to Read [00–4769]). Washington, DC: U.S. Government Printing Office.

New Standards. (2004). *Reading and writing grade by grade: Primary literacy standards for kindergarten through third grade.* Washington, DC: National Center on Education and the Economy.

Oberman, L.M., Hubbard, E.M., McCleary, J.P., Altschuler, E.L., Ramachandran, V.S., & Pineda, J.A. (2005). EEG evidence for mirror neuron dysfunction in autism spectrum disorders. *Brain Research and Cognitive Brain Research, 24,* 190–198.

Odom, S.L., Hoyson, M., Jamieson, B., & Strain, P.S. (1985). Increasing handicapped preschoolers peer social interactions: Cross-setting and component analysis. *Journal of Applied Behavior Analysis, 18,* 3–16.

Olsson, M.B., & Hwang, C.P. (2001). Depression in mothers and fathers of children with intellectual disability. *Journal of Intellectual Disability Research, 45,* 535–543.

O'Neill, R.E., Horner, R.H., Albin, R.W., Sprague, J.R., Storey, K., & Newton, J.S. (1997). *Functional assessment and program development for problem behavior* (2nd ed.). Pacific Grove, CA: Brooks/Cole Publishing Company.

O'Neill, R.E., Horner, R.H., Albin, R.W., Storey, K., & Sprague, J.R. (1990). *Functional analysis of problem behavior: A practical assessment guide.* Sycamore, IL: Sycamore Publishing.

Oram Cardy, J.E., Flagg, E.J., Roberts, W., Brian, J., & Roberts, T.P. (2005). Magnetoencephalography identifies rapid temporal processing deficit in autism and language impairment. *Neuroreport, 16,* 329–332.

Ozonoff, S., & Miller, J.N. (1995). Teaching theory of mind: A new approach to social skills training for individuals with autism. *Journal of Autism and Developmental Disorders, 25,* 415–433.

Ozonoff, S., & Cathcart, K. (1998). Effectiveness of a home program intervention for young children with autism. *Journal of Autism and Developmental Disorders, 28,* 25–32.

Parker, S.K., Schwartz, B., Todd, J., & Pickering, L.K. (2005). Thimersol-containing vaccines and autism spectrum disorder: A critical review of published original data. *Evidence Based Mental Health, 8,* 23.

Partington, J.W. (2006). *The assessment of basic language and learning skills-revised (ABLLS–R).* Pleasant Hills, CA: The Behavior Analysts.

Pearson, D.A., Loveland, K.A., Lachar, D., Lane, D.M., Reddoch, S.L., Mansour, R., & Cleveland, L.A. (2006). A comparison of behavioral and emotional functioning in children and adolescents with Autistic Disorder and PDD-NOS. *Child Neuropsychology, 12,* 321–333.

Peters, S.U., Beaudet, A.L., Madduri, N., & Bacino, C.A. (2004). Autism in Angelman's syndrome: Implications for autism research. *Clinical Genetics, 66,* 530–536.

Pickles, A., Starr, E., Kazak, S., Bolton, P., Papanikolaou, K., Bailey, A., et al. (2000). Variable expression of the autism broader phenotype: Findings from extended pedigrees. *Journal of Child Psychology and Psychiatry, 41,* 491–502.

Pinchot, P. (1948). French pioneers in the field of mental deficiency. *American Journal of Mental Deficiency, 3*(1), 128–137.

Piven, J., Chase, G.A., Landa, R., Wzorek, M., Gayle, J., Cloud, D., et al. (1992). Psychiatric disorders in the parents of autistic individuals. *Journal of the American Academy of Child and Adolescent Psychiatry, 30,* 370–371.

Piven, J., & Palmer, P. (2001) Psychiatric disorder and the broad autism phenotype: Evidence from a family study of multiple-incidence autism families. *American Journal of Psychiatry, 156,* 557–563.

Posey, D.J., & McDougle, C.J. (2000). The pharmacotherapy of target symptoms associated with autistic disorder and other pervasive developmental disorders. *Harvard Review of Psychiatry, 8,* 45–63.

Potter, Z., Manjii, H.K., & Rudorfer, M.V. (1998). Anxiolytics and antidepressants. In A.F. Shatzberg & C.B. Nemeroff (Eds.), *The American Psychiatric Press Textbook of Psychopharmacology* (p. 141). Washington, DC: American Psychiatric Publishing.

Prizant, B.M., & Wetherby, A.M. (1998). Understanding the continuum of discrete-trial traditional behavioral to social-pragmatic developmental approaches in communication enhancement for young children with autism/PDD. *Seminars in Speech and Language, 19,* 329–352.

Prizant, B.M., Wetherby, A.M., Rubin, E., & Laurent, A.C. (2003). The SCERTS™ Model: A transactional, family-centered approach to enhancing communication and socioemotional abilitys of children with autism spectrum disorder. *Infants and Young Children, 16,* 296–316.

Quill, K. (2000). *Do-watch-listen-say: Social and communication intervention for children with autism.* Baltimore: Paul H. Brookes Publishing Co.

Rapin, I. (1996). Neurological examination. In I. Rapin (Ed.), *Preschool children with inadequate communication: Developmental language disorder, autism, low IQ* (pp. 98–122). London: MacKeith Press.

Reaven, J., & Hepburn, S. (2003). Cognitive-behavioral treatment of obsessive-compulsive disorder in a child with Asperger syndrome: A case report. *Autism, 7,* 145–164.

Reichle, J., McEvoy, M., & Davis, C. (1999). *A replication and dissemination of a model of inservice training and technical assistance to prevent challenging behaviors in young children: Proactive approaches to managing challenging behavior in preschoolers;* http://ici2.umn.edu/preschoo behavior/strategy.htm

Reinhold, J.A., Molloy, C.A., & Manning-Courtney, P. (2005). Electroencephalogram abnormalities in children with autism spectrum disorders. *Journal of Neuroscience Nursing, 37,* 136–138.

Reiss, S., & Aman, M.G. (Eds.). (1998). *Psychotropic medications and developmental disabilities: The international consensus handbook.* Columbus: Nissonger Center, Ohio State University.

Research Units on Pediatric Psychopharmacology Autism Network. (2005). Risperidone treatment of autistic disorder: Longer-term benefits and blinded discontinuation after 6 months. *American Journal of Psychiatry, 162*(7), 1361–1369.

Rice, M.L. (2002). A unified model of specific and general language delay: Grammatical tense as a clinical marker of unexpected variation. In Y. Levy & J. Schaeffer (Eds.), *Language competence across populations: Toward a definition of specific language impairment* (pp. 63–95). Mahwah, NJ: Lawrence Erlbaum Associates.

Riggott, J. (2005) Mind Games. *Pasadena Weekly,* April 28, 2005, pages 14–17.

Risley, T. (1996). Get a life! Positive behavioral intervention for challenging behavior through life arrangement and life coaching. In L.K. Koegel, R.L. Koegel, & G. Dunlap (Eds.), *Positive behavioral support: Including people with difficult behavior in the community* (pp. 425–437). Baltimore: Paul H. Brookes Publishing Co.

Robbins, D.I., Fein, D., Barton, M.I., & Green, J.A. (2001). The modified checklist for autism in toddlers: An initial study investigating the early detection of autism and pervasive developmental disorders. *Journal of Autism and Developmental Disorders, 31*(2), 149–151.

Robbins, T.W. (1975). The potentiation of conditioned reinforcement by psychomotor stimulant drugs. A test of Hill's hypothesis. *Psychopharmacologia, 45,* 103–114.

Robbins, T.W., & Sahakian, B.J. (1979). "Paradoxical" effects of psychomotor stimulant drugs in hyperactive children from the standpoint of behavioural pharmacology. *Neuropharmacology, 18,* 931–950.

Rogers, S.J., & Lewis, H. (1989). An effective day treatment model for young children with pervasive developmental disorders. *Journal of the American Academy of Child and Adolescent Psychiatry, 28,* 207–214.

Romanczyk, R.G., Arnstein, L., Soorya, L.V., & Gillis, J. (2000). The myriad of controversial treatments for autism: A critical evaluation of efficacy. In S.O. Liliefield, S.J. Lynn, & J.M. Lohr (Eds.), *Science and pseudoscience in clinical psychology* (p. 363). New York: Guilford Press.

Rosenzweig, M.R., Bennett, E.L., & Diamond, M.C. (1972). Brain changes in response to experience. *Learning and Memory, 8,* 294–300.

Rourke, B.P. (1989). *Non-verbal learning disabilities: The syndrome and the model.* New York: Guilford Press.

Rourke, B.P. (1995). *Syndrome of nonverbal learning disabilities: Neurodevelopment manifestations.* New York: Guilford Press.

Rourke, B.P., & Tsatsanis, K.D. (2000). Nonverbal learning disability and Asperger's syndrome. In A. Klin, F.R. Volkmar, & S.S. Sparrow (Eds.), *Asperger's Syndrome.* New York: Guilford Press.

Royal College of Psychiatrists. (2001). *DC-LD: Diagnostic criteria for psychiatric disorders for use with adults with learning disabilities/mental retardation.* London: Author.

Rutter, M. (2005). Incidence of autism spectrum disorders: Changes over time and their meaning. *Acta Paediatrica, 94,* 2–15.

Sackett, D.L., Rosenberg, W.M., Gray, J.A., Haynes, R.B., & Richardson, W.S. (1996). Evidence-based medicine: What it is and what it isn't. *British Medical Journal, 312,* 71–72.

Sallows, G.O., & Graupner, T.D. (2005). Intensive behavioral treatment for children with autism: Four-year outcome and predictors. *American Journal on Mental Retardation, 110,* 417–438.

Sandman. C.A. (1988). B-endorphin disregulation in autistic and self-injurious behavior: A neurodevelopmental hypothesis. *Synapse, 2,* 193–199.

Sandman, C.A., Barron, J.L., Chicz-DeMet, A., & DeMet, E.M. (1990). Plasma B-endorphin levels in patients with self-injurious behavior and stereotypy. *American Journal on Mental Retardation, 95,* 84–92.

Sandman, C.A., Touchette, P., Lenjavi, M., Marion, S., & Chicz-DeMet, A. (2003). Beta-Endorphin and ACTH are dissociated after self-injury in adults with developmental disabilities. *American Journal of Mental Retardation, 108(6),* 414–424.

Sarakoff, R.A., Taylor, B.A., & Poulson, C.L. (2001). Children with autism to engage in conversational exchanges: Script fading with embedded textual stimuli. *Journal of Applied Behavior Analysis, 34,* 81–84.

Schopler, E. (1964). On the relationship between early tactile experiences and the treatment of an autistic and a schizophrenic child. *American Journal of Orthopsychiatry, 34,* 339–340.

Schopler, E., Reichler, R.J., Bashford, A., Lansing, M.D., & Marcus, L.M. (1979). *Psychoeducational profile—revised (PEP-R): Vol. 1.* Baltimore: University Park Press.

Scientific Learning Corporation; retrieved January 29, 2007, from http://www.scilearn.com/

Schreibman, L. (2005). *The science and fiction of autism.* Cambridge, MA: Harvard University Press.

Schultz, R.T., Gauthier, I., Klin, A., Fulbright, R.K., Anderson, A.W.,Volkmar, F., & Skudlarski P. (2000). Abnormal ventral temporal cortical activity during face discrimination among individuals with autism and Asperger syndrome. *Archives of General Psychiatry, 57,* 331–340.

Scolnick, B. (2005). Effects of electroencephalogram biofeedback with Asperger's syndrome. *International Journal of Rehabilitation Research, 28,* 159–163.

Shakespeare, W. (1594–7). *The Merchant of Venice* (Act I, Scene 1). Retrieved January 20, 2007, from http://library.educationworld.net/s15/als1.html

Shapira, N.A., Lessig, M.C., Lewis, M.H., Goodman, W.K., & Driscoll, D.J. (2004). Effects of topiramate in adults with Prader-Willi syndrome. *American Journal on Mental Retardation, 109,* 301–309.

Sherer, M., Pierce, K.L., Paredes, S., Kisacky, K.L., Ingersoll, B., & Schreibman, L. (2001). Enhancing conversation skills in children with autism via video technology. *Behavior Modification, 25,* 140–159.

Sichel, A.G., Fehmi, L.G., & Goldstein, D.M. (1995). Positive outcome with neurofeedback treatment. *Journal of Neurotherapy, 1,* 60–64.

Sicile-Kira, C. (2004). *Autism spectrum disorders: The complete guide to understanding autism, Asperger's syndrome, pervasive developmental disorder, and other ASDs.* New York: Perigee Trade.

Sidman, M. (1977). *Teaching some basic prerequisites for reading.* In P. Mittler (Ed.), *Research to practice in mental retardation: Vol. 2. Education and training* (pp. 353–360). Baltimore: University Park Press.

Sidman, M. (1986). *Functional analysis of emergent verbal classes.* In T. Thompson & M.D. Zeiler (Eds.), *Analysis and integration of behavioral units* (pp. 213–245). Hillsdale, NJ: Lawrence Erlbaum Associates.

Sigafoos, J., Drascow, E., Reichle, J., O'Reilly, M., Green, V.A., & Tait, K. (2004). Tutorial: teaching communicative rejecting to children with severe disabilities. *American Journal of Speech and Language Pathology, 13,* 31–42.

Sigafoos, J. (1999). Choice making and personal selection strategies. In J.K. Luiselli & M.J. Cameron (Eds.), *Antecedent control: Innovative approaches to behavioral support* (pp. 187–221). Baltimore: Paul H. Brookes Publishing Co.

Silay, Y.S., & Jankovic, J. (2005). Emerging drugs in Tourette syndrome. *Expert Opinion on Emerging Drugs, 10,* 365–380.

Silberberg, N., & Silberberg, M. (1968–1969). Case histories in hyperlexia. *Journal of School Psychology, 7,* 3–7.

Skinner, B.F. (1957). *Verbal behavior.* New York: Appleton Century Crofts.

Smalley, S.L., McCracken, J., & Tanguay, P. (1995). Autism, affective disorder and social phobia. *American Journal of Medical Genetics, 27,* 19–26.

Smathers, S.A., Wilson, J.G., & Nigro, N.A. (2003). Topiramate effectiveness in Prader-Willi syndrome. *Pediatric Neurolology, 28,* 130–133.

Smeeth, L., Cook, C., Fombonne, E., Heavey, L., Rodrigues, L.C., Smith, P.G., et al. (2004). MMR vaccination and pervasive developmental disorders: A case control study. *Lancet, 364,* 963–969.

Smith, V.K., & Dillenbeck, A. (2006). Developing and implementing early intervention plans for children with autism spectrum disorders. *Seminars in Speech and Language, 27,* 10–20.

Smith, T., Groen, A.D., & Wynn, J.W. (2000). Randomized trial of intensive early intervention for children with pervasive developmental disorder. *American Journal on Mental Retardation, 105,* 269–285.

Sofranoff, K., Attwood, T., & Hinton, S. (2005). A randomised controlled trial of a CBT intervention for anxiety in children with Asperger syndrome. *Journal of Child Psychology and Psychiatry, 46,* 1152–1160.

Sophocles. (442 BC). *Antigone.* Line 320; translated by Ian Johnston of Malaspina University-College, Nanaimo, BC, Canada; revised in May 2005. Retrieved January 18, 2007, from http://www.mala.bc.ca/~johnstoi/sophocles/antigone.htm

Sprague, J.R., & Horner, R.H. (1999). Low-frequency high-intensity problem behavior: Toward an applied technology of functional assessment and intervention. In A.C. Repp & R.H. Horner (Eds.), *Functional analysis of problem behavior: From effective assessment to effective support.* Belmont, CA: Wadsworth.

Staller, J. (2003). Aripiprazole in an adult with Asperger disorder. *Annals of Pharmacotherapy, 34,* 1628–1631.

Starr, E.M., Berument, S.K., Tomlins, M.., Papanikolaou, K., & Rutter, M. (2005). Brief report: Autism in individuals with Down syndrome. *Journal of Autism and Developmental Disorders, 35,* 665–673.

Stewart, R., Besset, A., Bebbington, P., Brugha, T., Lindesay, J., Jenkins, R., et al. (2006). Insomnia comorbidity and impact and hypnotic use by age group in a national survey population aged 16 to 74 years. *Sleep, 29,* 1391–1397.

Stone, W.L., Lemanek, K.L., Fishel, P.T., Fernandez, M.C., & Altemeier, W.A. (1990). Play and imitation skills in the diagnosis of autism in young children. *Pediatrics, 86,* 267–272.

Strain, P.S., & Cordisco, A. (1994). The LEAP program. In S.L. Harris & J.S. Handleman (Eds.), *Preschool education programs for children with autism* (pp. 115–126). Austin, TX: PRO-ED.

Strain, P.S., & Hoyson, M. (2000). On the need for longitudinal, intensive social skill intervention: LEAP follow-up outcomes for children with autism as a case-in-point. *Topics in Early Childhood Special Education, 20,* 116–122.

Strain, P.S., & Kohler, F.W. (1998). Peer-mediated social intervention for young children with autism. *Seminars in Speech and Language, 19,* 391–405.

Studdert-Kennedy, M. (1998). Move on FastForWord. *American Speech and Hearing Association, 40,* 7.

Studdert-Kennedy, M., & Mody, M. (1995). Auditory temporal perception deficits in the reading-impaired: A critical review of the evidence. *Psychonomic Bulletin and Review, 2,* 508–514.

Sturmey, P. (2005) Secretin is an ineffective treatment for pervasive developmental disabilities: A review of 15 double-blind randomized controlled trials. *Research in Developmental Disabilities, 26,* 87–97.

Sugai, G., & Tindal, G. (1993). Direct observation procedures and problem analysis. In *Effective school consultation: An interactive approach* (pp. 81–118). Pacific Grove, CA: Brooks/Cole.

Sundberg, M.L., & Partington, J.W. (1998). *Teaching language to children with autism or other developmental disabilities.* Danville, CA: Behavior Analysts, Inc.

Sweeney, E.J., Carbone, V.J., O'Brien, L., Zecchin, G., & Janecky, M.N. (2007). Transferring control of the mand to the motivating operation in children with autism. *Journal of Analysis of Verbal Behavior, 23.*

Symons, F.J., Butler, M.G., Sanders, M.D., Feurer, I.D., & Thompson T. (1999). Self-injurious behavior and Prader-Willi syndrome: Behavioral forms and body locations. *American Journal on Mental Retardation, 104*(3), 260–269.

Symons, F.J., Fox, N.D., & Thompson, T. (1998). Functional communication training and naltrexone treatment of self-injurious behavior: An experimental case report. *Journal of Applied Research and Intellectual Disabilities, 3,* 273–292.

Symons, F.J., Thompson, A., & Rodriguez, M.C. (2004). Self-injurious behavior and the efficacy of naltrexone treatment: A quantitative synthesis. *Mental Retardation and Developmental Disabilities Research Reviews, 10,* 193–200.

Szatmari, P. (2004). *A mind apart: Understanding children with autism and Asperger syndrome.* New York: Guilford Press.

Taylor, B., Miller, E., Farrington, C.P., Petropoulos, M.C., Favot-Mayaud, I., Li, J., & Waight, P.A. (1999). Autism and measles, mumps, and rubella vaccine: No epidemiological evidence for a causal association. *Lancet, 353,* 2026–2029.

Taylor, D.V., Rush, D., Hetrick, W.P., & Sandman, C.A. (1993). Self-injurious behavior within the menstrual cycle of women with mental retardation. *American Journal on Mental Retardation, 97,* 659–664.

Teitelbaum, O., Benton, T., Shah, P.K., Prince, A., Kelly, J.L., & Teitelbaum, P. (2004). Eshkol-Wachman movement notation in diagnosis: The early detection of Asperger's syndrome. *Proceedings of the National Academy of Sciences USA, 101,* 11909–11914.

Teitelbaum, P., Teitelbaum, O., Nye, J., Fryman, J., & Maurer, R.G. (1998). Movement analysis in infancy may be useful in early diagnosis of autism. *Proceedings of the National Academy of Sciences USA, 95,* 13982–13987.

Thiemann, K., & Goldstein, H. (2001). Social stories, written text cues, and video feedback: Effects on social communication of children with autism. *Journal of Applied Behavior Analysis, 34,* 425–446.

Thompson, T., Hackenberg, T., Cerutti, D., Baker, D., & Axtell, S. (1994). Opioid antagonist effects on self-injury in adults with mental retardation: Response form and location as determinants of medication effects. *American Journal on Mental Retardation, 99,* 85–102.

Thompson, T., & Butler, M.G. (2004). Prader Willi syndrome: Clinical behavior and genetic findings. In M.C. Wolraich (Ed.), *Disorders of learning and behavior: A practical guide to assessment and management.* Hamilton, Ontario: B.C. Decker.

Thompson, T., & Hollon, S.D. (2006). Behavioral and cognitive-behavioral interventions. In M.H. Ebert, P.T. Loosen, & B. Nurcombe (Eds.), *Current diagnosis and treatment in psychiatry* (2nd ed.). New York: Appelton & Lange.

Thompson, T., Moore, T., & Symons, F.J. (in press). Psychotherapeutic medications in positive behavior supports. In S. Odom, R. Horner, M. Snell, & J. Blacher (Eds.), *Handbook on developmental disabilities.* New York: Guilford Press.

Tobin, T.J. (2005). *Parents' guide to functional assessment* (3rd ed.). Educational and Community Supports, University of Oregon; retrieved January 18, 2007, from http://darkwing.uoregon.edu/~ttobin

Tobing, L.E., & Glenwick, D.S. (2002). Relation of the childhood autism rating scale-parent version to diagnosis, stress and age. *Research in Developmental Disabilities, 3,* 211–223.

Touchette, P.E., MacDonald, R.F., & Langer, S.N. (1985). A scatter plot for identifying stimulus control of problem behavior. *Journal of Applied Behavior Analysis, 18,* 343–351.

Tsai, L.V. (2001). *Taking the mystery out of medications in autism/Asperger's syndrome.* Arlington, TX: Future Horizons.

Turkeltaub, P.E., Flowers, D.L., Verbalis, A., Miranda, M., Gareau, L., & Eden, G.F. (2004). The neural basis of hyperlexic reading: An fMRI case study. *Neuron, 41,* 1–20.

Twatchman-Cullen, D. (1998). *A passion to believe: Autism and the facilitated communication phenomenon.* Boulder, CO: Westview Press.

Valdovinos, M.G., Napolitano, D.A., Zarcone, J.R., Williams, D.C., & Schroeder, S.R. (2002). Multimodal evaluation of risperidone for destructive behavior: functional analysis, direct observations, rating scales, and psychiatric impressions. *Experimental and Clinical Psychopharmacology, 10*(3), 268–275.

Valdovinos, M.G., Zarcone, J.R., Hellings, J.A., Kim, G., & Schroeder, S.R. (2004). Using the diagnostic assessment of the severely handicapped-II (DASH-II) to measure the therapeutic effects of risperidone. *Journal of Intellectual and Disability Research, 48,* 53–59.

Van den Heuvel, O.A., Veltman, D.J., Groenewegen, H.J., Cath, D.C., van Balkom, A.J., van Hartskamp, J., et al. (2005). Frontal-striatal dysfunction during planning in obsessive-compulsive disorder. *Archives of General Psychiatry, 62,* 301–309.

Vandercook, T., York, J., & Forest, M. (1989). MAPS: A strategy for building the vision. *Journal of the Association for Persons with Severe Handicaps, 14*(3), 205–215.

Vaughn, B., Fox, L., & Lentini, R. (2006). *Creating teaching tools for young children with challenging behavior: A user's manual.* Center for Evidence-Based Practice: Young Children with Challenging Behavior. The University of South Florida; retrieved January 18, 2007, from http://challengingbehavior.fmhi.usf.edu/index.html

Volkmar, F.R. (2005). *Handbook of autism and pervasive developmental disorders* (3rd ed.). Hoboken, NJ: Wiley.

Wagner, K.D. (2005). Pharmacotherapy for major depression in children and adolescents. *Progress in Neuropsychopharmacology and Biology, 29,* 819–826.

Wang, J., Li, F., Calhoun, J.H., & Mader, J.T. (2002). The role and effectiveness of adjunctive hyperbaric oxygen therapy in the management of musculoskeletal disorders. *Journal of Postgraduate Medicine, 48,* 226–231.

Whiteside, S.P., Port, J.D., & Abramowitz, J.S. (2004). A meta-analysis of functional neuroimaging in obsessive-compulsive disorder. *Psychiatry Research, 132,* 69–70.

Whiteside, S.P., Port, J.D., Deacon, B.J., & Abramowitz, J.S. (2006). A magnetic resonance spectroscopy investigation of obsessive-compulsive disorder and anxiety. *Psychiatry Research, 146,* 137–147.

Whittington, C.J., Kendall, T., Fonagy, P., Cottrell, D., Cotgrove, A., & Boddington, E. (2004). Selective serotonin reuptake inhibitors I childhood depression: Systematic review of published versus unpublished data. *Lancet, 363,* 1341–1345.

Wieder, S., & Greenspan, S.I. (2003). Climbing the symbolic ladder in the DIR model through floortime/interactive play. *Autism, 7,* 425–435.

Wilkinson, K.M., & McIlvane, W.J. (2001). Considerations in teaching graphic symbols. In J. Reichle, D. Beukelman, & J. Light (Eds.), *Exemplary strategies for beginning communicators: Implications for AAC* (pp. 273–321). Baltimore: Paul H. Brookes Publishing Co.

Witwer, A., & Lecavalier, L. (2005). Treatment incidence and patterns in children and adolescence with autism spectrum disorders. *Journal of Child and Adolescent Psychopharmacology, 15,* 671–681.

Wiznitzer, M. (2004). Autism and tuberous sclerosis. *Journal of Child Neurology, 19,* 675–679.

Woermann, F.G., Elst, L.T., Koepp, M.J., Free, S.L., Thompson, P.J., Trimble, M.R., et al. (2000). Reduction of frontal neocortical grey matter associated with affective aggression in patients with temporal lobe epilepsy: An objective voxel by voxel analysis of automatically segmented MRI. *Journal of Neurology, Neurosurgery and Psychiatry, 68,* 162–169.

Wolf, M.M., Risley, T.R., & Mees, H. (1964). Application of operant conditioning procedures to the behavioural problems of an autistic child. *Behaviour Research & Therapy, 1,* 305–312.

Woods, D.W., Hook, S.S., Spellman, D.F., & Friman, P.C. (2000). Case study: Exposure and response prevention for an adolescent with Tourette's Syndrome and OCD. *Journal of the American Academy of Child and Adolescent Psychiatry, 39,* 904–907.

Woods, D.W., Miltenberger, R.G., & Lumley, V.A. (1996). Sequential application of major habit reversal components to treat motor tics in children. *Journal of Applied Behavior Analysis, 29,* 483–493.

World Health Organization. (2006). *International statistical classification of diseases and related health problems* (10th Revision). Geneva: World Health Organization; retrieved January 18, 2007, from http://www.who.int/classifications/apps/icd/icd10online/

Zarcone, J.R., Hellings, J.A., Crandall, K., Reese, R.M., Marquis, J., Fleming, K., et al. (2001). Effects of risperidone on aberrant behavior of persons with developmental disabilities: I. A double-blind crossover study using multiple measures. *American Journal on Mental Retardation,106*(6), 525–538.

Zarcone, J.R., Lindauer, S.E., Morse, P.S., Crosland, K.A., Valdovinos, M.G., McKerhar, T.L., et al. (2004). Effects of risperidone on destructive behavior of persons with developmental disabilities: III. Functional analysis. *American Journal on Mental Retardation, 109*(4), 310–321.

Zwaigenbaum, L., Bryson, S., Rogers, T., Roberts, W.. Brian, J., & Szatmari, P. (2005). Behavioral manifestations of autism in the first year of life. *International Journal for Developmental Neuroscience, 23,*143–152.

Index

Page numbers followed by "f" indicate figures; those followed by "t" indicate tables.